Assessment and Treatment Planning for PTSD

Assessment and Treatment Planning for PTSD

B. CHRISTOPHER FRUEH

ANOUK L. GRUBAUGH

JON D. ELHAI

JULIAN D. FORD

WILEY
John Wiley & Sons, Inc.

Published by John Wiley & Sons, Inc., Hoboken, New Jersey.
Published simultaneously in Canada.

Library of Congress Cataloging-in-Publication Data:

    Assessment and treatment planning for PTSD [electronic resource]/B. Christopher
Frueh . . . [et al.].
      1 online resource.
    Includes bibliographical references and indexes.
    Description based on print version record and CIP data provided by publisher; resource not viewed.
      ISBN 978-1-118-26280-1 (mobipocket)—ISBN 978-1-118-23813-4 (epub)—
    ISBN 978-1-118-22473-1 (pdf)—ISBN 978-1-118-12239-6 (paperback) (print)
      I. Frueh, B. Christopher.
    DNLM: 1. Stress Disorders, Post-Traumatic. WM 172.5]
    616.85'21—dc23

                                2012016149

Contents

129651

Acknowledgments

Dr. Frueh is grateful for the support provided by the McNair Medical Institute of Houston, TX. Dr. Grubaugh is grateful for the institutional support of the Ralph H. Johnson Charleston Veterans Affairs Medical Center Research Service and the Medical University of South Carolina Department of Psychiatry. This work was conceived and developed during a meeting sponsored by The Menninger Clinic in Houston, TX. Thus, all authors are grateful to The Clinic for the support and resources it provided.

CHAPTER 1

Introduction and Overview

Posttraumatic stress disorder (PTSD) was officially introduced into the psychiatric nomenclature in 1980, with the publication of the *Diagnostic and Statistical Manual of Mental Disorders, Third Edition* (*DSM-III*) by the American Psychiatric Association (APA). Over the past 30 years, this disorder has changed the landscape of trauma and general stress studies, and it has contributed to the development of a wide range of sociopolitical, conceptual, and clinical issues and questions. The concept of posttraumatic reactions has been widely absorbed by the general public with regard to psychological adjustment after major traumatic events, as well as a wide range of other life stressors. Public awareness of PTSD has been furthered by extensive news coverage of recent national and international news events, including the 9/11 atrocities; the wars in Iraq and Afghanistan; terrorist attacks in London and Madrid; hurricanes, earthquakes, tsunamis, and other natural disasters; widely publicized cases of child sexual abuse among church officials and national sports heroes; and genocides in Africa and eastern Europe. Mainstream media publicity and films since the Vietnam War have also likely played a role in the layman's understanding of PTSD. A now common portrayal of returning combat veterans is that of the psychologically impaired victim-hero, found in Hollywood movies too numerous to count, such as *Taxi Driver* (1976), *Coming Home* (1978), *The Deer Hunter* (1979), *Born on the Fourth of July* (1989), and *In the Valley of Elah* (2007).

Undoubtedly, research on every nook and corner of this disorder has abounded in the past few decades, providing patients and their families, clinicians, health care administrators, and policy makers with a vastly better understanding of posttraumatic reactions—from both a psychopathological and a resilient standpoint—than we had before. Despite this expansion of our knowledge, there remain numerous unanswered questions and controversies as to how clinicians should evaluate, define, and treat psychiatric symptoms in the aftermath of trauma events. Clinicians are left in their practices with questions that lack practical directions based on solid empirical evidence. A good deal of pseudoscience and poor science in the field of traumatology, as well as a proliferation of clinical myths, misconceptions, and fads about traumatic reactions, has further muddied the water for clinicians. Toward this end, we have produced a volume intended to help the dedicated evidence-based mental health practitioner with clinical assessment and treatment planning for people—patients, clients, consumers, however one wishes to term or define them—suffering from posttraumatic reactions.

This opening chapter begins with a historical perspective on posttraumatic reactions, segues into a brief review of important conceptual questions and issues with regard to the diagnosis of PTSD, and concludes with a general overview of evidence-based practice in mental health care and a discussion of why such practice is so important for people suffering posttraumatic reactions.

HISTORICAL AND SOCIETAL PERSPECTIVES

The general notion that people are significantly affected, perhaps changed forever, by violent and horrific ordeals is not new. The postcombat reactions of warriors have been noted since ancient times throughout mythology and literature and in a variety of cultures (e.g., "Epic of Gilgamesh," writings of Homer and Shakespeare). Since the 19th century, different terms have been used to describe posttraumatic reactions for a variety of dangerous and frightening experiences. Frequently, these terms provided clues as to how the etiology or nature of the symptoms was viewed at the time. In the years following the U.S. Civil War, it was noted that many veterans reported symptoms of chronic chest pain, as well as fatigue, shortness of breath, and heart palpitations—yet physical abnormalities to explain these symptoms were often not to be found. Physicians and caretakers were puzzled by the syndrome, which, while somewhat common, had no obvious explanation. The observed functional syndrome became known as *soldier's heart* or *Da Costa's syndrome* for the surgeon who noted it in a series of case reports (Barnes, 1870). During World War I, the term *shell shock* was used to refer to a constellation of symptoms believed to be a neurological disorder caused by the sound of explosions and bright flashes of light from bursting artillery shells on the Western Front. *Combat fatigue* was a term used during World War II, when it was believed that combat reactions were caused by exposure to extreme stress and fatigue. During the 1970s, victims of sexual assault were often identified as suffering from a "rape trauma syndrome" (Burgess & Holmstrom, 1974) or "battered woman syndrome" (Walker, 1977).

In organized psychiatry, the concept of a specific category of life events causing a psychiatric disorder was first formalized in 1952, with the first edition of the *DSM*. Gross stress reaction (GSR) was defined as a "transient situational personality disorder" that could occur when essentially "normal" individuals experienced severe physical demands or extreme emotional stress. GSR was soon dropped from psychiatry's nosology in 1968, with the second edition of the *DSM*. Twelve years after the *DSM-II's* publication, a more narrow class of events—that is, trauma—was linked as the causative agent for a new and specific constellation of symptoms, and posttraumatic stress disorder was formally defined and included in the psychiatric nosology.

The diagnosis of PTSD, added to the *DSM* in 1980, was largely the result of attempts to account for the challenging impairment presented by Vietnam veterans at the time of their homecoming (Satel & Frueh, 2009; Shephard, 2001, 2004; Wessely & Jones, 2004). In the immediate post-Vietnam era, compensation for significant functional impairment was difficult to obtain other than for observable physical injuries and access to Veterans Administration (VA) medical services were possible only via a "war-related" disorder (Wessely & Jones, 2004). Veterans' advocates and antiwar activities were at the forefront of efforts to define and codify a "Vietnam syndrome," a psychiatric response to war unique among Vietnam veterans. At about the same time in the 1970s, the feminist movement was politically strong and gaining momentum. They successfully began to expose the violence that was common against women, which led to the development of a "rape trauma syndrome" (Burgess & Holmstrom, 1974). These two activist groups soon joined forces to make a common cause with mental health clinicians and researchers. Together, they worked to influence the development of the new diagnostic addition to the *DSM-III*. Thus, along with medical and psychological science, the development of the clinical conceptualization of PTSD was heavily influenced by socioeconomic and political forces (Mezey & Robbins, 2001; Shephard, 2001). For a more in-depth discussion on the origins of PTSD, see Shephard (2001), Summerfield (2001), Jones and Wessely (2007), Rosen and Frueh (2010), and Satel and Frueh (2009).

A Unique Psychiatric Disorder

PTSD is unique from the vast majority of psychiatric disorders in the *DSM* in that it is the rare disorder to include an etiological explanation (trauma)—and one that is actually part of its diagnostic criteria (Criterion A). Otherwise, for the most part, the *DSM* takes an atheoretical approach to quantifying and classifying mental disorders. The fact that PTSD cannot be diagnosed without the occurrence of a Criterion A event not only makes PTSD distinct from other psychiatric diagnoses, but it also renders it unique in the general field of stress studies (Breslau & Davis, 1987). As Rosen, Frueh, Elhai, Grubaugh, and Ford (2010) noted:

> Rather than all stressors creating an increased risk for a wide range of established conditions, there now was a distinct class of stressors that led to its own form of psychopathology. Thus, while any type of high stress could lead to increased risk of headaches, high blood pressure, or depression, only a Criterion A event such as combat, rape, or a life-threatening accident could lead to the distinct syndrome of PTSD. This assumption of a specific etiology, associated with a distinct clinical syndrome, provided the justification for a new field of "traumatology" to be carved out of general stress studies. (p. 7)

An Evolving Disorder

In the 30-plus years since its creation, the definition of PTSD has evolved steadily with each new revision of the *DSM*. Changes have been made to the definition of Criterion A, new symptoms have been added, and requirements regarding symptom onset and duration (Criterion E) have been modified.

In *DSM-III* (APA, 1980) the trauma criterion (Criterion A) was defined as: "Existence of a recognizable stressor that would evoke significant symptoms of distress in almost everyone" (p. 238). This stressor was described it as being outside the range of normal human experience. In *DSM-IV* (APA, 1994), Criterion A events are defined much more specifically:

> The person has been exposed to a traumatic event in which both of the following were present: (1) the person experienced, witnessed, or was confronted with an event or events that involved actual or threatened death or serious injury, or a threat to the physical integrity of self or others; (2) the person's response involved intense fear, helplessness, or horror. Note: in children, this may be expressed instead by disorganized or agitated behavior. (pp. 427–428)

Moreover, by 1994, empirical research showed that traumatic events were actually quite common to the human experience, so that aspect of the *DSM-III* definition was dropped from the definition.

The number of possible PTSD symptoms expanded from 12 in *DSM-III* to 17 in *DSM-IV* and included the addition of avoidance behaviors. Also added was the caveat in Criterion E that duration of the disturbance had to exceed 1 month. This revision to Criterion E in *DSM-IV* was paired with a new (but related) diagnosis: acute stress disorder (ASD). Like PTSD, ASD requires a Criterion A traumatic event and includes symptom criteria very similar to PTSD (Criteria B through D). ASD cannot be diagnosed unless symptoms and associated impairment lasts at least 2 days (so as to exclude those with immediate peritraumatic reactions, which are very common) and may not last more than 4 weeks past exposure to the traumatic stressor. In this way, ASD serves as a diagnosis for those suffering extreme traumatic stress reactions that occur too soon after trauma exposure to be classified as PTSD.

PTSD's defining criteria continue to be subject to much debate and discussion, and are likely to be revised in future editions of the *DSM*. We will return to further discussion of the future of PTSD in Chapter 12.

Important Conceptual Questions and Issues

Despite the proliferation of research on and expansion of clinical services for PTSD, much about the disorder remains misunderstood or unknown. In the sections that follow, we briefly introduce some of the important conceptual questions and issues regarding the diagnosis of PTSD that have implications for clinical assessment and treatment planning for people with significant traumatic event exposure.

Epidemiology of PTSD: Posttraumatic Morbidity Versus Resilience

There is now a widespread assumption on the part of many laypersons, journalists, and even clinicians that the majority of people who endure a traumatic experience, such as sexual assault, childhood abuse, a natural disaster, or wartime combat, will develop a psychiatric disorder as a direct result of the experience. However, the data actually tell a very different story. Most individuals will experience some short-term distress and may be affected in a variety of psychological ways. However, the majority of people who survive even the most horrific traumatic experiences do not develop PTSD or any other full-blown psychiatric disorder. That is, only a small minority of people will develop distress and functional impairment that rises to the level of a psychiatric disorder. Instead, long-term resilience is actually the norm rather than the exception for people after trauma (Bonanno, Westphal, & Mancini, 2011).

We now have a large body of epidemiological studies, conducted across a variety of populations, to inform our understanding of PTSD prevalence estimates (Breslau, Davis, Andreski, & Peterson, 1991; Davidson, Hughes, Blazer, & George, 1991; Dohrenwend et al., 2006; Norris, 1992; Smith et al., 2008). Data consistently show that exposure to potentially traumatic events (i.e., Criterion A) is quite common in the general population, with 60% to 80% of the population reporting exposure to various types of traumatic events (Breslau et al., 1991; Kessler, Sonnega, Bromet, Hughes, & Nelson, 1995). PTSD rates (point-prevalence) are consistently found to be in the 6% to 9% range for both civilians and military veterans. For those who develop PTSD, about 50% will remit within 3 months without treatment (Galea et al., 2002; Rothbaum, Foa, Riggs, Murdock, & Walsh, 1992). This is a robust finding that is specifically noted in *DSM-IV.* Individuals who are diagnosed with PTSD are at 3 times greater risk of meeting criteria again if exposed to a later traumatic stressor (Breslau, Peterson, & Schultz, 2008). In this way, PTSD can be a recurrent disorder after a first episode.

Psychiatric Comorbidity

Epidemiological studies also indicate that PTSD is not the only, or even the most likely, psychiatric reaction to follow trauma exposure. Fear, anxiety, sadness, anger, and guilt (among others) are common reactions to traumatic experiences. Other common reactions include physical or somatic complaints, such as insomnia, gastrointestinal symptoms, headaches, or sleep problems; social and relationship difficulties; and substance use, including alcohol and nicotine (Breslau et al., 1991; Bryant, 2010; Kessler et al., 1995). Major depression is probably the most common form of posttraumatic psychopathology, even more prevalent than PTSD. Moreover, among individuals who meet the diagnostic criteria for PTSD, a majority has additional psychiatric problems. Common co-occurring disorders with PTSD include depression, substance use disorders, panic attacks, and other anxiety disorders. Adding to the illness burden, people diagnosed with PTSD often present with significant medical comorbidity (e.g., chronic pain, cardiac difficulties) that is associated with increased use of health care services (Elhai, North, & Frueh, 2005; Schnurr & Green, 2004).

Individual Risk Factors

All of this raises the question: If only a small percentage (6% to 9%) of trauma–exposed people have PTSD, who is most likely to have it? A number of individual vulnerabilities and risk factors have been shown to be strong predictors of PTSD. Social support plays perhaps one of the most important buffering roles against psychiatric illness in the aftermath of trauma and stress. The converse of this is also true in that lower social support is associated with increased risk for PTSD (Andrews, Brewin, & Rose, 2003). Gender is another consistent risk factor. Females are at markedly increased risk of developing PTSD relative to men by a ratio of approximately two to one (Breslau et al., 1991, 1998; Tolin & Foa, 2006). Other significant PTSD risk factors are lower intelligence, lower education, lower socioeconomic status, prior history of poor social adjustment or psychiatric disorders, and substance abuse. Recent research also suggests that certain genetic phenotypes may interact with environmental stressors to affect the likelihood of PTSD after trauma (Koenen, 2007). At this point, genetic research on PTSD and other posttraumatic reactions is quite underdeveloped. This will undoubtedly change over the next 5 to 10 years, but it is unlikely that genetic variations will ever explain more than 35% of the risk for PTSD development.

The Etiological Nature of the Trauma

Inherent in the internal logic of the PTSD diagnosis is that trauma (Criterion A) causes the symptoms of the disorder. The belief in a specific etiology was fundamental to the very origins of PTSD, and provided the rationale to create a new psychiatric disorder that formed a unique class of stressors from more general life stressors. Accordingly, individuals who do not experience a traumatic event should not develop PTSD. However, empirical data has consistently shown otherwise—that non–Criterion A stressors (i.e., events not considered to be traumatic) can result in similar rates of PTSD (reviewed in Long & Elhai, 2009; Rosen & Lilienfeld, 2008). In fact, the assumption of a specific etiology for PTSD is so problematic, from a theoretical and empirical standpoint, that some investigators are starting to write about the "the Criterion A problem" (Weathers & Keane, 2007). This obviously has implications for our understanding and definition of the disorder, including how the field will characterize it in future editions of the *DSM*. Recent proposals have suggested everything from tighter definitions of what constitutes a traumatic event (Kilpatrick, Resnick, & Acierno, 2009) to the extreme of doing away with the gatekeeper function of Criterion A altogether (Brewin, Lanius, Novac, Schnyder, & Galea, 2009). At this point, it is somewhat of an open question as to whether "traumatic" stressors are in fact significantly unique and different from other life stressors (divorce, job loss, financial difficulty), or are better understood as points along a continuum of stressors (Dohrenwend, 2010). In the future, the field of trauma may converge with that of general stress studies.

PTSD Symptom Criteria: Symptom Overlap and Factor Structure

Another important question in the trauma field is: To what extent is PTSD a unique psychiatric disorder, and to what extent does it simply duplicate other diagnoses in the mood and anxiety disorders categories (McHugh & Treisman, 2007; Spitzer, First, & Wakefield, 2007)? This is not simply a lofty philosophical question. The answer has practical implications for our ability to understand and treat the syndrome of clinical symptoms that currently make up the disorder. Not only is PTSD highly comorbid with other *DSM* psychiatric disorders, but it also shares many symptoms with these other disorders. For example, criteria for diagnosing PTSD can be fully met with the right combination of symptoms pulled from the combined diagnoses of depression and specific phobia. See Rosen, Lilienfeld, Frueh, McHugh, and Spitzer (2010) for a detailed explanation for how this can be achieved. An additional related concern is that the core set of PTSD's symptoms have been demonstrated to be best conceptualized as general dysphoria or distress, common to other mood and anxiety disorders (Simms, Watson, & Doebbeling, 2002; Watson, 2005). Although initial studies on criteria sets that remove PTSD's overlapping symptoms find similar rates of prevalence and comorbidity (Elhai, Grubaugh, Kashdan, & Frueh, 2008; Ford, Elhai, Ruggiero, & Frueh, 2009; Grubaugh, Long, Elhai, Frueh, & Magruder, 2010), these findings do not resolve all concerns.

The factor structure of a disorder can provide us with information about how some symptoms are endorsed in a similar manner to each other and different from how other symptoms are endorsed. Factor analytic studies over the past 15 years have consistently shown that *DSM-IV*'s tripartite PTSD model (reexperiencing, avoidance/numbing, hyperarousal) does not adequately account for PTSD's factor structure (Elhai et al., 2008; Elhai & Palmieri, 2011; Yufik & Simms, 2010). This body of research reveals that two particular four-factor models best represent the PTSD construct across studies: (1) King, Leskin, King, and Weathers's (1998) model consisting of reexperiencing, effortful avoidance, emotional numbing, and hyperarousal factors; and (2) Simms, et al.'s (2002) model consisting of reexperiencing, effortful avoidance, dysphoria, and hyperarousal. These two models differ only in the placement of three PTSD symptoms: difficulty sleeping (PTSD's symptom D1), irritability (D2), and difficulty concentrating (D3). Symptoms D1 through D3 are part of the King et al. model's hyperarousal factor, but part of the Simms et al. model's dysphoria factor. Very recent confirmatory factor analytic findings demonstrated that separating the three symptoms into a separate factor significantly enhanced model fit for the two models, suggesting that these three symptoms represent a unique latent construct (Elhai et al. 2011).

Memory and Trauma

A common notion in the past was that memory for traumatic events functioned very differently from memory for ordinary experiences. Many clinicians also believed that major traumatic experiences were highly susceptible to being repressed. The explanation for this is that certain events are so horrific that the human mind cannot tolerate them and, therefore, represses them to the unconscious mind. From there, these unconscious traumatic memories cause havoc in the form of severe psychopathology, including symptoms of PTSD, "multiple personalities," borderline personality disorder, and other forms of psychiatric disturbance. This concept dates back to Sigmund Freud, has been the subject of several Hollywood movies (e.g., *Sybil*), and continues to exist today in some quarters. It has been the cornerstone of many high-profile lawsuits over the years, including those brought against the Catholic Church and day care centers. In fact, *DSM-IV* somewhat legitimizes this concept by including it as one of the 17 clinical symptoms of PTSD: "inability to recall an important aspect of the trauma." However, a large body of research from the fields of memory, learning, and cognition has failed to provide any support for this concept of a special mechanism for traumatic memory (McNally, 2003). This understanding has led to several dramatic revelations. For example, a very recent book by an investigative journalist

(Nathan, 2011) thoroughly discredited the case of Sybil, the famous patient with purported multiple personalities caused by childhood trauma (played by Sally Field in the movie). The evidence portrays a patient with other psychiatric disorders who was manipulated by her psychiatrist into reporting and playing out a series of symptoms that she did not actually experience.

Delayed-Onset PTSD

A feature of PTSD that has been included in the *DSM* is the concept of "delayed-onset" PTSD. According to this commonly held view, people can appear to be resilient after trauma but many years later can suffer a sudden onset of PTSD symptoms that is not attributable to any current stressor or illness. The stereotypical example of this is the combat veteran who is overcome suddenly with PTSD symptoms 20 or 30 years after the war is over. However, there is little empirical data to support the existence of delayed-onset PTSD. Several large epidemiological studies have reported zero or extremely low rates of delayed-onset PTSD in civilians and veterans (Breslau et al., 1991; Frueh, Grubaugh, Yeager, & Magruder, 2009). If, however, "delayed onset" is reconceptualized as a delay in seeking treatment, or subsequent exacerbation of prior symptoms by recent stressors occurring years after the original traumatic event, then the phenomenon may be somewhat more common (Andrews, Brewin, Philpott, & Stewart, 2007). One implication of this is that clinicians should be sure to take careful histories regarding a patient's course of symptoms and possible delays in seeking treatment, before applying the diagnostic qualifier of delayed onset.

The Forensic Aspect of PTSD

As indicated earlier, PTSD is one of the very few psychiatric disorders in the *DSM* that by definition includes an etiological criterion: traumatic event exposure. Because of this assumption of a specific cause for psychological suffering and impaired role functioning, the diagnosis of PTSD is commonly invoked among patients with claims for worker's compensation or disability or personal injury lawsuits (Taylor, Frueh, &

Asmundson, 2007). For example, the vast majority (> 90%) of veterans seeking treatment services within the Veterans Affairs (formerly Veterans Administration) system are also applying for disability payments, which creates a wide range of assessment and treatment considerations (Frueh, Grubaugh, Elhai, & Buckley, 2007; Worthen & Moering, 2011). The diagnosis provides an opening in tort litigation for plaintiffs to argue that subjective psychiatric symptoms are the direct result of an alleged traumatic event and not from other life stressors or personal vulnerabilities. Other major psychiatric disorders, including depression, anxiety, and addictions do not easily lend themselves to this. The *DSM-IV* specifically acknowledges this reality with a cautionary guideline for clinicians: "Malingering should be ruled out in those situations in which financial remuneration, benefit eligibility, and forensic determinations play a role" (APA, 1994, p. 467). This is a clinical assessment issue that we will address in a variety of ways in later chapters.

REFERENCES

American Psychiatric Association. (1980). *Diagnostic and statistical manual of mental disorders* (3rd ed.). Washington, DC: Author.

American Psychiatric Association. (1994). *Diagnostic and statistical manual of mental disorders* (4th ed.). Washington, DC: Author.

Andrews, B., Brewin, C. R., Philpott, R., & Stewart, L. (2007). Delayed-onset posttraumatic stress disorder: A systematic review of the evidence. *American Journal of Psychiatry, 164,* 1319–1326.

Andrews, B., Brewin, C. R., & Rose, S. (2003). Gender, social support, and PTSD in victims of violent crime. *Journal of Traumatic Stress, 16,* 421–427.

Barnes, J. K. (1870). *Medical and surgical history of the war of rebellion, 1861–1865.* Washington, DC: Government Printing Office.

Bonanno, G. A., Westphal, M., & Mancini, A. D. (2011). Resilience to loss and potential trauma. *Annual Review of Clinical Psychology, 7,* 1.1–1.25.

Breslau, N., & Davis, G. C. (1987). Posttraumatic stress disorder: The stressor criterion. *Journal of Nervous and Mental Disease, 175,* 255–264.

Breslau, N., Davis, G. C., Andreski, P., & Peterson, E. (1991). Traumatic events and posttraumatic stress disorder in an urban population of young adults. *Archives of General Psychiatry, 48,* 216–222.

Breslau, N., Kessler, R. C., Chilcoat, H. D., Schultz, L. R., Davis, G. C., & Andreski, P. (1998). Trauma and posttraumatic stress disorder in the community: The 1996 Detroit area survey of trauma. *Archives of General Psychiatry, 55,* 626–632.

Breslau, N., Peterson, E. L., & Schultz, L. R. (2008). A second look at prior trauma and the posttraumatic stress disorder effects of subsequent trauma: A prospective epidemiological study. *Archives of General Psychiatry, 65,* 431–437.

Brewin, C. R., Lanius, R. A., Novac, A., Schnyder, U., & Galea, S. (2009). Reformulating PTSD for *DSM-V:* Life after Criterion A. *Journal of Traumatic Stress, 22,* 366–373.

Bryant, R. A. (2010). Treating the full range of posttraumatic reactions. In G. M. Rosen & B. C. Frueh (Eds.), *Clinician's guide to postttraumatic stress disorder* (pp. 205–234). Hoboken, NJ: Wiley.

Burgess, A. W., & Holmstrom, L. L. (1974). Rape trauma syndrome. *American Journal of Psychiatry, 131,* 981–986.

Davidson, J. R. T., Hughes, D., Blazer, D. G., & George, L. K. (1991). Post-traumatic stress disorder in the community: An epidemiological study. *Psychological Medicine, 21,* 713–721.

Dohrenwend, B. P. (2010). Toward a typology of high-risk major stressful events and stituations in posttraumatic stress disorder and related psychopathology. *Psychological Injury and Law, 3,* 89–99.

Dohrenwend, B. P., Turner, J. B., Turse, N., Adams, B. G., Koenan, K. C., & Marshall, R. (2006). The psychological risks of Vietnam for U.S. veterans: A revisit with new data and methods. *Science, 313,* 979–982.

Elhai, J. D., Biehn, T. L., Armour, C., Klopper, J. J., Frueh, B. C., & Palmieri, P. A. (2011). Evidence for a unique PTSD construct represented by PTSD's D1–D3 symptoms. *Journal of Anxiety Disorders, 25,* 340–345.

Elhai, J. D., Grubaugh, A. L., Kashdan, T. B., & Frueh, B. C. (2008). Empirical examination of a proposed refinement to *DSM-IV* posttraumatic stress disorder symptom criteria using the National Comorbidity Survey Replication data. *Journal of Clinical Psychiatry, 69,* 597–602.

Elhai, J. D., North, T. C., & Frueh, B. C. (2005). Health service use predictors among trauma survivors: A critical review. *Psychological Services, 2,* 3–19.

Elhai, J. D., & Palmieri, P. A. (2011). The factor structure of posttraumatic stress disorder: A literature update, critique of methodology, and agenda for future research. *Journal of Anxiety Disorders, 25,* 849–854.

Ford, J. D., Elhai, J. D., Ruggiero, K. J., & Frueh, B. C. (2009). Refining the posttraumatic stress disorder diagnosis: Evaluation of symptom criteria with the National Survey of Adolescents. *Journal of Clinical Psychiatry, 70,* 748–755.

Frueh, B. C., Grubaugh, A. L., Elhai, J. D., & Buckley, T. C. (2007). U.S. Department of Veterans Affairs disability policies for PTSD: Administrative trends and implications for treatment, rehabilitation, and research. *American Journal of Public Health, 97,* 2143–2145.

Frueh, B. C., Grubaugh, A. L., Yeager, D. E., & Magruder, K. M. (2009). Delayed-onset posttraumatic stress disorder among veterans in primary care clinics. *British Journal of Psychiatry, 194,* 515–520.

Galea, S., Ahern, J., Resnick, H., Kilpatrick, D., Bucuvalas, M., Gold, J., & Vlahov, D. (2002). Psychological sequelae of the September 11 terrorist attacks in New York City. *New England Journal of Medicine, 346,* 982−987.

Grubaugh, A. L., Long, M. E., Elhai, J. D., Frueh, B. C., & Magruder, K. M. (2010). An examination of the construct validity of posttraumatic stress disorder with veterans using a revised criterion set. *Behaviour Research and Therapy, 48,* 909−914.

Jones, E., & Wessely, S. (2007). A paradigm shift in the conceptualization of psychological trauma in the 20th century. *Journal of Anxiety Disorders, 21,* 164−175.

Kessler, R. C., Sonnega, A., Bromet, E., Hughes, M., & Nelson, C. B. (1995). Posttraumatic stress disorder in the National Comorbidity Survey. *Archives of General Psychiatry, 52,* 1048−1060.

Kilpatrick, D. G., Resnick, H. S., & Acierno, R. (2009). Should PTSD Criterion A be retained? *Journal of Traumatic Stress, 22,* 374−383.

King, D. W., Leskin, G. A., King, L. A., & Weathers, F. W. (1998). Confirmatory factor analysis of the Clinician-Administered PTSD Scale: Evidence for the dimensionality of posttraumatic stress disorder. *Psychological Assessment, 10,* 90−96.

Koenen, K. C. (2007). Genetics of posttraumatic stress disorder: Review and recommendations for future studies. *Journal of Traumatic Stress, 20,* 737−750.

Long, M. E., & Elhai, J. D. (2009). Posttraumatic stress disorder's traumatic stressor criterion: History, controversy, clinical and legal implications. *Psychological Injury and Law, 2,* 167−178.

McHugh, P. R., & Treisman, G. (2007). PTSD: A problematic diagnostic category. *Journal of Anxiety Disorders, 21,* 211−222.

McNally, R. J. (2003). *Remembering trauma.* Cambridge, MA: Belknap Press of Harvard University Press.

Mezey, G., & Robbins, I. (2001). Usefulness and validity of post-traumatic stress disorder as a psychiatric category. *British Medical Journal, 323,* 561−563.

Nathan, D. (2011). *Sybil exposed: The extraordinary story behind the famous multiple personality case.* New York, NY: Free Press.

Norris, F. H. (1992). Epidemiology of trauma: Frequency and impact of different potentially traumatic events on different demographic groups. *Journal of Consulting and Clinical Psychology, 60,* 409−418.

Rosen, G. M., & Frueh, B. C. (2010). *Clinician's guide to posttraumatic stress disorder.* Hoboken, NJ: Wiley.

Rosen, G. M., Frueh, B. C., Elhai, J. D., Grubaugh, A. L., & Ford, J. D. (2010). Posttraumatic stress disorder and general stress studies. In G. M. Rosen & B. C. Frueh (eds), *Clinician's guide to posttraumatic stress disorder* (pp. 3−31). Hoboken, NJ: Wiley.

Rosen, G. M., & Lilienfeld, S. O. (2008). Posttraumatic stress disorder: An empirical analysis of core assumptions. *Clinical Psychology Review, 28,* 837−868.

Rosen, G. M., Lilienfeld, S. O., Frueh, B. C., McHugh, P. R., & Spitzer, R. L. (2010). Reflections on PTSD's future in *DSM-5*. *British Journal of Psychiatry, 197*, 343–344.

Rothbaum, B. O., Foa, E. B., Riggs, D. S., Murdock, T., & Walsh, W. (1992). A prospective examination of post-traumatic stress disorder in rape victims. *Journal of Traumatic Stress, 5,* 455–475.

Satel, S. L., & Frueh, B. C. (2009). Sociopolitical aspects of psychiatry: Posttraumatic stress disorder (pp. 728–733). In B. J. Sadock, V. A. Sadock, & P. Ruiz (Eds.), *Comprehensive textbook of psychiatry* (9th ed.). Baltimore, MD: Lippincott Williams & Wilkins.

Schnurr, P. P., & Green, B. L. (Eds.). (2004). *Trauma and health: Physical health consequences of exposure to extreme stress.* Washington, DC: American Psychological Association.

Shephard, B. (2001). *A war of nerves: Soldiers and psychiatrists in the twentieth century.* Cambridge, MA: Harvard University Press.

Shephard, B. (2004). Risk factors and PTSD: A historian's perspective. In G. M. Rosen (Ed.), *Posttraumatic stress disorder: Issues and controversies* (pp. 39–61). Chichester, U.K. Wiley.

Simms, L. J., Watson, D., & Doebbeling, B. N. (2002). Confirmatory factor analyses of posttraumatic stress symptoms in deployed and nondeployed veterans of the Gulf War. *Journal of Abnormal Psychology, 111*, 637–647.

Smith, T. C., Ryan, M. A. K., Wingard, D. L., Slymen, D. J., Sallis J. F., & Kritz-Silverstein, D. (2008). New onset and persistent symptoms of post-traumatic stress disorder self reported after deployment and combat exposures: Prospective population based US military cohort study. *British Medical Journal, 336*, 366–371.

Spitzer, R. L., First, M. B., & Wakefield, J. C. (2007). Saving PTSD from itself in *DSM-V. Journal of Anxiety Disorders, 21*, 233–241.

Summerfield, D. (2001). The invention of post-traumatic stress disorder and the social usefulness of a psychiatric category. *British Medical Journal, 322*, 95–98.

Taylor, S., Frueh, B. C., & Asmundson, G. J. G. (2007). Detection and management of malingering in people presenting for treatment of posttraumatic stress disorder: Methods, obstacles, and recommendations. *Journal of Anxiety Disorders, 21*, 22–41.

Tolin, D. F., & Foa, E. B. (2006). Sex differences in trauma and posttraumatic stress disorder: A quantitative review of 25 years of research. *Psychological Bulletin, 132*, 959–992.

Walker, L. E. (1977). Battered women and learned helplessness. *Victimology, 2*, 525–534.

Watson, D. (2005). Rethinking the mood and anxiety disorders: A quantitative hierarchical model for *DSM-V. Journal of Abnormal Psychology, 114*, 522–536.

Weathers, F. W., & Keane, T. M. (2007). The criterion A problem revisited: Controversies and challenges in defining and measuring psychological trauma. *Journal of Traumatic Stress, 20*, 107–121.

Wessely, S., & Jones, E. (2004). Psychiatry and the "lessons of Vietnam": What were they, and are they still relevant? *War & Society, 22,* 89–103.

Worthen, M. D., & Moering, R. G. (2011). A practical guide to conducting VA compensation and pension exams for PTSD and other mental disorders. *Psychological Injury and Law, 4*(3–4), 187–216.

Yufik, T., & Simms, L. J. (2010). A meta-analytic investigation of the structure of posttraumatic stress disorder. *Journal of Abnormal Psychology, 119,* 764–776.

CHAPTER 2

Using Evidence-Based Practices

As with every other sector of health care, there is now a widespread recognition that mental health care requires practice standards and professional accountability that are rooted in empirical evidence—that is, evidence-based practices, or EBPs, as we shall call them from here on (Frueh, Ford, Elhai, & Grubaugh, 2012; Institute of Medicine & National Research Council, 2001; Kazdin, 2008). EBPs and empirically supported treatments are a critical element of treatment standards for both child and adult mental health services (American Psychological Association, Presidential Task Force on Evidence-Based Practice, 2006; Barlow, 2000; Spring et al., 2008). Unfortunately, it is also well known that interventions used in clinical behavioral and mental health practice settings are not always carefully based on the best available empirical evidence (Cook, Schnurr, & Foa, 2004; Ferrell, 2009; Frueh, Cusack, Grubaugh, Sauvageot, & Wells, 2006; Gray, Elhai, & Schmidt, 2007; Henggeler, Sheidow, Cunningham, Donohue, & Ford, 2008; Stewart & Chambless, 2007). This very common problem is sometimes referred to as the *research-to-practice gap*. One of the goals of this book is to help reduce this "gap."

Over the remainder of this chapter we provide a brief—and hopefully painless—overview of EBP as it pertains to mental health care. We realize that many clinicians' eyes glaze over as they contemplate the ever-expanding alphabet soup of acronyms (e.g., CBT, PE, ACT, DBT, CPT, TMT) denoting the latest and greatest clinical intervention for this or that population or disorder. And while we are, perhaps, somewhat guilty ourselves of adding to this list with our own research activities, we are also exceedingly sympathetic to the sense of bewilderment, frustration, and anxiety experienced by many practitioners in regard to this topic.

Indeed, it can be quite difficult to follow all the latest developments in the field, let alone know where even to begin in selecting assessment instruments and treatment approaches. Nevertheless, we hope that over the next few pages, we will succeed in presenting not only a sufficient rationale for EBPs, but also a sensible and flexible approach to viewing and understanding the concept—and, of course, the remainder of this book is then intended to flesh out a wide range of evidence-based strategies relevant to the clinical assessment and treatment planning for posttraumatic stress disorder (PTSD).

EVIDENCE-BASED PRACTICE—WHAT IS IT AND WHY SHOULD WE CARE?

Certainly, we are all familiar with the notion that it is generally good in life to look for information to guide our decisions, especially the important ones. For example, who would buy a car, choose a vacation destination, or accept a new job without first attempting to make some sort of appraisal of the various options available? In fact, we live in a technological world, in which nearly every product for sale on the Internet comes with ratings made by individuals who bought these products, and many people use these ratings to inform their shopping decisions. Of course, virtually everyone seeks out some information to help guide their decision making. But how does one decide what information is most relevant or important?

In the case of a new automobile, there is an array of different information that might influence one's decisions: television commercials showing shiny new models; prior experience with a particular brand; observations made while driving of how other vehicles look or seem to perform; product reviews published in industry or consumer magazines; newspaper headlines about product recalls or problems; and so on. It is very likely that our decision will be influenced by several, if not most, of these sources of information. Yet, when we think about it, we realize that some of these sources deserve to be weighted heavier than others, while some pieces of information will raise doubts and questions that warrant further research on the matter before they can be resolved. For instance, while television advertisements may catch our attention and plant the seed of an attractive idea, and they may make appealing product claims, the savvy shopper will use this as a starting point. Do those "run-flat" tires really work well in practice? Does that mid-sized SUV really get 30 miles to the gallon? Does that shiny little sports car have good reliability? The savvy shopper will look for credible data—evidence—to answer these important questions as well as possible.

The search for evidence to guide decision making in buying a new automobile is not unlike the search for evidence to guide clinical decision making. And why are EBPs so critical to PTSD, other posttraumatic reactions, and the trauma field in general? The answer is that, in part, the mental health care field in general has come a little late to the EBP table. In order to align with standards in health care, expectations of patients and their families, standards of regulatory and licensing bodies, legal standards, and practices of insurance companies, mental health care practitioners should consider taking an EBP approach. More specifically, within the field of PTSD treatment, there is a long past history of harmful misconceptions and use of dubious treatment practices. Many well-intentioned interventions, both medications and psychotherapy, have produced findings of limited efficacy, no efficacy, or even outright harmful results for patients and their families. Often, new therapies are developed without a sound theoretical rationale and then disseminated before they have been evaluated adequately in clinical trials. A group of such treatments came to be known as the *power therapies*. These included thought-field therapy, the counting method, emotional freedom techniques, visual—kinesthetic dissociation, and several others—all with fantastic claims of nearly immediate and miraculous efficacy, and some of which are extremely financially expensive for clinicians to adopt. Not surprisingly, there is no empirically rigorous research—subjected to peer review—to support the use of these "therapies." This history should serve to remind practicing clinicians that they will serve their patients best by relying on empirically supported methods and practices (Cukor, Spitalnik, Difede, Rizzo, & Rothbaum, 2009).

At a recent clinical workshop for community practitioners, one of the authors had the following exchange with a member of the audience:

Audience Member: I'm not interested in the cognitive or behavioral therapies you've been talking about. Could you please tell us about some of the more exciting power therapies for PTSD?

Speaker: I'm not sure what you're referring to.

Audience Member: You know, the power therapies, like thought-field therapy.

Speaker: Well, I'm afraid I don't know much about the power therapies. The reason I've been talking about cognitive–behavioral therapies is that they are the interventions with the most, and best, scientific evidence of clinical efficacy for patients with PTSD.

Audience Member: Just because there is no evidence, doesn't mean a therapy is not effective.

Speaker: True . . . but it raises the question of why you would use an intervention for which there is no evidence, no research, and no data in support of its efficacy, especially when there are interventions that have been proven to work.

Audience Member: Researchers are biased.

Speaker: Maybe so. But we still have to look for the best possible evidence to guide our clinical decision making, right? If there is no evidence to support a treatment, then how can we justify using it?

Audience Member: But we already know they work!

Speaker: How do you know?

Audience Member: We just know. I've attended workshops; I've heard testimonials.

Speaker: That's a good place to start—but is it the best available evidence? How scientifically rigorous is it? How do they compare to the randomized controlled trials that have been conducted?

To define it more formally, EBP represents an approach to identify and appraise the best available scientific data in order to guide the choice of assessment and treatment practices. This involves making decisions about what data to review and how to identify it, and how to best integrate scientific evidence with clinical practice in the "real world." Clinicians must make a wide range of decisions, large and small, taking account of the many different practice settings, populations, providers, and other contextual variables that they face in their work. A variety of terms and definitions of EBP have been proposed by different people, many of them working in different fields from each other. Some people have suggested that the formal designation of a given intervention as an EBP requires strong empirical support from at least two randomized controlled trials (RCTs) that have been conducted by researchers who are independent from the development of the treatment, or seven to nine smaller experimental design studies, each with at least three subjects conducted by at least two independent researchers (Chambless & Hollon, 1998). These requirements were proposed in order to define specific treatment models as empirically supported treatments (ESTs). ESTs are a subcategory of EBP that focuses on specific treatment models, typically those that have been developed into clinician manuals, for which very good scientific evidence of either efficacy or effectiveness exists.

There are also other approaches to understanding EBPs. Some health care experts have pointed to the value of expert consensus panels, meta-analyses, and Cochrane database reviews to overcome the potential biases of individual or critical reviews (Spring et al., 2008). Also, national governments and some health insurance companies have developed very detailed EBP guidelines for the treatment of psychiatric disorders. Good examples of these in the trauma field are the United Kingdom's National Institute for Health and Clinical Excellence (NICE, 2005) and the United States' Institute of Medicine and National Research Council (2007) guidelines for treating PTSD and other posttraumatic disorders. These have been developed in order to guide (or mandate) efficacious mental health care practices.

In addition, the term *EBP* does not necessarily require, or even imply, the specific designation of particular treatment models as "evidence based." An alternative way to conceptualize EBP is to place less emphasis on intervention protocols or manualized treatments, and instead focus on empirically supported content-domain practice elements (Chorpita, Daleiden, & Weisz, 2005; Rosen & Davison, 2003). Such general practice elements might include the development of a therapeutic working alliance and enhancing patient motivation, teaching of skills for coping with severe psychiatric symptoms, or helping a patient to better process and manage distressing emotions.

In addition to all that we have described here, formal scientific data is not necessarily the only basis for determining what constitutes EBP. The American Psychological Association's Presidential Task Force on EBP (2006) proposed requiring evidence from clinicians' real-world observations and from client values and preferences. This is similar to what *Consumer Reports* obtains and presents in the course of their product reviews—including several past reviews of mental health practices. Placing value on these sources of information reflects an attempt to ensure that EBP not only produces quantifiable outcomes (e.g., results of scientific studies), but also will be of practical use for clinicians working in a variety of real-world clinical settings (First et al., 2003) and will be acceptable to (and respectful of) the recipients of these services.

Regardless of evidentiary parameters that are required to establish a mental or behavioral health practice as "evidence-based," EBP must be defined and presented in terms of very behaviorally specific practices that can be readily and reliably taught to clinicians so that they are able to use them in the ways intended. Treatment models and trans–theoretical practice elements involve a range of competencies that need to be operationalized and replicable. As Spring et al. (2008) noted, practitioner competencies for EBPs fall into four general areas: (1) assessment skills, (2) process skills (i.e., enhancing client motivation and the clinician–client "working alliance"), (3) communication skills for collaborative decision making, and (4) intervention skills.

There are two other concepts, alluded to earlier and related to EBPs, that are worth mentioning at this point: dissemination and implementation. *Dissemination* is the carefully focused distribution of scientific evidence and materials related to an intervention, practice, or clinical population to the relevant group of people who can make use of it (e.g., clinicians, administrators). *Implementation* refers to the specific strategies used to ensure successful adoption of any particular disseminated EBPs and integration into actual practice within clinical settings. Note that the conceptual framework provided by EBP allows for improved communication among professionals and disciplines, which hopefully—and ultimately—facilitates the effective dissemination and implementation of the very best available clinical practices.

THE PROCESS OF EVIDENCE-BASED PRACTICE

Because EBP is multifaceted, deriving and accumulating data from many different kinds of sources and disciplines, it also is constantly evolving as empirical knowledge is gained. Therefore, it should be obvious by now that EBP is not static, but instead is an ongoing process. This process, a central tenet of EBP, involves several steps (as perhaps best outlined by Spring et al., 2008):

1. **Ask** patient-centered questions that are relevant at the individual, community, or even the population level. For example: (a) Who are the patients with PTSD who do *not* respond favorably to relaxation training, and how can we adapt it to overcome the problems experienced by some patients? (b) What are the core symptoms of PTSD in children that should be addressed first? (c) What modifications in current treatment practices with combat veterans might increase the pace at which change occurs, in order to relieve their suffering and increase their functioning in the most timely and least costly manner?
2. **Identify and acquire** the best available scientific evidence to address these relevant questions. The evidence should include results of scientifically rigorous research (if it exists), observations of how clinicians deliver services, and preferences of patients that are relevant to effectively engaging and motivating them in treatment.
3. **Appraise the evidence critically** in order to make appropriate decisions about what and how best to implement in practice.
4. **Apply the evidence in practice**, taking into account a wide range of contextual and other relevant factors such as limitations in the available science, clinical context, patient values and preferences, and resources available.
5. **Assess outcomes**, adjust in an ongoing manner, and eventually disseminate if and when appropriate.

Appraising the Evidence in Evidence-Based Practice

Let's go back to step 3 in the preceding section. How should clinicians appraise the evidence, and what evidence should they look to? Since the goal is to make the most effective practice decisions for our patients, we should try to identify the best available empirical evidence. Once we have accomplished that, the evidence must then be critically appraised and integrated with other evidence that we have. Relevant data can take many forms, including single cases, time series, open trials, randomized clinical trials, meta-analyses, and consensus panels or agency guidelines.

Single-Case, Time Series, Open Trials

Case studies or small, nonrandomized treatment studies are often early first steps in the development and evaluation of new interventions or the application of established interventions to new populations or novel service delivery methods (such as psychotherapy offered online or through videoconferencing). Reports of this kind may provide valuable information about the feasibility of an intervention, acceptance of the intervention by patients and providers, and its potential for efficacy. Yes, by themselves, these types of reports rarely provide sufficient evidence to support an intervention as an EBP—they are merely a step in a larger scientific process. And, in fact, it's important to be mindful of the fact that many promising case studies or open trials are later not supported by more rigorous research studies. Studies of this sort are more prone to clinician or investigator bias, chance findings, or "cherry picking" of patients most likely to be helped by other interventions.

Randomized Clinical Trials (RCTs)

The standard for acknowledging an intervention as an EBP is typically at least two large randomized trials. These studies are designed to carefully control for a range of alternative factors, so that claims of causality for the treatment can be made. This is the standard required by the Food and Drug Administration (FDA) when approving medications for use with specific disorders. There are a number of important elements one can consider when evaluating the quality and applicability of an RCT (Borkovec & Castonguay, 1998; Chambless & Hollon, 1998). These include: (a) the study design itself;

(b) measures and outcome variables; (c) sample characteristics and size (also known as power); (d) clinician characteristics; (e) data analyses; (f) results and effect sizes (both statistical and clinical significance are important); and (g) any potential side effects or adverse event outcomes. Also see the Consolidated Standards for Reporting of Trials (CONSORT) statement, which was developed to ensure the quality of RCT reporting (Begg et al., 1996; CONSORT, 2009).

Clinical trials are often classified according to phase (I to IV). This is based on a system originally developed for medical and pharmaceutical studies. A Phase I clinical trial involves testing a treatment model or practice with a relatively small number of recipients. In pharmacotherapy research, this tends to range between 20 and 80 patients, all of whom who are assessed before and after the treatment in order to establish whether the treatment is safe and whether it is associated with sufficient benefits to warrant additional testing. Phase I clinical trials also may test different variations of the treatment, such as fewer or more sessions (comparable to the "dose" of a medicine), and the "mechanisms" by which the treatment achieves outcomes. Phase II clinical trials test the "efficacy" of a treatment by rigorously comparing its outcomes to those of usual clinical care (often known as *treatment as usual*) or relatively innocuous conditions that control for alternative possible sources of improvement. This is comparable to a placebo condition often used in medical research. Phase III trials of "effectiveness" are designed to test whether the intervention works outside of the laboratory in real-world practice settings (Frueh, Monnier, Elhai, Grubaugh, & Knapp, 2004). These studies may include a comparison with the best available alternative treatment, careful monitoring of side effects, and follow-up assessments to determine if the benefits are sustained over time. Finally, Phase IV trials represent postmarketing studies that are geared toward gathering more information about the risks, benefits, and optimal use of a given intervention, and are most common in pharmaceutical research.

Critical Reviews, Meta-Analyses, Consensus Panels, and Agency Guidelines

In additional to individual research studies, literature reviews can provide objective efforts to critically or quantifiably (e.g., meta-analyses) summarize and synthesize a large number of RCTs. Literature reviews can also help summarize what types of studies have been conducted and organize evidence to address a range of potential questions that extend beyond those addressed by a single RCT. This may include evaluation of short- and long-term efficacy, efficacy for specific subgroups (e.g., minorities), effectiveness in practice settings, comparisons across multiple interventions, research limitations and gaps in the extant literature that have yet to be studied, and directions for future research activities.

Keeping Up With the Scientific Literature

Our scientific knowledge is ever accumulating, growing, and advancing. New treatments and clinical practices are constantly under development in the mental and behavioral health field, with research supporting their efficacy and effectiveness often emerging quite rapidly. Therefore, staying true to the principles of EBP requires continuous effort. Most clinicians understand this, obviously, and it is the basis for "continuing education" requirements in the licensing standards of virtually every single mental health care discipline.

What About Cultural Competence in EBP?

By definition, the concept of EBP requires absolute respect for diversity and knowledge about the limitations of EBPs as they pertain to all special populations, ethnoracial groups, and cultural contexts (Spring et al., 2008; Whaley & Davis, 2007). Historically, ethnoracial minorities and many other groups of people (e.g., lesbian, gay, bisexual, and transgender; adults with severe mental illnesses; people living in rural areas; people with comorbid psychiatric disorders; prisoners) have not been very well represented in university-based clinical trials for mental health interventions. As a result, legitimate concerns have been raised about the validity of EBPs for many groups of people, and clinicians often question whether EBP standards are even relevant for a significant percentage of people.

Clinicians often have concerns regarding the appropriateness of EBPs for many patients. They may worry that interventions are not culturally competent, that there is the risk of compromising the therapeutic relationship when using potentially inflexible or "sterile" treatment manuals, that unique individual patient needs are not being met, that treatment credibility is undermined by a formulaic approach, and that service provision trends may reflect the interests of administrators or payers of services rather than their patients (Barlow, Levitt, & Bufka, 1999; Frueh et al., 2006; Hoagwood, Burns, Kiser, Ringeisen, & Schoenwald, 2001). This is certainly fair up to a point. There is no question that we need further research with more of the groups traditionally left out of clinical trials of interventions, and more of that work is currently being conducted around the world, in a wide variety of clinical settings. However, it is simply not feasible to conduct treatment outcome studies for every possible configuration of intervention, comorbidity, practice setting, and ethnoracial or cultural group. In fact, it is not even necessary. There is great value in using theoretically sound and empirically supported interventions for all groups as a starting point, at least. We do have to start somewhere, after all. So it makes sense, in the case of each individual patient, to start with the best available data to inform clinical decision making in their care.

What does this mean? It means that it is important to follow the EBP process outlined earlier: reviewing, synthesizing, and adapting the best available empirical data to make contextualized practice decisions that take into account limitations of the existing knowledge base and the unique needs and perspectives of each patient. Moreover, we believe that the perspectives of cultural competence and EBP are actually quite complementary to each other in that they each emphasize the importance of thoughtfully, and flexibly, adapting interventions from clinical trials for use with specific populations and clinical contexts (Whaley & Davis, 2007). In this view, available empirical data represent a foundation that all intervention efforts should be based on. Treatment manuals are not "cookbooks," and they do not provide a "step-by-step" guide that can be used rotely with *any* patient. Instead, they must always be tailored and refined—based on theory and evidence—usually on an ongoing basis, as needed to ensure that they are sensitive to and appropriate for each patient. This process requires taking into account relevant ethnic and cultural aspects of each patient's life—it requires being culturally competent.

In Conclusion

Thanks to more than 30 years of research on posttraumatic reactions, mental health clinicians now have the opportunity to benefit from relevant empirical data that can inform (at least partially) virtually every aspect of clinical assessment and treatment planning for people who have experienced significant trauma in their life. EBPs provide a common vocabulary and conceptual framework that can facilitate both research and high-quality practice in mental health care across the different disciplines involved, and this is especially important for the trauma field, which has been plagued by misconceptions, poor science, and pseudoscience since the early 20th century. EBPs are not a one-size-fits-all mandate for how to treat any given patient. In fact, as we described earlier, it is best to view evidence-based practice as an ongoing process that requires constant adaptation and refinement so as to ensure that interventions are relevant and effective for each individual patient. This framework and associated processes can help reduce the famous "gap" between research and practice, ensuring that patients receive the best possible care.

In the chapters that follow, we will address general issues in working with trauma survivors, specific assessment approaches for PTSD and other posttraumatic reactions, assessment of common comorbid psychiatric disorders, and ethnocultural and forensic considerations. We also include chapters on specific populations, including children and adolescents, veterans, and other underserved and understudied groups. We conclude the volume with chapters on treatment planning and patient feedback, treatment follow-up evaluations, and consideration of the future of PTSD in the *Diagnostic and Statistical Manual of Mental Disorders (DSM)* and new directions in the field of traumatology. We hope you enjoy the book and find it to be a valuable aid to your clinical practice.

References

American Psychological Association, Presidential Task Force on Evidence-Based Practice. (2006). Evidence-based practice in psychology. *American Psychologist, 61,* 271−285.

Barlow, D. H. (2000). Evidence-based practice: A world view. *Clinical Psychology: Science and Practice, 7,* 241−242.

Barlow, D. H., Levitt, J. T., & Bufka, L. F. (1999). The dissemination of empirically supported treatments: A view to the future. *Behaviour Research and Therapy, 37,* S147–S162.

Begg, C. B., Cho, M. K., Eastwood, S., Horton, R., Moher, D., Olkin, I., . . . Stroup, D. F. (1996). Improving the quality of reporting of randomized controlled trials: The CONSORT statement. *Journal of the American Medical Association, 276,* 637–639.

Borkovec, T. D., & Castonguay, L. G. (1998). What is the scientific meaning of empirically supported therapy? *Journal of Consulting and Clinical Psychology, 66,* 136–142.

Chambless, D. L., & Hollon, S. D. (1998). Defining empirically supported treatments. *Journal of Consulting and Clinical Psychology, 66,* 7–18.

Chorpita, B. F., Daleiden, E. L., & Weisz, J. R. (2005). Identifying and selecting the common elements of evidence-based interventions: A distillation and matching model. *Mental Health Services Research, 7,* 5–20.

Consolidated Standards for Reporting of Trials. (2009). Retrieved from www.consortstatement.org/

Cook, J. J., Schnurr, P. P., & Foa, E. B. (2004). Bridging the gap between posttraumatic stress disorder research and clinical practice: The example of exposure therapy. *Psychotherapy: Theory, Research, Practice, Training, 41,* 374–387.

Cukor, J., Spitalnick, J., Difede, J., Rizzo, A., & Rothbaum, B. O. (2009). Emerging treatments for PTSD. *Clinical Psychology Review, 29,* 715–726.

Ferrell, C. B. (2009). Reengineering clinical research science: A focus on translational research. *Behavior Modification, 23,* 7–23.

First, M., Pincus, H., Levine, J., Williams, J., Ustun, B., & Peele, R. (2003). Clinical utility as a criterion for revising psychiatric diagnoses. *American Journal of Psychiatry, 161,* 946–954.

Frueh, B. C., Cusack, K. J., Grubaugh, A. L., Sauvageot, J. A., & Wells, C. (2006). Clinician perspectives on cognitive-behavioral treatment for PTSD among public-sector consumers with severe mental illness. *Psychiatric Services, 57,* 1027–1031.

Frueh, B. C., Ford, J. D., Elhai, J. D., & Grubaugh, A. L. (2012). An overview of evidence-based practice in adult mental health. In P. Sturmey and M. Hersen (Eds.), *Handbook of evidence-based practice in clinical psychology: Vol. II. Adult disorders.* Hoboken, NJ: Wiley.

Frueh, B. C., Monnier, J., Elhai, J. D., Grubaugh, A. L., & Knapp, R. G. (2004). Telepsychiatry treatment outcome research methodology: Efficacy versus effectiveness. *Telemedicine Journal and E-Health, 10,* 455–458.

Gray, M. J., Elhai, J. D., & Schmidt, L. O. (2007). Trauma professionals' attitudes towards and utilization of evidence-based practices. *Behavior Modification, 31,* 732–748.

Henggeler, S. W., Sheidow, A. J., Cunningham, P. B., Donohue, B. C., & Ford, J. D. (2008). Promoting the implementation of an evidence-based intervention for adolescent marijuana abuse in community settings: Testing the use of intensive quality assurance. *Journal of Clinical Child and Adolescent Psychology, 37*, 682—689.

Hoagwood, K., Burns, B. J., Kiser, L., Ringeisen, H., & Schoenwald, S. K. (2001). Evidence-based practice in child and adolescent mental health services. *Psychiatric Services, 52*, 1179—1189.

Institute of Medicine & National Research Council. (2001). *Crossing the quality chasm: A new health system for the 21st century.* Washington, DC: National Academies Press.

Institute of Medicine & National Research Council. (2007). *Treatment of posttraumatic stress disorder: An assessment of the evidence.* Washington, DC: National Academies Press.

Kazdin, A. (2008). Evidence-based treatment and practice: New opportunities to bridge clinical research and practice, enhance the knowledge base, and improve patient care. *American Psychologist, 63*, 146—159.

National Institute for Health and Clinical Excellence. (2005). *The management of post traumatic stress disorder in primary and secondary care.* London: Author.

Rosen, G. M., & Davison, G. C. (2003). Psychology should list empirically supported principles of change (ESPs) and not credential trademarked therapies or other treatment packages. *Behavior Modification, 27*, 300—312.

Spring, B., Walker, B., Brownson, R., Mullen, E., Newhouse, R., Satterfield, J., . . . Hitchcock, K. (2008). *Definition and competencies for evidence-based behavioral practice (EBBP).* Chicago, IL: Council for Training in Evidence-Based Behavioral Practice.

Stewart, R. E., & Chambless, D. L. (2007). Does psychotherapy research inform treatment decisions in private practice? *Journal of Clinical Psychology, 63*, 267—281.

Whaley, A. L., & Davis, K. E. (2007). Cultural competence and evidence-based practice in mental health services: A complementary perspective. *American Psychologist, 62*, 563—574.

CHAPTER 3

Working With Trauma Survivors

In this chapter, we describe clinical considerations that are essential to the assessment and treatment planning of posttraumatic stress disorder (PTSD) and posttraumatic reactions. First, guidelines for the assessment and clinical interpretation of client's histories of exposure to psychological trauma will be discussed. These include the role and nature of trauma history in PTSD assessment and treatment planning, and distinguishing trauma history versus PTSD and posttraumatic reactions. Second, important considerations will be discussed for the assessment and clinical interpretation of PTSD symptoms and the full and subthreshold syndrome of PTSD, as well as other traumatic stress-related symptoms, disorders, and syndromes. The chapter concludes with a discussion of issues related to the communication of assessment findings to clients, other professionals, and third parties (e.g., legal authorities, insurers, child protective services). The guidelines for assessment of trauma recently formulated by the American Psychological Association's Division of Trauma Psychology (APA Guidelines; Armstrong et al., 2011) will be referred to in order to inform readers based on the most current thinking of clinical experts on the assessment of traumatic stress and PTSD (see Table 3.1).

ASSESSING TRAUMA HISTORY

The first challenge for mental health, counseling, marriage and family therapy, social work, and substance abuse professionals in assessment and treatment planning for PTSD is to determine whether the client's presenting problems in fact involve traumatic stress reactions. While it is helpful to determine if a client has experienced traumatic stressors, this is necessary but *not alone sufficient* for the more fundamental determination that PTSD (or other associated traumatic stress-related symptoms) should be addressed in treatment. Thus, the first mistake with regard to PTSD that should be assiduously avoided in clinical assessment and treatment planning is to either fail to assess the client's trauma history (and thereby omit the potentially indicated follow-up assessment of PTSD) *or* to identify a trauma history and assume without further evidence that PTSD is present and requires treatment.

TABLE 3.1	**SAMPLE ITEMS FROM THE TRAUMATIC EVENTS SCREENING INSTRUMENT (TESI)**

These questions are about stressful experiences that may have happened at any time in your life. For each that has occurred to you, please indicate *how old you were* (this may be more than one age if it happened for a long time or several times) and *if you felt afraid, helpless, or horrified* at the time or soon after. You also can "pass" if you'd rather not answer.

1.1. Have you ever *been in* a really bad accident, a fall, or a fire where you could have died or been badly hurt?

0 ☐ NO
1 ☐ YES

IF YES (check **all** that apply)

1 ☐ Before you were 6 years old?
2 ☐ Before you were 18 years old?
3 ☐ Age 18 or older?
4 ☐ In the past year?

Did paramedics treat you or did you go to a hospital emergency room?

0 ☐ NO
1 ☐ YES

Did you have to stay overnight in a hospital?

0 ☐ NO
1 ☐ YES

FHH: During or afterward, did you feel intense fear, helpless, or horrified (emotionally shocked, stunned, confused, or sickened)?

☐ NO
☐ YES

1.2. Have you ever *seen* a really bad accident, a fall, or a fire where someone could have been killed or badly hurt?

0 ☐ NO

1 ☐ YES

If YES (check **all** that apply)

1 ☐ Before you were 6 years old?

2 ☐ Before you were 18 years old?

3 ☐ Age 18 or older?

4 ☐ In the past year?

FHH: During or afterward, did you feel intense fear, helpless, or horrified (emotionally shocked, stunned, confused, or sickened)?

0 ☐ NO

1 ☐ YES

1.3. Have you ever been in a life-threatening storm (like a tornado or hurricane) or severe earthquake or flood?

0 ☐ NO

1 ☐ YES

IF YES (check **all** that apply)

1 ☐ Before you were 6 years old?

2 ☐ Before you were 18 years old?

3 ☐ Age 18 or older?

4 ☐ In the past year?

FHH: During or afterward, did you feel intense fear, helpless, or horrified (emotionally shocked, stunned, confused, or sickened)?

0 ☐ NO

1 ☐ YES

1.4. Has an immediate family member, romantic partner, or someone else *you were very close to* ever died *unexpectedly*?

0 ☐ NO

1 ☐ YES

If YES, who was this?

☐ Parent

☐ Partner/spouse

☐ Other family member

☐ Other adult (teacher, clergy, etc.)

☐ Close friend

Was the death due to:

1 ☐ An accident

2 ☐ An illness

(continues on next page)

(continued)

    3 ☐ Assault or murder

    3 ☐ Suicide

    5 ☐ Other causes: _____

    When did this happen? (check all that apply)

    1 ☐ Before you were 6 years old?

    2 ☐ Before you were 18 years old?

    3 ☐ Age 18 or older?

    4 ☐ In the past year?

    FHH: During or afterward, did you feel intense fear, helpless, or horrified (emotionally shocked, stunned, confused, or sickened)?

    0 ☐ NO

    1 ☐ YES

1.5. Have you ever had a really bad illness where you could have died or been permanently physically harmed?

    0 ☐ NO

    1 ☐ YES

    IF YES (check **all** that apply)

    1 ☐ Before you were 6 years old?

    2 ☐ Before you were 18 years old?

    3 ☐ Age 18 or older?

    4 ☐ In the past year?

    Did paramedics treat you or did you go to a hospital emergency room?

    0 ☐ NO

    1 ☐ YES Did you have to stay overnight in a hospital?

    0 ☐ NO

    1 ☐ YES

    FHH: During or afterward, did you feel intense fear, helpless, or horrified (emotionally shocked, stunned, confused, or sickened)?

    0 ☐ NO

    1 ☐ YES

1.6. As a child (before age 18), were you ever completely separated from the adult(s) you felt closest to?

    0 ☐ NO

    1 ☐ YES

    IF YES:

    Who was this?

    1 ☐ Parent

      ☐ Other family member

      ☐ Other adult (teacher, clergy, etc): _____

How long were you separated?

____ months ____ years

How old were you? (check all that apply)

1 ☐ Younger than 6 years old?

2 ☐ 6–12 years old?

3 ☐ 13–17 years old?

FHH: During or afterward, did you feel intense fear, helpless, or horrified (emotionally shocked, stunned, confused, or sickened)?

0 ☐ NO

1 ☐ YES

1.7. Have you ever had a child of yours taken away from you?

0 ☐ NO

1 ☐ YES

If Yes, what year did this happen? ____

Was this done:

☐ By the police, a judge, or DCF

☐ By your spouse/partner

☐ Another family member

☐ By a stranger

FHH: During or afterward, did you feel intense fear, helpless, or horrified (emotionally shocked, stunned, confused, or sickened)?

0 ☐ NO

1 ☐ YES

Were you and your child reunited?

0 ☐ NO

1 ☐ YES

Age Code:

1 ☐ Before 18 years old

2 ☐ 18 years old or older

3 ☐ past year

2.1 Has someone ever tried to kill you or hurt you really badly? Like by attacking you with a gun, knife, or weapon? Or like by hitting you really hard or by strangling, choking, biting or burning you? Or mugged you?

0 ☐ NO

1 ☐ YES

If YES, who was this?

1 ☐ Parent

2 ☐ Partner/spouse

3 ☐ Sibling

(continues on next page)

(*continued*)

    4 ☐ Other adult family member

    5 ☐ Other adult

    6 ☐ Other child/teenager

    If YES (check all that apply)

    1 ☐ Before you were 6 years old?

    2 ☐ Before you were 18 years old?

    3 ☐ Age 18 or older?

    4 ☐ In the past year?

    FHH: During or afterward, did you feel intense fear, helpless, or horrified (emotionally shocked, stunned, confused, or sickened)?

    0 ☐ NO

    1 ☐ YES

2.2 Has someone ever said they'd kill you or hurt you really badly, and you thought they really might do it?

    0 ☐ NO

    1 ☐ YES

    If YES, who was this?

    1 ☐ Parent

    2 ☐ Partner/spouse

    3 ☐ Sibling

    4 ☐ Other adult family member

    5 ☐ Other adult

    6 ☐ Other child/teenager

    IF YES (check all that apply)

    1 ☐ Before you were 6 years old?

    2 ☐ Before you were 18 years old?

    3 ☐ Age 18 or older?

    4 ☐ In the past year?

    FHH: During or afterward, did you feel intense fear, helpless, or horrified (emotionally shocked, stunned, confused, or sickened)?

    0 ☐ NO

    1 ☐ YES

3.1 Have you ever seen or heard people *in your family* threatening, fighting, beating up, or attacking each other where you thought they might kill or really hurt each other? Or using weapons like guns or knives to hurt each other?

    0 ☐ NO

    1 ☐ YES

    If YES, who was this?

1 ☐ Parent

2 ☐ Partner/spouse

3 ☐ Sibling

4 ☐ Other adult family member

5 ☐ Other child/teen family member

If YES (check all that apply)

1 ☐ Before you were 6 years old?

2 ☐ Before you were 18 years old?

3 ☐ Age 18 or older?

4 ☐ In the past year?

FHH: During or afterward, did you feel intense fear, helpless, or horrified (emotionally shocked, stunned, confused, or sickened)?

0 ☐ NO

1 ☐ YES

3.2 Have you ever been in a close relationship with someone who made you fear for your life or feel helpless and trapped?

0 ☐ NO

1 ☐ YES

If YES, who did this?

1 ☐ Parent

2 ☐ Spouse

3 ☐ Other family member

4 ☐ Other significant adult (teacher, clergy)

5 ☐ A friend

IF YES (check all that apply)

1 ☐ Before you were 6 years old?

2 ☐ Before you were 18 years old?

3 ☐ Age 18 or older?

4 ☐ In the past year?

FHH: During or afterward, did you feel intense fear, helpless, or horrified (emotionally shocked, stunned, confused, or sickened)?

0 ☐ NO

1 ☐ YES

3.3 Were you ever emotionally shamed, humiliated, or made to feel horrible about yourself by someone close to you?

0 ☐ NO

1 ☐ YES

If YES, who did this?

(*continues on next page*)

(*continued*)

    1 ☐ Parent

    2 ☐ Spouse

    3 ☐ Other family member

    4 ☐ Other significant adult (teacher, clergy)

    5 ☐ A friend

    IF YES (check all that apply)

    1 ☐ Before you were 6 years old?

    2 ☐ Before you were 18 years old?

    3 ☐ Age 18 or older?

    4 ☐ In the past year?

    FHH: During or afterward, did you feel intense fear, helpless, or horrified (emotionally shocked, stunned, confused, or sickened)?

    0 ☐ NO

    1 ☐ YES

3.4 Have you ever had an abortion or miscarriage?

    0 ☐ NO

    1 ☐ YES

    If YES, how old were you (1st time)? _____

    2 ☐ Before you were 18 years old?

    3 ☐ Age 18 or older?

    4 ☐ In the past year?

    FHH: During or afterward, did you feel intense fear, helpless, or horrified (emotionally shocked, stunned, confused, or sickened)?

    0 ☐ NO

    1 ☐ YES

4.1 Have you ever seen or heard people *outside your family* fighting, beating up, or attacking each other where you thought they might kill or really hurt each other? Or using weapons like guns or knives to hurt each other?

    0 ☐ NO

    1 ☐ YES

    IF YES (check all that apply)

    1 ☐ Before you were 6 years old?

    2 ☐ Before you were 18 years old?

    3 ☐ Age 18 or older?

    4 ☐ In the past year?

    FHH: During or afterward, did you feel intense fear, helpless, or horrified (emotionally shocked, stunned, confused, or sickened)?

    0 ☐ NO

    1 ☐ YES

4.2 Have you ever been in a war (or in the military) and almost been killed, or seen people get badly hurt or die?

0 ☐ NO

1 ☐ YES

IF YES (check **all** that apply)

1 ☐ Before you were 6 years old?

2 ☐ Before you were 18 years old?

3 ☐ Age 18 or older?

4 ☐ In the past year?

Were you a soldier?

0 ☐ NO

1 ☐ YES

FHH: Did you feel intense fear, helpless, or horrified (shocked, stunned, confused, or sickened)?

0 ☐ NO

1 ☐ YES

4.3 Have you ever lost your home or had to permanently leave your home due to disaster, war, violence, or homelessness?

0 ☐ NO

1 ☐ YES

If YES (check all that apply)

1 ☐ Before you were 6 years old?

2 ☐ Before you were 18 years old?

3 ☐ Age 18 or older?

4 ☐ In the past year?

Was this due to a:

1 ☐ Natural disaster

2 ☐ A fire or explosion

3 ☐ War

4 ☐ Other violence _____

5 ☐ Homelessness: _____

FHH: During or afterward, did you feel intense fear, helpless, or horrified (emotionally shocked, stunned, confused, or sickened)?

0 ☐ NO

1 ☐ YES

The next question is about unwanted sexual experiences that can happen to children or adults. You may not have reported this to the police or told family or friends. The person doing this might have been a friend, a date, or even a family member.

(continues on next page)

(continued)

5.1 Has someone ever made you see or do something sexual against your wishes or when you were helpless?

0 ☐ NO

1 ☐ YES

IF YES (check all that apply)

1 ☐ Before you were 6 years old?

2 ☐ Before you were 18 years old?

3 ☐ Age 18 or older?

4 ☐ In the past year?

Who did this?

1 ☐ Parent

2 ☐ Partner/spouse

3 ☐ Sibling

4 ☐ Other adult family member

5 ☐ Other adult

6 ☐ Other child/teenager

FHH: During or afterward, did you feel intense fear, helpless, or horrified (emotionally shocked, stunned, confused, or sickened)?

0 ☐ NO

1 ☐ YES

6.1 Have there been other events where you or someone else was killed or could have died or been very badly hurt?

If these events do not fit in any of the other questions, please briefly describe:

_____

0 ☐ NO

1 ☐ YES

If YES (check all that apply)

1 ☐ Before you were 6 years old?

2 ☐ Before you were 18 years old?

3 ☐ Age 18 or older?

4 ☐ In the past year?

FHH: During or afterward, did you feel intense fear, helpless, or horrified (emotionally shocked, stunned, confused, or sickened)?

0 ☐ NO

1 ☐ YES

In the Public Domain. Copies may be obtained from Julian Ford, PhD (jford@uchc.edu).

What Is a Traumatic Stressor?

Although it may seem obvious that some types of events "must be" psychologically traumatic, in fact how to define a traumatic stressor (as opposed to other stressors or adversities) has been a point of great controversy in the mental health field for more than 30 years, since the PTSD diagnosis was first codified in the *Diagnostic and Statistical Manual of Mental Disorders* (*DSM*; American Psychiatric Association, 1980). The core features of a traumatic stressor as proposed in the most recent version of the *DSM* (www.dsm5.org) are exposure either directly or as a witness to actual or threatened death or serious injury, or to sexual violation. With two exceptions, this exposure must be firsthand. The exceptions are that (1) learning that a close relative or friend experienced an actual or threatened death or serious injury, or (2) repeatedly being exposed to gruesome evidence of death or serious injury (most typically by emergency medical, child protective services, or military personnel), may be psychologically traumatic even though the events are not directly experienced or witnessed.

Thus, in order to be considered potentially psychologically traumatic, a stressor must confront the person not only with upsetting or disturbing events or circumstances, but more specifically with the reality of death or serious physical or sexual harm. Substantial research indicates that PTSD involves neurobiological alterations associated with fear that are not found in healthy individuals or those with related anxiety or affective disorders (Heim & Nemerof, 2009; Jovanovic & Ressler, 2011). The phrase "seeing my life pass before my eyes" expresses the shocking and potentially terrifying or horrifying sense of acute recognition of the possibility of death or a permanently and painfully altered life that is the essence of traumatic stressors. Such stressors may shatter the illusions of security and invulnerability that support healthy functioning and coping with nontraumatic stressors (Updegraff, Silver, & Holman, 2008).

The technical definition of a traumatic stressor stands in contrast to the colloquial use of the term *trauma*, which includes a wider range of adverse or stressful life events. Studies have reported evidence that PTSD diagnostic prevalence and severity may be equally or more often met by people who report encountering nontraumatic stressors as by those who report exposure to traumatic stressors (reviewed in Long & Elhai, 2009). A study with children concluded that "low-magnitude" (nontraumatic) stressors should be assessed as potential contributors to PTSD because, despite being four times less likely to lead to subclinical PTSD or distressing memories than traumatic stressors, nontraumatic stressors were 4 times *more likely to occur* in a 3-month prospective period than traumatic stressors (Copeland, Keeler, Angold, & Costello, 2010). Thus, while identifying a traumatic stressor is necessary in order to establish a diagnosis of PTSD, clinicians should be alert to the possibility that PTSD symptoms may occur for people who experience stressors that are impactful despite not being traumatic.

However, the clinical significance of PTSD symptoms in the absence of a traumatic stressor has not been established. Studies comparing the neurobiology and functional impairment of persons with comparable levels of PTSD symptoms who do or do not report a traumatic event will be needed, at a minimum, before it can be determined whether "PTSD" with and without an antecedent traumatic stressor can be considered clinically equivalent. A study with representative samples of adolescents and adults found that almost all persons meeting the symptom criteria for PTSD also reported a Criterion A1 event (Kilpatrick, Resnick, & Acierno, 2009). Exposure to stressors that are not evidently traumatic may be followed by symptoms that are similar to PTSD, especially if the events involve loss in close relationships or occur to a person who has been exposed to traumatic events at other times in his or her life (reviewed in Long & Elhai, 2009). Thus, what seems to be PTSD due to nontraumatic stressors may be better understood clinically and treated therapeutically as symptoms of anxiety or dysphoria. The memory-based therapies that have the strongest evidence base for the treatment of PTSD (see below) may be less indicated in those cases than therapies aimed at enhancing anxiety or mood management.

Should Subjective Peritraumatic Distress Be Assessed?

The *DSM-5* proposes to remove the subjective component (i.e., Criterion A2: intense fear, helplessness, or horror) that was part of the *DSM-IV* definition of a traumatic stressor. Analyses of PTSD data from the National

Comorbidity Replication Study have shown that Criterion A2 was almost completely redundant with the other symptom criteria for PTSD (i.e., 98.6% of participants who met A2 also met all other PTSD symptom criteria) and minimally altered the estimated prevalence of PTSD (Karam et al., 2010). However, individuals reporting A2 subjective reactions were almost 100 times more likely to meet all other PTSD symptom criteria (9.7%) than those who did not (0.1%) (for similar findings, see Boals & Scheuttler, 2009). A prospective study of emergency room admissions found that almost one in four patients who met criteria for PTSD 3 months later did not report subjective distress sufficient to qualify for Criterion A2 soon after the event (O'Donnell, Creamer, McFarlane, Silove, & Bryant, 2010). Those persons tended to report "subthreshold" (milder) A2 reactions, other emotional reactions (e.g., anger, guilt, dissociation), or were amnesic for the injury events. Other studies have found that a different subjective reaction, peritraumatic dissociation, was more consistently predictive of subsequent PTSD than peritraumatic distress— and peritraumatic hyperarousal also was found to be predictive of PTSD in several studies (Sugar & Ford, 2012). These findings suggest that subjective peritraumatic distress as defined in the *DSM-IV* is not necessary for a diagnosis of PTSD, but that a broader range of peritraumatic emotional reactions (including distress, dissociation, and hyperarousal) should be assessed with acute survivors of psychological trauma in order to identify those persons who are at highest risk of subsequently developing PTSD.

Why Assess Trauma History?

Almost two thirds of all adults (and also children; see Chapter 7) are exposed to a traumatic stressor at some point in their lives (Breslau, 2009), and an even higher proportion of adults and children in mental health treatment have trauma histories (approaching 90% by most estimates). Thus, on a purely probability basis, it is more efficient to take the time and effort to assess trauma history than to simply assume that most treatment-seeking individuals have a trauma history and therefore should be assessed for PTSD symptoms. This is a good case for universal assessment of PTSD symptoms in mental health clinics and practices, but it is not a logical basis for omitting assessment of trauma history. Assessing trauma history provides both the client and the clinician with several types of valuable information.

In the first place, as noted previously, we do not know if PTSD symptoms in the absence of a traumatic stressor cause the same degree of functional impairment as PTSD symptoms linked to a traumatic stressor. The potentially profound difference in the biology of traumatic versus nontraumatic stressors, due to the severity of threat to life, limb, and privacy involved in traumatic stressors, suggests that even apparently identical "stress" symptoms may reflect very different biological and psychological alterations that may require different treatment interventions. As previously noted, the memory/narrative therapies that are well validated for PTSD psychotherapy may be particularly important for PTSD related to traumatic events, but they have not been tested empirically (to establish whether they are needed, as well as if they are efficacious) with PTSD symptoms related to nontraumatic stressors. Anxiety management and affect regulation models of psychotherapy that do not include memory processing may be more efficient and less stressful for clients whose "PTSD" symptoms are not associated with traumatic stressors than emotionally challenging approaches such as prolonged exposure or cognitive processing therapy.

Second, traumatic stressors take many different forms that have different types and degrees of impact on the health and functioning of survivors (Breslau, 2009; Mol et al., 2005). For example, the most prevalent types of traumatic stressors such as severe accidents or exposure to disasters tend to be less likely to lead to PTSD or other severe psychiatric disorders and chronic impairment than less common traumatic stressors such as sexual or physical violence or abuse (Breslau, 2009; Kessler, 2000). On a more nuanced basis, it is not the general type of traumatic stressor that is most associated with morbidity—both etiology and maintenance (Schnurr, Lunney, & Sengupta, 2004)—but the specific risk factors that are involved in each individual episode of exposure to traumatic stressors (e.g., temporary versus permanent loss of home and community; intentional vs. negligent vs. accidental harm). When trauma is layered on prior trauma—for example, adult domestic violence following prior experiences of childhood abuse—the cumulative impact of revictimization tends to be greater than when a trauma-naïve individual experiences a similar traumatic stressor (Duckworth & Follette, 2011).

Therefore, it is important to determine not only whether a traumatic stressor has occurred, but also its specific nature and the risk factors involved, as well as (per the earlier discussion regarding peritraumatic stress reactions) the severity of its immediate impact on the individual.

Third, an often overlooked element in a complete trauma history is the other side of the coin from traumatic stress and posttraumatic impairment: How did the individual adapt in order to cope with the threat and harm (Ford, 2009), and what personal and interpersonal resources helped protect and bolster her or his resilience or recovery (Layne et al., 2008)? "Protective" or "resilience" factors such as self-efficacy and social support (Hobfoll et al., 2007; Yehuda & Flory, 2007) are as important to assess as the nature of stressors when obtaining a trauma history. Including these more positive elements in the assessment should not be done to suggest to clients that their traumatic experiences were not as distressing or difficult to recover from as they seem, but instead to help clients to recognize and draw upon their intra- and interpersonal resources by illuminating that aspect of the traumatic circumstances as well as the trauma itself.

A fourth reason to assess trauma history is that exposure to traumatic stressors has been shown to increase the risk of many psychiatric disorders, not just PTSD (D'Andrea, Ford, Stolbach, Spinazzola, & van der Kolk, 2012; Dedert et al., 2009; Zlotnick et al., 2008). Although PTSD is commonly accompanied by comorbid psychiatric disorders (Breslau, 2009), psychiatric disorders that occur in the absence of PTSD have been found to be more likely to occur for individuals with (versus without) a history of exposure to traumatic stressors (Dedert et al., 2009; Seng, D'Andrea, & Ford, in press). When clients present with symptoms consistent with disorders other than PTSD, the role that traumatic stressors may play in the severity or chronicity of those other disorders' symptoms will be missed if trauma history is overlooked because PTSD symptoms do not seem to be apparent or prominent. This may lead to missed opportunities to utilize psychotherapies that have shown evidence of efficacy in reducing not only PTSD but also other psychiatric disorders' symptom severity (Courtois & Ford, 2009). This is the flip side of the precaution described by the APA Guidelines (point 4), which states that clinicians should always consider that symptoms that seem to be related to exposure to a traumatic stressor may be due entirely or in large part to other factors (e.g., genetic vulnerability, social learning, nontraumatic stressors). It is equally important that clinicians consider that symptoms that seem clearly to reflect a psychiatric disorder that does not appear to be due to exposure to traumatic stressors may be caused or exacerbated by past (or recent) trauma exposure.

A fifth reason to assess trauma history is for the safety of the client. As stated in point 5 of the APA Guidelines, in the process of conducting a trauma history assessment, clinicians may obtain information indicating that a client currently is exposed to ongoing traumatic stressors. This may be due to being in an abusive or violent relationship or community, which often is not discussed—or only briefly and superficially checked on (e.g., "Are you feeling unsafe in any relationship currently? Have you ever been abused?")—and overlooked as a result. A thorough trauma history provides the client with a much more specific set of questions that tend to elicit more complete disclosures by clearly defining potential types of traumatic stressors (rather than using vague terms such as "feeling unsafe" or "abuse"). This can provide a crucial opportunity for the clinician to help the client to develop realistic plans for her or his current safety.

How to Sensitively Assess Trauma History

Traumatic events are rarely, if ever, easy for a client to discuss. In fact, many clinicians report being at least somewhat reluctant to ask clients about their trauma histories for fear of "opening Pandora's box" (Frueh, Cusack, Grubaugh, Sauvageot, & Wells, 2006). The distress that often accompanies disclosure of traumatic memories (which may take the form of dissociative detachment as well as overt anxiety, dysphoria, anger, grief, guilt, or shame) can seem overwhelming to the client—and to the clinician. In rare instances, this may lead to a crisis (e.g., episodes of acute suicidality, worsened PTSD or psychiatric symptoms, or substance use relapse) requiring urgent safety interventions. In those cases, it most often is the underlying instability of a client's psychological state that is the determining factor: crises occur not primarily due to the discussion of trauma memories, but when that discussion elicits distress that tips the balance for a client who (whether this is obvious or not) already is on the verge of a deterioration of clinical status or crisis. Clinical inquiry about clients' trauma histories therefore should be done in a manner that helps clients to not only honestly disclose troubling memories but, moreover, to manage their emotions so as to avoid increasing feelings of fear, dysphoria, or helplessness. Ideally, a trauma history assessment helps the client to experience a sense of accomplishment and potentially even personal growth. This occurs when clients learn that it is possible, with the guidance of a clinician, to discuss troubling past experiences without becoming emotionally overwhelmed or flooded with intrusive memories of past traumas. Trauma history assessment also can enable clients not only to disclose troubling memories but to achieve a sense of increased understanding of the past events that bolsters their self-confidence in the present.

These general principles have specific implications for clinical practice. First, before beginning a trauma history assessment, the clinician should always assess the client's current psychological state and personal circumstances, in order to identify potential instability that could lead to deterioration of clinical status or crisis if traumatic memories are discussed. It is important also to learn of any past episodes, in treatment or in other walks of life, in which the client was unable to function or went into crisis. Knowing the circumstances surrounding such serious problems can enable the clinician to compare this to the client's present circumstances and determine if bolstering the client's resources, coping skills, or emotion regulation skills should precede the discussion of past potentially traumatic events. However, if the client's vulnerabilities are due at least in part to intrusive reexperiencing of troubling trauma memories, a careful and sensitive discussion of those events can greatly increase the client's sense of personal control and serve as an important first step toward fully processing and recovering from traumatic events.

Relatedly, there are several considerations that enter into doing trauma history assessment in a careful and sensitive manner. Perhaps surprisingly, the most important factor is not what the clinician says or does when conducting a trauma history assessment, but the state of mind of the clinician. Approaching a trauma history with trepidation can lead to inadvertent nonverbal messages to the client that this may not be safe or that the client may not be able to handle the discussion. This can create a vicious cycle in which the clinician's anxieties lead to the adverse outcome that he or she expects, as a result of eliciting or intensifying the client's anxiety. However, if the clinician is indifferent to the potential distress that discussing trauma history may elicit for the client, or impatient with a client who is avoidant or seems to need a lot of reassurance in talking about troubling memories, this also may increase the client's anxiety.

The optimal state of mind for the clinician, in general and specifically in assessing trauma history, is one of cautious confidence and empathic interest. Caution is warranted because of the potential stressfulness for the client of discussing traumatic memories, and can best be put into practice by being attentive to the client's state of mind and emotional stability in order to monitor the client's ability to cope successfully when the discussion does prove stressful. Confidence can be reassuring to the client, when this is based on the clinician's realistic trust in his or her own expertise and on a genuine belief that discussing the trauma history can be both safe and helpful for the client. This, of course, means that the clinician must feel as much, if not more, confidence as the client does in being able to safely and effectively conduct the trauma assessment. It also means that the clinician must approach the assessment with the expectation that the client has the psychological resources to be able to choose what, and how much, to disclose about troubling memories. The clinician's responsibility is to ask about past traumatic experiences in a down-to-earth but precise manner, without either pressing for more details than the client is comfortable disclosing or permitting the client to become unmanageably emotionally involved in disclosure.

We acknowledge that clinicians who are less seasoned or those new to working with trauma victims may shy away from asking sensitive questions about a client's possible history of traumatic events or posttraumatic emotional reactions. Some clinicians may fear offending the client or, worse yet, drudging up traumatic memories that could emotionally harm the client. We urge the clinician to inquire about previous traumatic events, despite a possible reluctance to do so, for multiple reasons. First, a substantial proportion of the general population has experienced at least one psychological trauma—probably in the 50% to 60% prevalence range (Kessler, Sonnega, Bromet, Hughes, & Nelson, 1995); and information about trauma exposure history can be quite relevant to the client's presenting mental health problems. Second, an extensive research literature has demonstrated that querying and discussing traumatic event exposure is not harmful to clients, and that they often perceive such inquiries as being beneficial to them (reviewed in Newman & Kaloupek, 2004). Would a clinician in our modern day shy away from asking a client about suicidal ideation, for the fear of instilling suicidal thoughts in the client? Of course not—although they used to. As such, the clinician should not shy away from inquiring about previous traumas with the client. Again, exposure therapy for PTSD, one of the most empirically supported treatments for the disorder, involves actively discussing one's trauma in vivid detail (reviewed in Ponniah & Hollon, 2009).

However, there is a fine line between querying and encouraging discussion of previous trauma, and being too forceful about such discussion with a client who is not yet ready for it. It is best to explicitly state that the client should disclose only what he or she feels ready and able to disclose. If, after many weeks or months of treatment, the client still is unwilling to discuss his or her trauma exposure that is clearly relevant to the presenting problem, the clinician can gently nudge the client to discuss difficult traumatic memories. In that case, the clinician may begin by reminding the patient that effortful avoidance of trauma-related stimuli is in fact a hallmark symptom of PTSD, further indicating that such avoidance is part of the etiology of PTSD and serves to maintain the disorder (Foa & Kozak, 1986).

Empathy is crucial in collecting a detailed trauma history. Empathy is an attitude of valuing and wanting to understand the client's perspective, in order to genuinely communicate to the client that her or his point of view should be examined carefully and taken seriously. As such, empathy is akin to but very different from sympathy—not so much a sense of compassion for or resonance with clients as a respect for and desire to understand and help them to understand their own thoughts and emotions (Allen, Fonagy, & Bateman, 2008). To the extent that the clinician is genuinely interested in learning not just the facts but the unique personal significance that past events have for each client, this empathic stance establishes a therapeutic context for the trauma history of respectful personal exploration. Indeed, clients can benefit from realizing that a trauma history assessment is not a rote recitation of past events but an opportunity for them as well as the therapist to more fully understand what happened in traumatic past events and what this meant to them then and means to them now.

The clinician's state of mind in conducting a trauma assessment thus sets the stage for explaining the assessment to the client and conducting the assessment with the client in a manner that is reassuring, informative, and motivating for the client. The intention to be sensitive and respectful to, and genuinely interested in, the meaning of traumatic events for the client must be translated into corresponding words and actions. This can be done in several ways. Rather than asking the client only to describe what happened, the assessor should also ask what thoughts and emotions the client experienced during the events and afterward. Rather than assuming that the client actually was helpless or ineffective in the midst of traumatic events—which is a common self-perception on the part of trauma survivors (Foa, Ehlers, Clark, Tolin, & Orsillo, 1999)—the assessor should ask the client what she or he did before, during, and after traumatic events in order to attempt to cope and mitigate the harm, protect self or others, and recover. This line of inquiry enables clients to recognize ways in which they were able to maintain some degree of agency and control in the face of life-threatening or otherwise harmful or overwhelming events.

However, it is important not to inadvertently allow the assessment to pressure the client to "produce" a coherent understanding of the meaning of traumatic events or a recollection of personal efficacy. Asking questions such as those shown in Table 3.1 about whether several specific potentially traumatic events occurred creates a useful baseline assessment. Inquiring about the client's thoughts, feelings, and actions before, during, or after these events provides a foundation for later therapeutic interventions designed to help clients fully reconstruct traumatic memories with a more coherent understanding and fuller appreciation of their efficacy as well as the distressing or demoralizing aspects of past traumatic events.

But how should a clinician typically bring up the topic of psychological trauma with a client in the first place? The way in which this issue is broached is quite important. Psychological trauma should probably not be one of the first topics queried by the clinician within an initial interview, given the sensitivity of the topic, but can be raised after some discussion of other areas of assessment. Often, we recommend starting assessment by collecting a general psychosocial history that would not be too sensitive to discuss (e.g., medical, social, familial histories) before inquiring about trauma exposure.

When trauma exposure is to be assessed, the clinician should probably discuss the rationale for such line of inquiry—namely, that obtaining this information can be informative in conceptualizing the patient's mental health picture. We find it helpful in easing into trauma query by normalizing the experience of trauma exposure for the patient, by introducing the notion that traumatic events are tragic that unfortunately occur to many people, and that sometimes result in distressing emotional reactions that are quite normal given the circumstances. Using such a preface that is empathic and normalizing can go a long way to helping the patient feel more comfortable in discussing previous trauma exposure, and in developing therapeutic rapport over such potentially sensitive discussion. Finally, we should note that disclosing traumatic events hinges on the ability of the patient to be physically safe from any repercussions of such disclosure. Honest disclosure would be extremely difficult with the patient's perpetrator present in the evaluation room, or in some cases, living with or still associating with the patient.

Next, the specific questions that the clinician asks the client when conducting a trauma history assessment are crucial not only to elicit accurate and useful information, but moreover to behaviorally convey the attitude of cautious confidence and empathic interest. Two mistakes to avoid are using overly global language, and adopting the tone of an interrogation. With regard to the former concern, asking clients about "abuse," "neglect," "trauma," "battering," "betrayal," "violation," or other loaded colloquial terms is likely to elicit denial or overly general responses. While it may be important to determine if a client *felt* abused, neglected, traumatized, battered, betrayed, or violated, it is best to begin by ascertaining what actually happened before inquiring about the personal meaning of those events—and to not suggest meanings to the client by using those highly charged terms unless a client spontaneously describes thoughts and feelings at the time of or after a potentially traumatic event that clearly imply such appraisals. Each individual defines these colloquial terms very differently, as well, leading to problems when a client makes the overinclusive assumption, for example, that *abuse* refers to any conflictual interpersonal interaction, or an overrestrictive assumption that it refers only to childhood sexual abuse.

Thus, in inquiring about previous trauma exposure, it is essential that the clinician uses terms that are tied to specific behaviors defined by law, rather than academic or colloquial terms that may be ambiguous. For example, while some individuals correctly know that "rape" is defined legally as forced sexual penetration, they may mistakenly believe that such an experience does not qualify as "rape" if the perpetrator is an acquaintance, or if the victim was on a date with the perpetrator prior to the rape, or if the victim was voluntarily intoxicated, and so on. As such, the client may not answer such a question with precise accuracy based on legal definitions of trauma exposure. Instead, we recommend that the clinician uses a standardized measure of previous trauma exposure—specifically, one that uses behaviorally specific terminology that maps onto legal definitions of traumatic events.

For example, rather than asking, "Were you physically abused when you were a child," it would be better to ask a question such as "When you were less than 18 years old, did anyone ever hit, slap, shove, kick, burn, or punch you in a way that left a mark/bruise or led you to miss school or go to the doctor?" (adapted from Resnick, Best, Kilpatrick, Freedy, & Falsetti, 1993). There are numerous advantages of the latter version of the question. First, it specifies a time frame for "childhood," which may be of interest for clarification by the clinician. Second, such query indexes specific physically abusive acts from which the client may identify as having occurred to him or her; without cueing the client into such specific abusive acts, the client may otherwise unintentionally neglect to endorse "physical abuse," despite having experienced one of these abusive acts. Finally, the latter query clarifies, based on consequences, the minimum threshold for the severity of such an act in order for endorsing it, to separate a minor and legal "spanking" from a more serious event that can lead to serious physical consequences.

Therefore, when conducting a trauma history assessment, clinicians are advised to use the behavioral and nonjudgmental language provided by a number of structured trauma history assessment measures (see, for example, Table 3.1). Although it may seem overly graphic to use terms such as *hit, kicked, beaten, stabbed*, or *burned*, clients tend to appreciate the directness and clarity of (and understand) those specific nontechnical descriptors. This approach cues the client to recall incidents that are most likely to have been traumatic, while also reducing the risk that important potentially traumatic events will be overlooked because they do not come to mind or are avoided by the client. Structured trauma history instruments also remind the clinician to inquire about the client's peritraumatic characteristics and reactions (whether for diagnostic purposes or to ascertain the likely emotional impact of the event(s)) and the chronology of the events in the client's life. They also can be used in a conversational manner rather than as a lock-step questionnaire, which permits the clinician to move flexibly through the different types of potentially traumatic events (rather than being bound to go in the exact order of the instrument's items) while still being very clear and efficient in helping the client to recall potentially traumatic events. Peritraumatic characteristics may include variables such as: (a) severity and frequency with which traumatic stressors occurred; (b) the client's emotional, cognitive, and biological reactions during the trauma; (c) age and developmental period in which the stressor occurred; (d) other person(s) directly or indirectly involved during and after the event(s); and (e) social support and/or social pressures placed upon the patient during and after the event(s). These characteristics can serve as risk or protective factors and are addressed in several of the trauma history instruments discussed below.

Concerning the second mistake, it is important to make the trauma history assessment an exploration and not an interrogation. Although time often is limited, it is unwise to go through a series of trauma history questions rapidly without providing the client with an opportunity to periodically pause and reflect on the personal impact and meaning of the recalled events—or simply to take a break and allow the incubation phase of the creative process to help him or her reintegrate the memory (i.e., implicit therapeutic processing). However, it is equally unwise to encourage or allow a client to dwell obsessively on troubling past events. This can lead to emotional turmoil and confusion rather than to memory processing or integration. Therapeutic narrative memory processing may be indicated in treatment, but in the initial assessment phase it is best to limit this to relatively brief periods of reflection sufficient to enable the client to recognize that the event is sufficiently significant to warrant further therapeutic examination. Neither the client nor the clinician should become so focused on "getting the memory out" or "finding out everything that happened" that the assessment becomes an external or self-interrogation.

Fourth, it is important to clarify for each client that there is no psychological assessment that can objectively prove that a traumatic event actually occurred (APA Guidelines, point 3). Of particular importance, a trauma history assessment is *not* intended to enable the client to uncover or recover forgotten or "repressed" traumatic memories (McNally, 2007). It is entirely possible that some memories of traumatic experiences are not accessible to conscious retrieval for several reasons, including difficulty in verbal/declarative memory processes associated with victimization-related PTSD (Bremner et al., 2003), and normal memory processes (e.g., insufficient consolidation in long-term memory, decay of memory traces, or cognitive overload of working memory; Veltmeyer et al., 2009). None of these limitations on memory retrieval necessarily require, or even involve, the psychic defense of repression. Even if they did, it would be contraindicated therapeutically to attempt to break through or break down a self-protective psychic defense in order to find a "lost" memory.

Trauma history assessors should never attempt to be memory detectives or archeologists of the mind, searching for buried secrets or truths. Nor should they attempt to definitively confirm the veracity of a memory of a traumatic event, with one exception. Forensic evaluations and expert legal testimony may involve determination of the likely nature and truthfulness of self-reported trauma memories, but in such cases specialized forensic expertise is needed (see Chapter 7). The goal of a clinical trauma history is a systematic review of the full range of potentially traumatic events and to identify likely traumatic exposures that will serve as a focus for planning services.

One area of particular controversial concern regarding traumatic memories is the matter of repressed memories of child sexual abuse when these memories are raised by adult clients. It is difficult to determine clinically if any memory, including a memory of traumatic events, was "repressed" rather than simply not being easily accessible in one's memory. It also is difficult to determine if a memory was "recovered" as opposed to being constructed in one's mind (McNally, 2003). Clinicians are advised to not encourage clients to search for "repressed" memories; again, clinicians are not typically trained in, nor typically serve in the capacity of, forensic detective work. For any "newly recovered" memory that the client reports, the clinician should not validate this memory as definitely true or false; yet they should also not invalidate claims of "recovered" memories outright. Often, the clinician will feel most comfortable, especially in a high-stakes clinical situation, such as when legal involvement is ongoing or imminent, in corroborating trauma exposure using medical, educational, military, police department, or other records.

When and With Whom to Assess Trauma History   Trauma history assessment usually begins with an open-ended exploration of the client's current circumstances and psychosocial history, which should be done in a manner that enhances client engagement, motivation, and trust rather than as an exhaustive (and, for the client, exhausting and potentially threatening) review of specific potentially traumatic events. In the course of this preliminary survey, the clinician can provide the client with a rationale for more detailed trauma history assessment—for example, "In order for us to plan the best approach to treatment for you, it is important for me to have a good understanding of the kinds of difficult or stressful experiences that you've had or are having in your life and how these experiences have affected and may still be affecting you, as well as how you handled them at the time and how you're dealing with them now." It tends to be anxiety reducing for most clients if the assessor explains that it is not necessary to talk in detail about any troubling past or current experiences, and that the client should feel free to decline to disclose (e.g., by saying "I prefer to pass on that question") any experience that she or he does not feel ready to acknowledge. This establishes an agreement that disclosure is fully voluntary, while also indirectly suggesting that some traumatic events may be disclosed at a later time if and when the client feels "ready" based on developing trust in the assessor or changes in life circumstances or symptoms that provide a sufficient sense of safety to permit disclosure. The clinician should always assume that a trauma history is a work in progress, based not only on the client's willingness to disclose but also on the client's potentially increasing understanding of the impact that events have had upon her or him (which often is minimized at the outset of therapy).

When assessment is done with an adult, the client usually is the primary informant for a trauma history. However, clients with severe psychiatric or cognitive/developmental impairment may have difficulty in providing accurate or complete historical information or in managing the emotional distress and mental confusion that can occur when discussing troubling memories. In such cases it is optimal to get the client's self-report—often incrementally in small amounts over a number of interviews—but also (with the client's consent) to obtain collateral information from other informants (e.g., family members, case managers, health care providers) and institutional or medical records. It is important to remember, however, that no form of collateral data can be assumed to be "objective" and complete, because other individuals may not know many events that have happened in a client's life even if they know them well, and formal records often have gaps and inaccuracies despite their appearance of being definitive.

When assessment is done with a child or adolescent, it is optimal to get trauma history data from knowledgeable informants, such as family members or other caregivers who may be in a better position to recognize the impact that events have had upon the client or to feel able to disclose troubling experiences. The correspondence between parents and children in reporting trauma history is generally relatively low (Daviss et al., 2000; Ford et al., 1999)—with each informant often reporting a subset of potentially traumatic events that the other does not view or is reluctant to acknowledge as sufficiently harmful or distressing to the child to warrant reporting. There is no evidence-based guideline for whether to interview or administer a questionnaire to the child/youth and adult(s) regarding trauma history separately or conjointly. This remains an individual clinical decision, which should be based on an assessment of the child's and adult's preferences, apparent comfort in being asked and responding to sensitive questions together with or apart from each other, and ability to emotionally self-regulate with or apart from each other. With older children or adolescents, it often—but by no means always—is developmentally most appropriate to offer to privately discuss (or help them go through a questionnaire that reviews) their trauma history, while also separately (with the youth's knowledge, and if possible, assent) querying the adult(s).

Obtaining collateral information on the patient's emotional condition is helpful as well. Family collateral informants can be helpful in establishing the presence and severity of symptoms that cannot be observed easily in treatment sessions, such as sleep impairment, nightmares, anhedonia, and distress when encountering reminders of the patient's traumatic event. Some symptoms, however, may also be observed in session and used to supplement the client's report of symptoms. For example, the clinician may observe and note instances of exaggerated startle, if an unexpected noise is heard outside of the clinic office, or difficulty concentrating when the patient reviews clinic paperwork. Records such as from a hospital, police reports, school, work, the military, or other sources, may corroborate trauma exposure and symptoms as well. Such data provide additional information beyond simply relying on the patient's self-report. Later, in Chapter 7, we will discuss the issue of symptom overreporting in the PTSD evaluation, and the need for the clinician to retain a healthy skepticism in evaluating a PTSD patient, when external rewards may be present that could incentivize distorted symptom endorsements.

Clinical Interpretation and Use of Trauma History

The ultimate result of trauma history assessments is a set of hypotheses about the nature and type(s) of potentially traumatic events that have occurred—or are still occurring—in a client's life. Clinically, it is important to know not only what happened but also how the client reacted and coped during and after the traumatic events. This is the case despite the strong likelihood that the *DSM-5* definition of a traumatic stressor will no longer require the *DSM-IV* Criterion A2—that the individual felt intense fear, helplessness, or horror. Criterion A2 has not been deemed useful in diagnosing PTSD because it is not predictive of subsequent PTSD status. However, this is not because peritraumatic reactions do not play a role in PTSD, but instead because, across several studies, virtually everyone who develops PTSD also endorses Criterion A2, and many people who endorse Criterion A2 do *not* develop PTSD (Anders, Frazier, & Frankfurt, 2011). The fact that peritraumatic reactions are essentially synonymous with PTSD thus actually highlights, rather than diminishes, the importance of assessing peritraumatic reactions of distress, dissociation, or hyperarousal. In addition, evidence-based approaches to conducting trauma memory processing in treatment explicitly include a detailed review of peritraumatic reactions during the exposure or cognitive processing of memories of traumatic stressor experiences.

PTSD treatments also seek to enhance the client's sense of efficacy and personal control by helping the client to learn experientially—through trauma memory narrative reconstruction in sessions and the *in vivo* facing of trauma reminders in the everyday environment that trigger troubling emotions and memories—that she or he has the inner resources and strengths to face and resolve those memories and the distress they elicit. This is much harder to accomplish when clients recall only the distress or dissociation that they experienced during traumatic events, than when they are able to have a more balanced and complete recollection that includes ways in which they were able to cope effectively despite experiencing understandable peritraumatic fear, helplessness, horror, or related distress (e.g., anger, grief, shame) or dissociation in the midst of traumatic events. Some clinicians and theorists have proposed that people can grow personally as a result of experiencing traumatic events, and while this possibility remains controversial (Ford, Tennen, & Albert, 2008) it is clear that in treatment clients can experience a sense of renewal, forgiveness, and resolution that is more than a simple reduction of anxiety or distress. Such "posttraumatic growth," whether occurring spontaneously or through treatment, often begins with a recognition by the client that she or he handled traumatic events with a degree of courage, determination, and character that is a counterbalance to the feeling of being a helpless victim.

It is essential to distinguish between traumatic events and stressors that, despite being significantly upsetting for a client, did *not* pose a survival threat to the client directly (e.g., life-threatening accidents, disaster, violence, or abuse) or indirectly (e.g., as a witness or significant other of others who are killed or severely physically harmed or abused). Stressors that are not traumatic may have a powerful influence on client's lives, for example, coping with poverty or other financial pressures, stigma and discrimination, or family conflict and divorce. When such stressors actually lead to severe physical harm or abuse, or to death or the threat of death, they may cross over the line and engender the biological and psychosocial survival reactions that are the hallmark of traumatic stressors. However, this distinction is important clinically because of differences in the indicated approaches to treatment for the sequelae of traumatic versus other stressors. Clients who are affected by nontraumatic stressors tend to respond well to changes in lifestyle (e.g., exercise/activity, stress inoculation/anxiety management) and social support (e.g., interpersonal psychotherapy, enhanced contact with friends and family). Those approaches to treatment have not been found to be as efficacious in addressing PTSD as interventions that help clients to change how they cognitively and emotionally process trauma memories (Cahill, Rothbaum, Resick, & Follette, 2009; Cloitre et al., 2010; Ford, Steinberg, & Zhang, 2011). Thus, distinguishing between traumatic versus other stressors can help clinicians to better target and deliver effective psychotherapy.

Note that the nature of a threat to survival may differ substantially, depending on the individual's age, gender, knowledge, and socioeconomic supports or adversities. Children may not experience some objectively life-threatening events as traumatic because they do not have the experience and knowledge to fully appraise the events and their consequences: for example, children diagnosed with cancer are less likely to experience traumatic stress reactions than their older family members and caregivers (Alderfer, Cnaan, Annunziato, & Kazak, 2005). However, young children may experience chronic domestic violence or caregiver depression as a threat to their survival where an adolescent or adult in similar circumstances might feel able to protect and care for themselves sufficiently to be distressed but not traumatized. However, the individual's developmental history of exposure to potentially traumatic stressors also always must be taken into account in evaluating the traumagenicity of exposure: an adolescent or adult who witnessed terrifying or potentially life-threatening family violence in early childhood may experience less extreme interpersonal violence as a survival threat based on the sensitization to threat caused by the early life trauma (see Duckworth & Follette, 2011, on retraumatization).

A final key take-home point regarding trauma history assessment is that exposure to traumatic events does not automatically imply that PTSD will occur. Epidemiological (Breslau, 2009) and prospective clinical (Hobfoll et al., 2007) studies have demonstrated that the *vast majority* of people who are exposed to traumatic stressors do *not* develop PTSD. They almost always experience peritraumatic reactions during or soon after traumatic exposure, but—with the exception of individuals who are victimized by abuse or multiple types of violence (Kessler et al., 1995)—the vast majority (> 75%) of trauma survivors never develop PTSD. Thus, trauma exposure *per se* should never be used as the sole justification for a clinical diagnosis of PTSD nor its treatment.

Beyond the 17 Cardinal PTSD Symptoms   Assessing comorbid and associated symptoms is essential in order to define the specific nature of each individual's PTSD as well as to establish differential diagnosis(es) (Weathers, Keane, & Foa, 2008). Exposure to traumatic stressors is associated with increased risk of a wide range of psychosocial, behavioral, and physical health problems for children (D'Andrea et al., 2012) and adults (Anda et al., 2006; van der Kolk, Roth, Pelcovitz, Sunday, & Spinazzola, 2005). Anxiety may occur not only as PTSD hyperarousal and hypervigilance symptoms, but also in the form of worry, rumination, phobias, obsessions, and panic. Dysphoria may manifest not only as anhedonia, social detachment, emotional numbing, and irritability (which are symptoms of depressive disorders as well as PTSD), but also in the form of hopelessness, psychomotor retardation, and suicidality. Intrusive reexperiencing symptoms are not limited to PTSD's unwanted memories, flashbacks, and triggered reminders but also may take the form of reactive aggression; somatization; psychoses; reenactments involving addiction, anorexia or bulimia, or sexual dysfunction; complicated bereavement; or pathological dissociative states. Substance abuse, including alcohol and nicotine, are also common posttraumatic behavioral reactions.

When these comorbid symptoms or associated features of PTSD were present prior to the first apparent exposure to traumatic stressors, it is important to determine if they actually began in the aftermath of earlier traumatic circumstances (e.g., caregiver deaths or separations, abuse, or witnessing family violence in early childhood). Traumatic accidents, losses, illness, and victimization often are unreported or unrecognized clinically despite being prevalent among, and having a substantial impact on, infants and toddlers (Briggs-Gowan, Carter, et al., 2010; Briggs-Gowan, Ford, Fraleigh, McCarthy, & Carter, 2010). Symptoms that were present prior to trauma exposure also may be significantly exacerbated by posttraumatic reactions. When preexisting symptoms are severe, their intensity and associated impairment may lead assessors to overlook or underestimate the contribution of PTSD symptoms. This can lead to missed opportunities to include PTSD in the treatment plan and overtreatment or unsuccessful treatment of the preexisting comorbid or associated symptoms. For example, an adolescent who has had problems with oppositionality and isolation since early childhood may be able to function sufficiently well to stay in school and out of trouble with the law until becoming severely depressed and having episodes of violent behavior in states of dissociation after experiencing the loss of a primary relationship due to violence. The chronic conduct and affective symptoms may lead an assessor to conclude that this youth suffers from externalizing and depressive disorders rather than PTSD, when all three types of disorders may require treatment rather than just the preexisting ones.

PTSD and its symptoms also may be overlooked or minimized in importance when there are evident symptoms of Axis II personality disorders. Psychological trauma, particularly when interpersonal violence or victimization and the breakdown or destruction of primary relationships are involved in formative developmental periods (e.g., abuse and domestic violence in early childhood, war violence as a combatant or civilian in late adolescence and early adulthood), is a risk factor for the development of personality disorders (Golier et al., 2003). Associated features of PTSD in the *DSM-IV* (e.g., emotion dysregulation, dissociation, preoccupation with somatic complaints, dependency and conflict in relationships) are cardinal features of several personality disorders. Therefore, although adults who present with personality disorder symptoms should not be assumed to have trauma histories or PTSD, they should be carefully assessed for PTSD and its associated features in order to identify those for whom treatment may be most complete and effective if traumatic stress reactions are addressed as well as characterological problems.

Two additional foci for PTSD assessment that go beyond the primary PTSD symptoms are somatization and cognitive impairment (see Table 3.2, #12 and #19). As noted previously, a preoccupation with physical health problems has been identified in the *DSM-IV* as an associated feature of PTSD. Recall that during the U.S. Civil War physicians identified a syndrome of cardiac symptoms that became known as "soldier's heart." Somatization disorders are a distinct diagnostic category from PTSD or other anxiety disorders that include distress due to illness, body system breakdowns, or pain that either cannot be explained medically or are inexplicably severe or refractory to treatment. Before concluding that somatic symptoms should be exclusively diagnosed and treated as somatoform disorders, it is important to determine whether somatization symptoms may be due to traumatic stress reactions that involve a particular form of emotion dysregulation that is consistent with PTSD's emotional numbing symptoms (i.e., overregulation of affect; van Dijke et al., 2011).

Limitations in intellectual capacities have been shown to be a risk actor for PTSD (Koenen et al., 2009), and PTSD often is accompanied by cognitive impairments among adults and children even in the absence

TABLE 3.2	**EXCERPTS FROM THE AMERICAN PSYCHOLOGICAL ASSOCIATION DIVISION OF TRAUMA PSYCHOLOGY ASSESSMENT GUIDELINES**

General Principles

1. Research indicates that many treatment-seeking or clinically referred children, adolescents, and adults have experienced traumatic events in their lives. These traumas may produce lasting symptoms and psychosocial problems, exacerbate or interact with other comorbid psychological difficulties, and even impact the effectiveness of treatment. For this reason, trauma history and trauma-related symptomatology should be evaluated whenever possible, whether during the clinical intake process or in the context of formal psychological assessment.
2. Assessors should be aware that the most common response to trauma is short-lived distress that may not necessitate intervention, other than social support and access to resources. Short-term distress to a negative event, therefore, is insufficient to justify a diagnosis of PTSD.
3. Assessors should clarify with clients that assessments cannot determine whether or not a particular event actually occurred. Trauma evaluations can only indicate whether the findings are consistent with trauma exposure.
4. Since many factors can affect assessment results, all likely hypotheses should be explored before coming to conclusions about the role that trauma may play in any given client's symptom, problem, or disorder.
5. In some instances, the nature of the account might lead the interviewer to understand that (at least in the eyes of the client) the trauma is ongoing. Whenever this is the case, the clinician must attend to potential safety issues and directly address, when possible, instances of acute danger to the client or others. Assessors should be familiar with the APA ethical guidelines (list) and relevant laws on responding to such situations.

VI. Domains to Assess

6. Trauma assessments should include psychosocial history, availability of social support, mental health and treatment history, mental health history of first-degree relatives, social and occupational functioning, current medical illnesses, and current life stress. When possible, evaluation of traumatized children should include adults who have ongoing contact with the child, such as parents, caretakers, and teachers, since each separate source can provide important information. Standardized measures are available for collecting and comparing reports from different sources.
7. Core posttraumatic symptoms of reexperiencing, avoidance, emotion dysregulation (e.g., numbing, persistent negative emotion states), and hyperarousal should be assessed routinely at the start of treatment and periodically during treatment. Dissociative symptoms should also be assessed. . . .
8. Duration and severity of responses to any past traumatic stressors should also be assessed for their possible effects on present reactions, both by a measure that specifically lists a wide range of traumatic stressors and open questions about other past events that caused prolonged upset.

9. Aspects of the traumatic exposure, cognitive, emotional, and physical resources of the individual, psychological context (prior and current psychopathology), past trauma exposure, and social resources and support should be assessed in terms of their influence on the presence and severity of symptoms and on likely prognosis.

10. When psychological disorders do follow trauma exposure, they may or may not include PTSD or a dissociative disorder. Other potential outcomes include major depression (with or without psychotic features), an anxiety disorder other than PTSD (e.g., panic disorder), substance use disorders, a somatoform disorder, personality disorders, and extreme anger responses that may justify diagnoses such as intermittent explosive disorder or oppositional defiant disorder. For some vulnerable individuals, trauma exposure may be followed by a psychotic disorder (e.g., brief psychotic disorder with marked stressor).

11. Clients who present with a history of repeated interpersonal traumas during childhood should be assessed for Axis II disorders, affect and impulse regulation difficulties, and problems with interpersonal relations, attention, somatic functioning, and cognition (including dissociation).

12. When somatization is observed or suspected, or whenever somatic symptoms are a prominent part of the clinical picture, the psychologist should not immediately conclude that a somatization disorder is the only possible explanation. Trauma exposure can be associated with a wide range of potentially serious medical problems. . . . In such cases, the client should be referred for . . . medical evaluation.

13. Clients' responses to traumatic stress should be considered in the context of their gender, ethnic, cultural, and racial identity, socioeconomic status, and sexual orientation, as well as cultural contexts that may help determine both their interpretation of traumatic events and how they express trauma-related distress. When the assessor differs from the client on one or more of these identity factors, the potential impact of such differences on the client's reporting style and behavior . . . should be considered. . . .

VII. Assessment Methods

14. When possible, both a general clinical interview and a set of measures should be used to assess response to traumatic stress. Optimally, the measures would include a general personality or psychopathology measure and a PTSD symptom measure or broader measure of trauma responses that includes PTSD symptoms. The evaluation of sexually abused children [should] involve at least one test or scale measuring sexual behavior or symptoms. If caretakers do not want the child to be asked such questions, appropriate caretaker report measures can be used.

15. Recording qualitative data from observations, in addition to test or scale scores, can help the assessor recognize and track clients' trauma-related responses that may only be ascertained by, for example, direct observation of the client's intonation, facial expressions, or body posture and reactions.

16. Tests that include a measure of overreporting and underreporting are preferable to those with no validity scales. In a test battery, not all tests need include validity scales as long as at least one does. . . . [A]n invalid response to an assessment measure does not indicate whether or not the test-taker has been traumatized, only that his or her test responses are not interpretable without further evaluation of the reasons for the invalidity score. Validity scores may be influenced by trauma. . . .

(continues on next page)

(continued)

17. Given the limited sensitivity and specificity of PTSD scales that are part of broad general personality or psychopathology measures, the presence or absence of elevated PTSD scales should not be overinterpreted, nor should they be the only basis for selecting follow-up tests of trauma exposure. The common use of a test is not a sufficient justification for its choice in a battery in the absence of research supporting reliability and validity for the purposes proposed.

18. Whenever possible, disorder-specific structured interviews should be used to confirm any diagnosis given. When this is not feasible, a careful *DSM-IV*-driven diagnostic interview may suffice. Psychological testing should include, and be substantially based upon, psychometrically valid, reliable, and stable tests that are developmentally and culturally appropriate. The availability of norms is a critical consideration in selection of tests, and specific attention should be given to the nature of these norms when the results are interpreted (e.g., Is the client arguably part of the population upon which the test was normed? Are the norms based on clinical or nonclinical samples?). Optimally, tests used will have general population norms available, and will have established validity for trauma-exposed populations. A diagnosis cannot be made solely based on cutting scores or elevated T-scores.

19. Cognitive testing is often an important component of a trauma assessment battery, in order to determine the client's overall level of intellectual functioning. It also may be valuable in determining the likely performance of the individual in occupational or educational systems, given potential impacts of trauma on attention, working memory, and executive function. . . .

VIII. Optimizing Therapeutic Aspects of Trauma Assessment

20. Trauma assessment, like any other assessment process, is subject to relational issues and dynamics that can affect clients' cooperativeness as well as their ability to emotionally tolerate the procedure. Traumatized children may be particularly mistrustful of a newly introduced assessor and consequently deny symptoms. [Assessors] should take time to develop a good working alliance so that clients feel respected and safe enough to talk about potentially stigmatizing symptoms and traumatic experiences that are, or were, overwhelming, shaming, or terrorizing. . . .

21. Clients will feel more respected, be more cooperative, and feel more satisfied with their assessment when clinicians provide feedback that helps them and their families begin to understand and cope with the painful and otherwise inexplicable effects of trauma. . . . If appropriate, feedback can be given to young children in the form of fables and stories that offer greater understanding and hope of overcoming trauma.

22. Traumatic experiences, by their very nature, create a sense of powerlessness in terms of one's ability to control one's external and internal environment. Assessors can avoid reinforcing traumatic powerlessness by helping clients to understand the purpose of the assessment process, enabling them to have some control over pacing, and encouraging them to monitor and share their reactions with the assessor as the testing proceeds.

23. Tests and assessment interactions themselves can "trigger" traumatic memories, leading to a host of reactions, including emotional flooding, anger, shame, avoidance, sensations of physical pain, and cognitive disorganization. However, in order to plan treatment, some specifics of trauma exposure typically must be known,

such as frequency of exposure and the nature and severity of traumatic event(s). These details can be elicited via nonsuggestive questions such as a free report, or in response to a trauma history measure or structured interview. When possible, clients should be encouraged to detail their thoughts during the traumatic incident and the interpretations that they later made about self, other, and world. Discussion of the event(s) should include beliefs, assumptions, prior history with the perpetrator, and emotional reactions to traumatic event(s). Assessors should be attentive to and prepared to help clients manage and recover from distress that arises during assessment. To minimize distress during reporting about trauma exposure, clients should be encouraged to keep their eyes open and to avoid reporting sensory details or speaking about the trauma in the present tense.

24. If eliciting details of trauma exposure via free report appears to be causing extreme distress, it may be possible to obtain the information using a series of closed-ended questions or a measure of trauma history. In some cases, the nature of the trauma will be known from external sources (crime reports or governmental records of torture), and treatment planning may begin tentatively before the client is able to discuss the material in an explicit way.

25. Assessors should be aware of the possibility of unconsciously conspiring with the client to avoid the most frightening and aversive facets of the trauma. Alternatively, the assessor may become fascinated with the unusual and frightening facet of a trauma story, and ask for detail that goes beyond clinical necessity. . . . Further, trauma assessment can arouse intense empathetic emotions and physical reactions in assessors. For this reason, it is important for assessors to develop their own professional support system in order to avoid losing their objectivity. . . .

Reprinted with permission of lead author Judith Armstrong, PhD (see Armstrong et al., 2011).

of physical injuries or illness that could directly cause neurological conditions (Marx, Doron-Lamarca, Proctor, & Vasterling, 2009; Saigh, Yasik, Oberfield, Halamandaris, & Bremner, 2006). Cognitive impairment may lead to difficulties in recalling, recognizing, describing, or emotionally tolerating detailed discussion of traumatic memories or PTSD symptoms. In addition, cognitive impairment may require adaptations in PTSD treatment in order to accommodate deficits in declarative and working memory (e.g., in trauma memory, narrative portions of therapy) and processing (e.g., in cognitive therapy).

CONCLUSION

PTSD assessment requires specific knowledge and techniques that are not routinely offered in preprofessional or continuing professional education in the mental health, social work, and counseling fields (Courtois & Gold, 2009). In addition to familiarity with and the ability to evaluate the psychometric status of trauma history and PTSD assessment instruments (see Chapters 3 and 4), assessors must be prepared to make often subtle judgments about the nature and impact that exposure to traumatic stressors and living with PTSD and associated or comorbid symptoms have had—and continue to have—on each individual client's life and development. They also must be sensitive to the emotional difficulties that inquiring about traumatic memories and PTSD symptoms may pose for clients, yet also able to convey a sense of confidence in both the assessment process and the client which can empower clients to participate fully and safely in a thorough and systematic assessment (see Table 3.2, #20, #22, #23, #25). And they must be able to summarize the findings of the assessment in nontechnical—but accurate and not "dumbed-down"—language, in order to provide the client (and, as clinically and ethically indicated, key significant others in the client's personal life and treatment) with an understanding of how coping with traumatic stressors appears to have led to symptoms that can be remedied with evidence-based treatments for PTSD and associated disorders (Table 3.2, #21). This is a tall order, but—with the knowledge base provided by this book and professional training designed to provide guidance in the application of that knowledge in real-world clinical practice—well within the capacity of most professionals who conduct psychosocial or psychiatric assessments in which PTSD should be screened, ruled in or out, and carefully described when it is (or was) present.

A final concluding caveat regarding safety: Clinical risk management is essential for the professional as well as for the client when assessing clients with trauma histories and traumatic stress disorders. Kinsler, Courtois, and Frankel (2009) offer a detailed discussion of the ethical and legal issues that may arise. Safety depends not only on assessors' technical knowledge and therapeutic skills, but also on their fulfilling the role of a mandated reporter (e.g., of child or elder abuse), and ensuring client privacy and confidentiality of treatment and clinical records.

REFERENCES

Alderfer, M. A., Cnaan, A., Annunziato, R. A., & Kazak, A. E. (2005). Patterns of posttraumatic stress symptoms in parents of childhood cancer survivors. *Journal of Family Psychology, 19*(3), 430–440.

Allen, J. G., Fonagy, P., & Bateman, A. W. (2008). *Mentalizing in clinical practice.* Washington, DC: American Psychiatric Publishing.

American Psychiatric Association. (1980). *Diagnostic and statistical manual of mental disorders.* Washington, DC: Author.

Anda, R. F., Felitti, V. J., Bremner, J. D., Walker, J. D., Whitfield, C., Perry, B. D., . . . Giles, W. H. (2006). The enduring effects of abuse and related adverse experiences in childhood: A convergence of evidence from neurobiology and epidemiology. *European Archives of Psychiatry and Clinical Neuroscience, 256,* 174–186.

Anders, S. L., Frazier, P. A., & Frankfurt, S. B. (2011). Variations in Criterion A and PTSD rates in a community sample of women. *Journal of Anxiety Disorders, 25,* 176–184.

Armstrong, J., Brand, B., Briere, J., Carlson, E., Dalenberg, C., Finn, S., . . . Cole, N. (2011). *Division 56 guidelines for clinicians regarding the assessment of trauma.* Washington, DC: American Psychological Association.

Boals, A., & Schuettler, D. (2009). PTSD symptoms in response to traumatic and non-traumatic events: The role of respondent perception and A2 criterion. *Journal of Anxiety Disorders, 23,* 458–462.

Bremner, J. D., Vythilingam, M., Vermetten, E., Southwick, S. M., McGlashan, T., Nazeer, A., . . . Charney, D. S. (2003). MRI and PET study of deficits in hippocampal structure and function in women with childhood sexual abuse and posttraumatic stress disorder. *American Journal of Psychiatry, 160,* 924–932.

Breslau, N. (2009). The epidemiology of trauma, PTSD, and other posttrauma disorders. *Trauma Violence & Abuse, 10*(3), 198–210.

Briggs-Gowan, M. J., Carter, A. S., Clark, R., Augustyn, M., McCarthy, K. J., & Ford, J. D. (2010). Exposure to potentially traumatic events in early childhood: Differential links to emergent psychopathology. *Journal of Child Psychology and Psychiatry, 51,* 1132–1140.

Briggs-Gowan, M. J., Ford, J. D., Fraleigh, L., McCarthy, K., & Carter, A. S. (2010). Prevalence of exposure to potentially traumatic events in a healthy birth cohort of very young children in the northeastern United States. *Journal of Traumatic Stress, 23,* 725–733.

Cahill, S. P., Rothbaum, B. O., Resick, P., & Follette, V. (2009). Cognitive behavior therapy for adults. In E. B. Foa, T. M. Keane, M. J. Friedman, & J. A. Cohen (Eds.), *Effective treatments for PTSD* (2nd ed., pp. 139–222). New York, NY: Guilford Press.

Cloitre, M., Stovall-McClough, K. C., Nooner, K., Zorbas, P., Cherry, S., Jackson, C. L., . . . Petkova, E. (2010). Treatment for PTSD related to childhood abuse: a randomized controlled trial. *American Journal of Psychiatry, 167,* 915–924.

Copeland, W. E., Keeler, G., Angold, A., & Costello, E. J. (2010). Posttraumatic stress without trauma in children. *American Journal of Psychiatry, 167,* 1059–1065.

Courtois, C. A., & Ford, J. D. (Eds.). (2009). *Treating complex traumatic stress disorders: An evidence-based guide.* New York, NY: Guilford Press.

Courtois, C. A., & Gold, S. N. (2009). The need for inclusion of psychological trauma in the professional curriculum: A call to action. *Psychological Trauma: Theory, Research, Practice, and Policy, 1*, 3–23.

D'Andrea, W., Ford, J. D., Stolbach, B., Spinazzola, J., & van der Kolk, B. (2012). Phenomenology of symptoms following interpersonal trauma exposure in children: An empirically-based rationale for enhancing diagnostic parsimony. *American Journal of Orthopsychiatry.*

Daviss, W. B., Mooney, D., Racusin, R., Ford, J. D., Fleischer, A., & McHugo, G. J. (2000). Predicting posttraumatic stress after hospitalization for pediatric injury. *Journal of the American Academy of Child & Adolescent Psychiatry, 39*, 576–583.

Dedert, E. A., Green, K. T., Calhoun, P. S., Yoash-Gantz, R., Taber, K. H., Mumford, M. M., . . . Weiner, R. D. (2009). Association of trauma exposure with psychiatric morbidity in military veterans who have served since September 11, 2001. *Journal of Psychiatric Research, 43*, 830–836.

Duckworth, M., & Follette, V. (Eds). (2011). *Retraumatization.* New York, NY: Routledge.

Foa, E. B., Ehlers, A., Clark, D. M., Tolin, D. F., & Orsillo, S. M. (1999). The Posttraumatic Cognitions Inventory (PTCI): Development and validation. *Psychological Assessment, 11*(3), 303–314.

Foa, E. B., & Kozak, M. J. (1986). Emotional processing of fear: Exposure to corrective information. *Psychological Bulletin, 99*, 20–35.

Ford, J. D. (2009). Neurobiological and developmental research: Clinical implications. In C. Courtois & J. D. Ford (Eds.), *Treating complex traumatic stress disorders: An evidence-based guide* (pp. 31–58). New York, NY: Guilford Press.

Ford, J. D., Racusin, R., Daviss, W. B., Ellis, C. G., Thomas, J., Rogers, K., Reiser, J., Schiffman, J., & Sengupta, A. (1999). Trauma exposure among children with oppositional defiant disorder and attention deficit-hyperactivity disorder. *Journal of Consulting and Clinical Psychology, 67*, 786-789.

Ford, J. D., Steinberg, K. L., & Zhang, W. (2011). A randomized clinical trial comparing affect regulation and social problem-solving psychotherapies for mothers with victimization-related PTSD. *Behavior Therapy, 42*, 560–578.

Ford, J. D., Tennen, H., & Albert, D. (2008). Post-traumatic growth: A contrarian view. In P. A. Linley & S. Joseph (Eds.), *Trauma, recovery, and growth* (pp. 297–324). Hoboken, NJ: Wiley.

Frueh, B. C., Cusack, K. J., Grubaugh, A. L., Sauvageot, J. A., & Wells, C. (2006). Clinician perspectives on cognitive–behavioral treatment for PTSD among public-sector consumers with severe mental illness. *Psychiatric Services, 57*, 1027–1031.

Golier, J. A., Yehuda, R., Bierer, L. M., Mitropoulou, V., New, A. S., Schmeidler, J., . . . Siever, L. J. (2003). The relationship of borderline personality disorder to posttraumatic stress disorder and traumatic events. *American Journal of Psychiatry, 160*, 2018–2024.

Heim, C., & Nemeroff, C. B. (2009). Neurobiology of posttraumatic stress disorder. *CNS Spectrums, 14*(1 Suppl 1), 13–24.

Hobfoll, S. E., Watson, P., Bell, C. C., Bryant, R. A., Brymer, M. J., Friedman, M. J., . . . Ursano, R. J. (2007). Five essential elements of immediate and mid-term mass trauma intervention: Empirical evidence. *Psychiatry, 70*(4), 283–315.

Jovanovic, T., & Ressler, K. J. (2011). How the neurocircuitry and genetics of fear inhibition may inform our understanding of PTSD. *American Journal of Psychiatry, 167,* 648–662.

Karam, E. G., Andrews, G., Bromet, E., Petukhova, M., Ruscio, A. M., Salamoun, M., . . . Kessler, R. C. (2010). The role of criterion A2 in the *DSM-IV* diagnosis of posttraumatic stress disorder. *Biological Psychiatry, 68,* 465–473.

Kessler, R. C. (2000). Posttraumatic stress disorder: The burden to the individual and to society. *Journal of Clinical Psychiatry, 61*(Suppl 5), 4–12.

Kessler, R. C., Sonnega, A., Bromet, E., Hughes, M., & Nelson, C. B. (1995). Posttraumatic stress disorder in the National Comorbidity Survey. *Archives of General Psychiatry, 52,* 1048–1060.

Kilpatrick, D. G., Resnick, H. S., & Acierno, R. (2009). Should PTSD Criterion A be retained? *Journal of Traumatic Stress, 22,* 374–383.

Kinsler, P. J., Courtois, C. A., & Frankel, A. S. (2009). Therapeutic alliance and risk management. In C. A. Courtois & J. D. Ford (Eds.), *Treating complex traumatic stress disorders: An evidence-based guide* (pp. 183–201). New York: Guilford Press.

Koenen, K. C., Moffitt, T. E., Roberts, A. L., Martin, L. T., Kubzansky, L., Harrington, H., . . . Caspi, A. (2009). Childhood IQ and adult mental disorders: A test of the cognitive reserve hypothesis. *American Journal of Psychiatry, 166,* 50–57.

Layne, C., Beck, C., Rimmasch, H., Southwick, J., Moreno, M., & Hobfoll, S. (2008). Promoting "resilient" posttraumatic adjustment in childhood and beyond. In D. Brom, R. Pat-Horenczyk, & J. D. Ford (Eds.), *Treating traumatized children: Risk, resilience, and recovery* (pp. 13–47). London, UK: Routledge.

Long, M. E., & Elhai, J. D. (2009). Posttraumatic stress disorder's traumatic stressor criterion: History, controversy, clinical and legal implications. *Psychological Injury and Law, 2,* 167–178.

Marx, B. P., Doron-Lamarca, S., Proctor, S. P., & Vasterling, J. J. (2009). The influence of pre-deployment neurocognitive functioning on post-deployment PTSD symptom outcomes among Iraq-deployed Army soldiers. *Journal of the International Neuropsychology Society, 15,* 840–852.

McNally, R. J. (2003). Progress and controversy in the study of posttraumatic stress disorder. *Annual Review of Psychology, 54,* 229–252.

McNally, R. J. (2007). Dispelling confusion about traumatic dissociative amnesia. *Mayo Clinic Proceedings, 82*(9), 1083–1090.

Mol, S. S. L., Arntz, A., Metsemakers, J. F. M., Dinant, G.-J., Bilters-Van Montfort, P. A. P., & Knottnerus, J. A. (2005). Symptoms of post-traumatic stress disorder after non-traumatic events: Evidence from an open population study. *British Journal of Psychiatry, 186,* 494–499.

Newman, E., & Kaloupek, D. G. (2004). The risks and benefits of participating in trauma-focused research studies. *Journal of Traumatic Stress, 17,* 383−394.

O'Donnell, M. L., Creamer, M., McFarlane, A. C., Silove, D., & Bryant, R. A. (2010). Should A2 be a diagnostic requirement for posttraumatic stress disorder in *DSM-V? Psychiatry Research, 176,* 257−260.

Ponniah, K., & Hollon, S. D. (2009). Empirically supported psychological treatments for adult acute stress disorder and posttraumatic stress disorder: A review. *Depression and Anxiety, 26,* 1086−1109.

Resnick, H. S., Best, C. L., Kilpatrick, D. G., Freedy, J. R., & Falsetti, S. A. (1993). *Trauma assessment for adults* [Unpublished interview protocol]. Medical University of South Carolina, Department of Psychiatry, Crime Victims Research and Treatment Center, Charleston, SC.

Saigh, P. A., Yasik, A. E., Oberfield, R. A., Halamandaris, P. V., & Bremner, J. D. (2006). The intellectual performance of traumatized children and adolescents with or without posttraumatic stress disorder. *Journal of Abnormal Psychology, 115,* 332−340.

Schnurr, P. P., Lunney, C. A., & Sengupta, A. (2004). Risk factors for the development versus maintenance of posttraumatic stress disorder. *Journal of Traumatic Stress, 17,* 85−95.

Seng, J., D'Andrea, W., & Ford, J. D. (in press). Psychological trauma history and empirically derived psychiatric syndromes in a community sample of women in prenatal care. *Psychological Trauma.*

Sugar, J., & Ford, J. D. (2012). Peritraumatic reactions and posttraumatic stress disorder in psychiatrically impaired youth. *Journal of Traumatic Stress, 25*(1), 41−49.

Updegraff, J. A., Silver, R. C., & Holman, E. A. (2008). Searching for and finding meaning in collective trauma: results from a national longitudinal study of the 9/11 terrorist attacks. *Journal of Personality and Social Psychology, 95,* 709−722.

van der Kolk, B. A., Roth, S., Pelcovitz, D., Sunday, S., & Spinazzola, J. (2005). Disorders of extreme stress. *Journal of Traumatic Stress, 18,* 389−399.

van Dijke, A., Ford, J. D., van der Hart, O., van Son, M., van der Heijden, P., & Bühring, M. (2011). Childhood traumatization by primary caretaker and affect dysregulation in patients with borderline personality disorder and/or somatoform disorder. *European Journal of Psychotraumatology, 2.* doi: 10.3402/ejpt.v2i0.5628

Veltmeyer, M. D., Clark, C. R., McFarlane, A. C., Moores, K. A., Bryant, R. A., & Gordon, E. (2009). Working memory function in post-traumatic stress disorder: An event-related potential study. *Clinical Neurophysiology, 120,* 1096−1106.

Weathers, F., Keane, T., & Foa, E. (2008). Assessment and diagnosis of adults. In E. Foa, T. Keane, M. Friedman, & J. Cohen (Eds.), *Effective treatments for PTSD* (pp. 23−61). New York, NY: Guilford Press.

Yehuda, R., & Flory, J. D. (2007). Differentiating biological correlates of risk, PTSD, and resilience following trauma exposure. *Journal of Traumatic Stress, 20,* 435−447.

Zlotnick, C., Johnson, J., Kohn, R., Vicente, B., Rioseco, P., & Saldivia, S. (2008). Childhood trauma, trauma in adulthood, and psychiatric diagnoses: results from a community sample. *Comprehensive Psychiatry, 49*(2), 163−169.

CHAPTER 4

Assessing PTSD

The previous chapter covered important considerations in assessing trauma and PTSD. In this chapter, we focus on additional important issues and practical methods in assessing posttraumatic stress disorder (PTSD). We begin by discussing the aims and overall strategies in assessing PTSD. Next, we discuss specific strategies and methods assessing a history of traumatic event exposure (which is required for a PTSD diagnosis). Finally, we discuss issues in assessing for the presence of specific PTSD symptoms in order to diagnose PTSD, along with assessment strategies and practical methods for conducting such evaluations.

We generally recommend a top-down approach to assessing psycho-pathology in general, and we illustrate this approach by referring to a funnel that one might use to precisely pour liquid into a container that has a narrow top. That is, just as the top of a funnel is wide and broad, we first recommend broadly assessing the client's mental health by querying numerous mental health conditions in addition to PTSD. Just as the funnel begins narrowing in its middle, for disorders that the client screened positive for, we would narrow our query to the frequency and intensity of those disorders' symptoms in order to gather more comprehensive information about those conditions (discussed in the next chapter). As the funnel further narrows toward its base, we next recommend narrowing our assessment by querying the client about his or her exposure to diverse types of traumatic events; specific traumatic events that are endorsed by the client can be further queried by further narrowing the line of inquiry to details of the particular traumatic event(s) experienced. Finally, if at least one traumatic event is endorsed by the client, the clinician would narrowly query the client about specific symptom criteria of PTSD. We discuss this approach of narrowing in on a query of trauma exposure and PTSD in more detail in this chapter; we discuss narrowing in on other disorders and conditions in the next chapter.

ASSESSING TRAUMA HISTORY

Strategies for Trauma History Assessment

We recommend the following specific steps in inquiring about past and current trauma exposure. First, as discussed in the previous chapter, the clinician should use a preface statement that orients the client to the query of previous traumatic events, normalizing such experiences for the client by pointing out that they regrettably occur with some frequency in the general population, while conveying empathy about the possible occurrence of such events. The clinician should confidently broach this topic and need not be apologetic for raising a sensitive query.

Second, the clinician should use a psychometrically sound, standardized interview or self-report instrument that assesses previous trauma exposure. The ideal measure should list a variety of events that would meet the definition of a traumatic stressor within the *DSM-IV*'s PTSD Criterion A1, with instructions for the client to indicate any events of this nature that have occurred to him or her. The list of events itself should use behaviorally specific terms to identify traumatic events, limiting ambiguity to a minimum. A measure with follow-up probing questions for traumatic events that are endorsed is helpful in gathering information on traumatic event–related characteristics, as well as in establishing whether the event meets PTSD's traumatic stressor criterion in *DSM-IV* (Criterion A). Objective corroboration of any endorsed traumas that may be relevant to ongoing legal or forensic involvement should be sought.

Third, if the client endorsed only one traumatic event, the clinician should consider this event as the "index trauma," informing the client that the clinician will subsequently query the client about particular symptoms (of PTSD) from that index trauma. If the client endorsed more than one type of traumatic event and/or more than one specific incident of one or more types of traumatic events, the clinician should attempt to elicit from the client which traumatic incident the client would consider to currently cause the most emotional distress; that event would become the client's index trauma. It is true that for some clients, it would be difficult to select one particular index trauma—how does a client select a specific most distressing combat firefight from the daily firefights in which he or she was engaged in the war zone, for example? Nonetheless, the clinician should encourage the client to attempt to select the traumatic incident that is most distressing, even if (a) the client does not particularly believe that any traumatic incidents experienced were very distressing or (b) it is difficult to relatively rate distress from one serious incident over another. Later in this chapter, we further discuss linking PTSD symptom queries to one's index traumatic event.

Instruments

Several instruments have been developed to assess a history of trauma exposure. Some of these instruments are standardized interviews, which have the advantage of allowing the clinician to probe ambiguous responses, but may tie up clinic resources. Other instruments are self-administered/ self-report measures that may tie up few clinic resources but lack the built-in ability for probing responses. Previous papers have comprehensively reviewed these instruments for adults (Briere, 2004) and children (Ohan, Myers, & Collett, 2002). One may wonder how to choose a particular trauma history instrument, with numerous options from which to choose. We suggest using a measure that has documented evidence of reliability and validity, has coverage of a broad enough diversity of traumatic events, uses behaviorally specific items, and, if it is an interview-based measure, has a relatively short administration time.

A few notable trauma history instruments for adults are worth mentioning, all of which are self-report measures. The Traumatic Life Events Questionnaire queries exposure to 23 traumatic events, and has been comprehensively investigated for its reliability and validity (Kubany et al., 2000). The Trauma Assessment for Adults (Resnick, Best, Kilpatrick, Freedy, & Falsetti, 1993) includes 13 items querying trauma exposure, and has demonstrated reliability and validity (Gray, Elhai, Owen, & Monroe, 2009). Finally, the 18-item Traumatic Event Screening Instrument for Adults (Ford & Fournier, 2007) and 12-item Stressful Life Events Screening

Questionnaire (Goodman, Corcoran, Turner, Yuan, & Green, 1998) have documented psychometric properties as well.

For children, relatively fewer instruments have been developed to assess previous trauma exposure. The Traumatic Events Screening Interview has versions that may be directly administered as an interview to children (TESI-C) or to the child's parent (TESI-PRR), as well as a self-report version (TESI-C/SR) (e.g., Ford, Hartman, Hawke, & Chapman, 2008). Additionally, the Dimensions of Stressful Events Rating Scale contains 50 items of trauma exposure in an interview format, taking about 15 to 30 minutes of administration time (Fletcher, 1996).

Technical Considerations: Response Validity

Relevant to clients with legal involvement, some individuals may underreport or overreport their trauma exposure. Acierno, Kilpatrick, and Resnick (1999) discussed situations in which one may underreport trauma exposure, including when the alleged perpetrator lives with and even financially supports the victim, fear of retribution by the perpetrator, fear of stigma or blame as a trauma victim, lack of encouragement to disclose, past negative experiences from disclosing trauma, and fear of emotional consequences. Reasons to overreport trauma exposure can involve attempts at obtaining monetary compensation from litigation or disability claims, reducing criminal penalties, and attention seeking (Taylor, Frueh, & Asmundson, 2007). These issues are described in more detail in Chapter 7.

The issue of overreporting (e.g., malingering, factitious claims) will be addressed as a legal/forensic as well as clinical concern in Chapter 7. However, for different reasons, underreporting is equally problematic and generally less often detected. Weathers, Keane, and Foa (2008) report that some of the PTSD symptoms are "negative" in nature; that is, they reflect the absence of a positive state or actions rather than the more obvious presence of pathological psychological states or behavior. PTSD Criterion C symptoms characterized as dysphoria and emotional numbing are obvious exemplars, but active avoidance symptoms also often are underreported and go undetected when they involve a forgoing of behavior rather than more obvious active attempts to escape danger or distress. For example, many individuals who meet all other criteria for PTSD do not view themselves as intentionally avoiding reminders of past traumatic events because their avoidance has become so habitual and second nature that they no longer recognize how they have stopped going certain places, talking about certain subjects, doing certain activities, or even thinking about certain topics as a way to avoid experiencing emotional distress or disturbing memories.

It also is important to remember that anhedonia, emotional numbing, amnesia, and social detachment may be the downstream results of previous active attempts at avoidance, which may persist in subtle forms of which the individual no longer is aware because he or she has become so emotionally shut down that reminders no longer elicit sufficient distress to warrant consciously activated avoidance. Severe and chronic positive (e.g., reexperiencing) and negative (e.g., dysphoria and emotional numbing) PTSD symptoms also may engender an attitude of helplessness, which can obscure continued attempts to intentionally avoid troubling memories or emotional distress. Therefore, PTSD assessment should assess whether the person has reduced involvement in or contact with people, places, activities, conversations, thoughts, or emotions for any reason, and rather than limiting inquiry to specific intentional attempts to avoid potential reminders of past traumatic events.

Assessing PTSD Symptom Criteria

In some ways, the assessment of PTSD is simpler than the assessment of trauma history. Once a likely trauma history has been established, PTSD requires that three types of symptoms occur and cause impairment in functioning for at least a month (i.e., intrusive reexperiencing, avoidance and emotional numbing, and hyperarousal). In the *DSM-5*, the middle set of symptoms is proposed to be divided into two groups, active avoidance and negative alterations in cognition or mood—but PTSD's essential structure and symptoms are largely unchanged. There is a large collection of questionnaires and semistructured interviews that have been validated for the assessment of PTSD and its symptoms (see Chapter 3) and for symptoms of comorbid mental and physical health disorders (see Chapter 5; Nader, 2008; Weathers et al., 2008).

Connecting PTSD Symptom Inquiries to an Index Trauma

In the context of an evaluation for PTSD, if a patient endorses no history of traumatic events, there is no compelling reason to query PTSD symptoms. After all, a diagnosis of PTSD requires that the individual has experienced a traumatic event, so the absence of a trauma history automatically renders the individual to not be diagnosed with PTSD. We should provide the warning that some clinicians, in our experience, believe that even in the absence of a trauma history, if the client essentially meets the minimum symptom criteria for PTSD, he or she should be diagnosed with PTSD. This notion appears to be based on the "if it quacks like a duck" argument; that is, some believe that if a client's presentation very much appears like PTSD, then he or she should be so diagnosed. However, there are substantial problems with this argument.

Specifically, individuals may endorse symptoms of PTSD, despite having no history of traumatic events. In fact, research demonstrates that when queried about PTSD symptoms, individuals without a trauma history demonstrate equivalent severity of PTSD symptoms as compared with individuals with a trauma history (reviewed in Long & Elhai, 2009). What can account for this seeming paradox where individuals without a "traumatic" event history can have significant symptoms of "posttraumatic" stress disorder? The answer lies in the fact that not all of PTSD's symptoms are specific or unique to PTSD. Several PTSD symptoms overlap precisely with symptoms found in other anxiety and mood disorders. For example, PTSD's problems with sleep and concentration overlap with both generalized anxiety disorder and major depressive disorder. PTSD's irritability additionally overlaps with generalized anxiety disorder, and PTSD's anhedonia additionally overlaps with major depression. And other PTSD symptoms, while not strictly overlapping with mood and anxiety disorders, are conceptually related by virtue of their focus on distress, dysphoria, and misery (e.g., social detachment, restricted affect, sensing a foreshortened future).

Let us take, for example, a hypothetical individual who has never experienced a psychological trauma but has recently started a change in schedule that affects his or her sleep, such as by taking a nightshift job or caring for a newborn baby. Such a sleep schedule change may evoke symptoms that happen to be part of the PTSD diagnosis, such as difficulty sleeping, which in turn can evoke difficulty concentrating and irritability during the daylight hours (because of diminished sleep), and feeling detached from others (because of isolation involved with such a job or new caregiver status). Thus, despite no traumatic stressor being endorsed, the individual already endorsed four of the required six PTSD symptoms for the diagnosis. Yet we would not diagnose this individual with PTSD because the presentation does not fall within the intended meaning of the PTSD construct. It is precisely because of situations such as this that the traumatic stressor criterion must be satisfied in order to accurately diagnose someone with the disorder, without resulting in misdiagnosis.

As we discussed earlier in this chapter, assessing PTSD for a client who endorses only one instance of a traumatic event is quite straightforward—the clinician would inquire about PTSD that stems from that traumatic incident. However, most individuals who have experienced trauma report multiple traumatic incidents and multiple types of traumatic events (Kessler, Sonnega, Bromet, Hughes, & Nelson, 1995). Children who experience several types of victimization (e.g., bullying, abuse, family violence) tend to have particularly extensive and severe PTSD and related symptoms (Cloitre et al., 2009; Finkelhor, Turner, Ormrod, & Hamby, 2010; Ford, Elhai, Connor, & Frueh, 2010). This is true as well for adults who are revictimized in multiple ways in childhood and later in life (Briere, Kaltman, & Green, 2008). It is essential to ensure that PTSD evaluation is conducted based on a particular index trauma, rather than inquiring about symptoms globally from multiple traumatic events. After all, the assignment of a *DSM-IV* PTSD diagnosis requires that the minimum number of symptoms be endorsed from at least one specific traumatic incident. If the client endorsed only some (but not the minimum required) symptoms for PTSD from a specific traumatic incident, but endorses the remaining minimum required symptoms from another traumatic incident(s) in order to meet the minimum threshold for PTSD, *DSM-IV* requirements would indicate that this is not a sufficient condition for meeting PTSD's diagnosis.

So, the client must be queried about PTSD in relation to a specific index trauma. However, clinic resources would be depleted if PTSD were to be assessed separately in relation to each traumatic incident endorsed. In order to provide the client with the fairest manner in which to meet full

PTSD diagnostic criteria, while also minimizing the burden of evaluation, the patient should be given the opportunity to connect their PTSD ratings to the traumatic event that is most likely to result in a PTSD diagnosis. Therefore, we recommend assessing PTSD symptoms in relation to a patient's traumatic stressor that is self-nominated as the event that is currently most distressing or upsetting.

Alternatively, as discussed in Chapter 7, if it is necessary to evaluate PTSD from a specific trauma relevant to litigation, that specific trauma would represent the index trauma from which PTSD symptoms are queried.

We provide the caveat, however, that asking clients to sequester their PTSD symptom ratings to a specific index trauma does not come without limitations. For some PTSD symptoms, it may be easy to separate whether the symptom comes from a specific trauma (e.g., rape) versus another type of trauma (e.g., disaster)—for example, nightmares can be more clearly linked to the content and affect of one particular trauma over another. However, it may be difficult to distinguish whether that same symptom stemmed from a rape in childhood versus a rape in young adulthood. Other symptoms that reflect more general distress (e.g., concentration problems, anhedonia) may be particularly difficult for the patient to indicate from which traumatic incident the symptom was caused. Weathers et. al. (2008) suggest helping such individuals to identify specific examples of particularly troubling events rather than asking them to attempt to relate symptoms to the totality of their traumatic exposure. It also can be clarifying to ask whether symptoms became noticeably worse at certain points in the individual's life, because traumatic events may exacerbate previously milder symptoms as well as leading to the initial onset of previously nonexistent symptoms.

Defining PTSD Symptoms Accurately

Weathers et. al. (2008) also note that many PTSD symptoms are neither clearly defined nor well understood by most clinicians, notably flashbacks, psychogenic amnesia, and a sense of foreshortened future. Also, they note that symptoms within each PTSD domain often are overlapping and difficult to distinguish from one another (e.g., unwanted memories, nightmares, and flashbacks; anhedonia, emotional numbing, and social detachment; hyperarousal and startle). In some cases, symptoms in different PTSD domains overlap as well (e.g., nightmares and sleep disturbance). Careful attention to the exact wording of each PTSD symptom in the American Psychiatric Association's *Diagnostic and Statistical Manual* can help to clarify each symptom, but clinicians and researchers also should refer to carefully constructed diagnostic interviews (e.g., the Clinician-Administered PTSD Scale [CAPS] for adults, for which there also is a child and adolescent version; Nader, 2008) for specific questions designed to identify and discriminate the PTSD symptoms.

Time Since the Trauma

It is crucial for the clinician to ensure that at least 1 month has elapsed since posttraumatic stress disorder symptoms began in order to diagnose a patient with PTSD, according to criteria requirements in the *DSM-IV.* Some clinicians who evaluate a trauma victim less than 1 month (rather than the required 30 days) after symptoms had their onset may be tempted to diagnose the patient with PTSD, under the assumption that symptoms will continue past the 30 days. However, this assumption may not be tenable, as many trauma victims are resilient and return to premorbid functioning before the 30-day minimum requirement for the PTSD diagnosis. If the clinician believes that the patient meets the required symptoms for PTSD, but it has been less than 30 days since the onset of symptoms, the clinician is advised to assign a better fitting diagnosis such as adjustment disorder or acute stress disorder, until such time as the patient satisfies the full criteria for PTSD including the time frame requirement.

Labeling a PTSD Symptom as Clinically Significant

Diagnosis or Symptom Severity? A first consideration in determining how to approach the assessment of PTSD with an individual client is whether this is being done to formulate a clinical diagnosis or to measure the severity of symptoms for the purpose of screening to determine likely eligibility for treatment or for a study, to establish an initial baseline of the nature and extent of traumatic stress symptoms, or to monitor changes in symptoms over the course of treatment or time. Questionnaires tend to be most efficient for screening and to assess the nature and severity of PTSD symptoms, but they cannot solely determine a PTSD diagnosis.

Diagnosis requires clinical judgment, even when well-standardized diagnostic interviews are used. For example, the CAPS (Weathers et al., 2008) provides detailed, layperson-friendly questions and follow-up probes and operational definitions to clarify the exact frequency and intensity of each PTSD symptom. However, rather than being a rote set of questions that is asked verbatim, the CAPS is designed in a semistructured manner that requires the assessor to make judgments such as: Exactly how often did the symptom occur in the current or worst past month? Was the symptom at all manageable, and, if so, how much effort did the individual have to make in order to cope when it occurred? How much impairment in relationships, work or school, and personal life did the symptom cause, and did these problems lead to serious legal, financial, residential, career, or avocational problems? Thus, PTSD diagnosticians must be prepared to efficiently and sensitively inquire about and record not only whether symptoms occurred but their impact on the individual and the degree to which the individual was able to cope and function when symptoms occurred.

Thus, clinicians should consider not only whether PTSD symptoms are present, but also the severity of reported problems. Clinicians may be tempted to use a "yes"/"no" symptom query format, but such a dichotomous format would make it impossible to track a patient's progress over time through the course of treatment. Additionally, without information on the severity of a symptom, it cannot be easily determined if a reaction should be considered "clinically significant." For example, imagine asking a patient about recent nightmares, to which the patient responds affirmatively; yet if the clinician had asked about how often the nightmares were occurring, perhaps the patient would have indicated a frequency of less than once per month, probably not frequent enough to be considered a significant symptom. Of course, there is no universal agreement on which various levels of symptom severity meet criteria for being a "significant symptom," and *DSM-IV* provides little assistance in arriving at such a determination. Thus, clinical judgment often is required; however, use of standardized instruments with behavioral anchor-points in the symptoms' response options helps with narrowing in on such a consensus.

Gauging PTSD symptom severity can be achieved not only by querying symptom frequency (e.g., nightmares occurring once per month vs. once per week), but also how intensely they occur (e.g., nightmares keeping the client awake for 1 hour vs. 3 hours after). From a clinical standpoint, the impact on a client's well-being and functioning can be altered by different combinations of frequency and intensity. Compare, for example, a flashback that occurs once every few months but is so intense that the client requires acute psychiatric hospitalization, with a series of moderately disabling flashbacks that occur several times a week. Treatment for these two "comparably severe" PTSD symptoms is likely to be quite different (e.g., crisis prevention as a focus in the first case, exposure therapy in the latter case). Though the need for assessing both frequency and intensity of PTSD symptoms has been debated (Elhai, Palmieri, Biehn, Frueh, & Magruder, 2010). Nonetheless, it is important to carefully define symptom "severity" in each PTSD case with specific reference to frequency and intensity, rather than simply labeling symptoms as more or less severe.

Screening for PTSD   In light of the extensive prevalence of exposure to traumatic stressors, not only among people with serious mental health and addictive disorders but also in community and health care populations, screening for possible PTSD or related posttraumatic stress problems is a crucial first step before more detailed diagnostic or symptom assessments can be done. PTSD has been shown to be associated with medical and mental health and psychosocial problems among vulnerable groups such as schoolchildren, adult and pediatric medical patients, pregnant women, community mental health patients, and youth and adults in the social services and criminal justice systems (Frueh, Grubaugh, Cusack, & Elhai, 2009; Ko et al., 2008). Therefore, screening for PTSD may be particularly important with individuals involved in these systems, and their involvement provides ready opportunities to conduct this screening if efficient and validated measures are available. This combination of need and opportunity led to the development of a very brief—four item—self-report screening questionnaire, the Primary Care PTSD Screen (PC-PTSD), which has been validated in primary medical care (Ouimette, Wade, Prins, & Schohn, 2008), substance abuse treatment (Kimerling,

Trafton, & Nguyen, 2006), and criminal justice (Ford, Trestman, Wiesbrock, & Zhang, 2009) populations.

The design of the PC-PTSD is instructive because it does not attempt to verify the exact nature of past exposure to traumatic events, but instead focuses on the four fundamental domains of PTSD symptoms: (1) intrusive reexperiencing; (2) active avoidance of reminders; (3) hyperarousal and hypervigilance; and (4) emotional numbing and social detachment. While the exact number of items that must be answered "Yes" in order to identify an individual as in need of further assessment for PTSD will differ depending on the specific group and setting in which screening is being done, the validation studies cited above consistently have found that endorsing two or more of the items is associated with an elevated risk of PTSD. Note that the PC-PTSD does require a link between symptoms and past potentially traumatic experience, in order to identify PTSD rather than other anxiety or affective disorders with similar symptoms:

The Primary Care PTSD Screen (PC-PTSD)

In your life, have you ever had any experience that was so frightening, horrible, or upsetting that, *in the past month*, you . . .

1. Have had nightmares about it or thought about it when you did not want to?
2. Tried hard not to think about it or went out of your way to avoid situations that reminded you of it?
3. Were constantly on guard, watchful, or easily startled?
4. Felt numb or detached from others, activities, or your surroundings?

When screening or other sources of referral lead to a request for more extensive PTSD assessment, the next challenge after conducting the trauma history portion of the assessment is to determine not only what PTSD and associated symptoms are (or were) present, but also: (a) the likelihood that symptoms are linked to traumatic stress exposure, (b) the specificity of each symptom, (c) the severity of and degree of impairment caused by the symptoms, and (d) whether symptoms are either under- or overreported.

Assessing Impairment   Symptoms tend to be associated with worse impairment in functioning and well-being as they become more frequent and severe, but this is not a one-to-one relationship. Symptoms that occur infrequently may have a devastatingly negative impact. For example, even a one flashback can lead to highly dangerous (e.g., risky, addictive, violent or violence-eliciting, promiscuous) behavior. A flashback involving strange visual and auditory experiences or derealization and depersonalization also may lead to the misdiagnosis of psychosis, and to restrictive treatment (e.g., psychiatric hospitalization and antipsychotic medication). However, the persistent strain of apparently mild nightmares and sleep disturbance can lead to slow but steady escalation of other PTSD symptoms (e.g., irritability, impaired concentration, hypervigilance, anhedonia, social detachment) and eventually to severe impairment. Therefore, regardless of their apparent frequency or intensity, it is crucial to carefully assess how PTSD symptoms affect functioning in social and educational/vocational roles, as well as in psychological and physical well-being.

Strategies for Assessing PTSD Symptoms

The primary strategy in assessing PTSD symptoms begins with first orienting the patient to the index trauma that s/he selected from the trauma exposure assessment. The clinician would then query the patient about current PTSD symptoms that are specifically linked to the index trauma.

In terms of strategy for the specific PTSD assessment instrument chosen, the clinician should use a sound measure that has been comprehensively reviewed for its psychometric properties. For a diagnostic evaluation, a structured diagnostic interview for PTSD is preferred over a self-report PTSD instrument. A diagnostic interview allows for clinician judgment in interpreting particular symptoms as clinically meaningful, as well as allowing for the patient to ask for clarification on the meaning of items. A self-report measure does not allow for clinical judgment or clarification, and typically does not include items to approximate all the criteria for a PTSD diagnosis, including functional impairment and the timing requirements. Preferably, an instrument that allows not only for binary responses to PTSD symptoms ("yes" vs. "no"), but also allows for precise dimensionality of response choices that are based on behavioral anchor points, is recommended.

Instruments

Many PTSD diagnostic interviews and self-report instruments are available. Of course the interviewer-administered instruments may tie up clinic resources, while the self-report instruments can be completed by patients in a clinic waiting room. Most measures include at least the 17 *DSM-IV* PTSD symptom-items required for the diagnosis. These measures are reviewed extensively in other sources (Briere, 2004; Norris & Hamblen, 2004).

For adults, we first discuss interviewer-administered instruments that would be required for assigning a PTSD diagnosis. Arguably, the most precise diagnostic interview for PTSD is the CAPS (Blake et al., 1995). The CAPS is packaged with a brief checklist to assess traumatic event history (the Life Events Checklist), and is the only standardized diagnostic interview that assesses for both the frequency and severity of each *DSM-IV* PTSD symptom. The CAPS also has the advantage of precise rating, which is facilitated by its inclusion of response options for each symptom that are behaviorally anchored, thus ensuring high interrater reliability (Weathers, Keane, & Davidson, 2001). The only disadvantage is that its administration time ranges from roughly 40 to 60 minutes. Less time-consuming alternatives to the CAPS would be the PTSD Symptom Scale−Interview (PSS-I; Foa & Tolin, 2000) and Structured Interview for PTSD (SI-PTSD; Davidson, Kudler, & Smith, 1997), which each take half the administration time as the CAPS because they do not address both the frequency *and* intensity of symptoms. The PSS-I and SI-PTSD both have fairly precise behaviorally anchored response options and adequate psychometric properties. Finally, another option is to use general structured or semistructured diagnostic interviews for *DSM-IV* mental disorders (e.g., Structured Clinical Interview for *DSM-IV*, discussed in Chapter 5), for which there is a PTSD module; however, these interviews merely assess the presence/ absence of symptoms, rather than their frequency or intensity.

Also for adults, numerous self-report PTSD measures are available, which can be useful in screening for PTSD, or tracking treatment outcomes. Some of the more widely used self-report measures of PTSD, all of which have documented psychometric properties and at least include the 17 *DSM-IV* PTSD symptoms, include the PTSD Checklist (Weathers, Litz, Herman, Huska, & Keane, 1993), PTSD Symptom Scale-Self Report

(Foa, Riggs, Dancu, & Rothbaum, 1993), and Posttraumatic Diagnostic Scale (Foa, Cashman, Jaycox, & Perry, 1997). Other widely used PTSD measures (Elhai, Gray, Kashdan, & Franklin, 2005) that include more than the 17 *DSM-IV* PTSD items are the Impact of Event Scale—Revised (Weiss & Marmar, 1997) and multiscale Trauma Symptom Inventory (TSI; Briere, 1995) and TSI-2 (Briere, 2011).

Fewer instruments are available for children in assessing PTSD. The CAPS for Children and Adolescents (CAPS-CA; Nader et al., 1996) is patterned after and offers the same unique features of the adult CAPS, taking 30 to 120 minutes in administration time. The Children's PTSD Inventory (Saigh et al., 2000) takes only 15 to 20 minutes to administer. Other notable possibilities include PTSD modules of the Diagnostic Interview for Children and Adolescents—Revised (DICA-R), Diagnostic Interview Schedule for Children (DISC), and other structured or semistructured child diagnostic interviews (Ohan et al., 2002) discussed in Chapter 5.

For children age 6 and 7 or older, the Child PTSD Symptom Scale (Foa, Johnson, Feeny, & Treadwell, 2001) is a child version of the PDS, mapping well onto *DSM-IV* PTSD items (making it unique relative to other child PTSD measures). Other instruments adapted from the adult TSI for children include the Trauma Symptom Checklist for Children (Briere, 1996) and Trauma Symptom Checklist for Young Children (Briere, 2005).

CONCLUSION

In this chapter, we discussed special considerations in evaluating patients for trauma exposure, including caveats about recalling traumatic memories. We discussed the use of standardized trauma exposure instruments used to query traumatic event experiences. Strategies and issues in querying PTSD from an index trauma event were discussed, along with standardized PTSD instruments and considerations in their use. The strategies discussed here should allow the clinician to confidently evaluate a patient for a history of trauma exposure and PTSD.

REFERENCES

Acierno, R., Kilpatrick, D. G., & Resnick, H. S. (1999). Posttraumatic stress disorder in adults relative to criminal victimization: Prevalence, risk factors, and comorbidity. In P. A. Saigh & J. G. Bremner (Eds.), *Posttraumatic stress disorder: A comprehensive text* (pp. 44–68). Boston, MA: Allyn & Bacon.

Blake, D. D., Weathers, F. W., Nagy, L. M., Kaloupek, D. G., Gusman, F. D., Charney, D. S., & Keane, T. M. (1995). The development of a clinician-administered PTSD scale. *Journal of Traumatic Stress, 8,* 75–90. doi: 10.1002/jts.2490080106

Briere, J. (1995). *Trauma Symptom Inventory professional manual.* Odessa, FL: Psychological Assessment Resources.

Briere, J. (1996). *Trauma Symptom Checklist for Children: Professional manual.* Odessa, FL: Psychological Assessment Resources.

Briere, J. (2004). *Psychological assessment of adult posttraumatic states: Phenomenology, diagnosis, and measurement.* Washington, DC: American Psychological Association.

Briere, J. (2005). *Trauma Symptom Checklist for Young Children: Professional manual.* Odessa, FL: Psychological Assessment Resources.

Briere, J. (2011). *Trauma Symptom Inventory-2 professional manual.* Odessa, FL: Psychological Assessment Resources.

Briere, J., Kaltman, S., & Green, B. L. (2008). Accumulated childhood trauma and symptom complexity. *Journal of Traumatic Stress, 21,* 223–226.

Cloitre, M., Stolbach, B. C., Herman, J. L., van der Kolk, B., Pynoos, R., Wang, J., & Petkova, E. (2009). A developmental approach to complex PTSD: Childhood and adult cumulative trauma as predictors of symptom complexity. *Journal of Traumatic Stress, 22,* 399–408.

Davidson, J. R. T., Kudler, H. S., & Smith, R. (1997). Structured Interview for PTSD (SIP): Psychometric validation for *DSM-IV* criteria. *Depression and Anxiety, 5,* 127–129. doi: 10.1002/(SICI)1520-6394(1997)5:3<127::AID-DA3>3.0.CO;2-B

Elhai, J. D., Gray, M. J., Kashdan, T. B., & Franklin, C. L. (2005). Which instruments are most commonly used to assess traumatic event exposure and posttraumatic effects? A survey of traumatic stress professionals. *Journal of Traumatic Stress, 18,* 541–545. doi: 10.1002/jts.20062

Elhai, J. D., Palmieri, P. A., Biehn, T. L., Frueh, B. C., & Magruder, K. M. (2010). Posttraumatic stress disorder's frequency and intensity ratings are associated with factor structure differences in military veterans. *Psychological Assessment, 22,* 723–728. doi: 10.1037/a0020643

Finkelhor, D., Turner, H., Ormrod, R., & Hamby, S. L. (2010). Trends in childhood violence and abuse exposure: evidence from 2 national surveys. *Archives of Pediatric and Adolescent Medicine, 164,* 238–242.

Fletcher, K. (1996). Psychometric review of Dimensions of Stressful Events (DOSE) Ratings Scale. In B. H. Stamm (Ed.), *Measurement of stress, trauma, and adaptation* (pp. 144–151). Lutherville, MD: Sidran Press.

Foa, E. B., Cashman, L., Jaycox, L., & Perry, K. (1997). The validation of a self-report measure of posttraumatic stress disorder: The Posttraumatic Diagnostic Scale. *Psychological Assessment, 9,* 445–451. doi: 10.1037/1040-3590.9.4.445

Foa, E. B., Johnson, K. M., Feeny, N. C., & Treadwell, K. R. H. (2001). The Child PTSD Symptom Scale: A preliminary examination of its psychometric properties. *Journal of Clinical Child Psychology, 30*, 376–384. doi: 10.1207/S15374424JCCP3003_9

Foa, E. B., Riggs, D. S., Dancu, C. V., & Rothbaum, B. O. (1993). Reliability and validity of a brief instrument for assessing post-traumatic stress disorder. *Journal of Traumatic Stress, 6*, 459-473. doi: 10.1002/jts.2490060405

Foa, E. B., & Tolin, D. F. (2000). Comparison of the PTSD Symptom Scale–Interview version and the Clinician-Administered PTSD Scale. *Journal of Traumatic Stress, 13*, 181–191. doi: 10.1023/A:1007781909213

Ford, J. D., Elhai, J. D., Connor, D. F., & Frueh, B. C. (2010). Poly-victimization and risk of posttraumatic, depressive, and substance use disorders and involvement in delinquency in a national sample of adolescents. *Journal of Adolescent Health, 46*, 545–552.

Ford, J. D., & Fournier, D. (2007). Psychological trauma, post-traumatic stress disorder, and health-related functioning of low-income urban women receiving community mental health services for severe mental illness. *Journal of Psychiatric Intensive Care, 3*, 27–34. doi: 10.1017/S1742646407001094

Ford, J. D., Hartman, J. K., Hawke, J., & Chapman, J. (2008). Traumatic victimization, posttraumatic stress disorder, suicidal ideation, and substance abuse risk among juvenile justice-involved youths. *Journal of Child and Adolescent Trauma, 1*, 75–92. doi: 10.1080/19361520801934456

Ford, J. D., Trestman, R. L., Wiesbrock, V. H., & Zhang, W. (2009). Validation of a brief screening instrument for identifying psychiatric disorders among newly incarcerated adults. *Psychiatric Services, 60*, 842–846.

Frueh, B. C., Grubaugh, A. L., Cusack, K. J., & Elhai, J. D. (2009). Disseminating evidence-based practices for adults with PTSD and severe mental illness in public-sector mental health agencies. *Behavior Modification, 33*, 66–81.

Goodman, L., Corcoran, C., Turner, K., Yuan, N., & Green, B. L. (1998). Assessing traumatic event exposure: General issues and preliminary findings for the Stressful Life Events Screening Questionnaire. *Journal of Traumatic Stress, 11*, 521–542. doi:10.1023/A:1024456713321

Gray, M. J., Elhai, J. D., Owen, J. R., & Monroe, J. R. (2009). Psychometric properties of the Trauma Assessment for Adults. *Depression and Anxiety, 26*, 190–195. doi: 10.1002/da.20535

Kessler, R. C., Sonnega, A., Bromet, E., Hughes, M., & Nelson, C. B. (1995). Posttraumatic stress disorder in the National Comorbidity Survey. *Archives of General Psychiatry, 52*, 1048–1060.

Kimerling, R., Trafton, J. A., & Nguyen, B. (2006). Validation of a brief screen for posttraumatic stress disorder with substance use disorder patients. *Addictive Behaviors, 31*, 2074–2079.

Ko, S. J., Ford, J. D., Kassam-Adams, N., Berkowitz, S. J., Wilson, C., Wong, M., . . . Layne, C. M. (2008). Creating trauma-informed systems: Child welfare, education, first responders, health care, juvenile justice. *Professional Psychology-Research and Practice, 39*, 396−404.

Kubany, E. S., Haynes, S. N., Leisen, M. B., Owens, J. A., Kaplan, A. S., Watson, S. B., & Burns, K. (2000). Development and preliminary validation of a brief broad-spectrum measure of trauma exposure: The Traumatic Life Events Questionnaire. *Psychological Assessment, 12*, 210−224. doi: 10.1037/1040-3590.12.2.210

Long, M. E., & Elhai, J. D. (2009). Posttraumatic stress disorder's traumatic stressor criterion: History, controversy, clinical and legal implications. *Psychological Injury and Law, 2*, 167−178. doi: 10.1007/s12207-009-9043-6

Nader, K. (2008). *Understanding and assessing trauma in children and adolescents: Measures, methods and youth in context.* New York, NY: Routledge.

Nader, K., Kriegler, J. A., Blake, D. D., Pynoos, R. S., Newman, E., & Weather, F. W. (1996). *Clinician-Administered PTSD Scale, Child and Adolescent Version.* White River Junction, VT: National Center for PTSD.

Norris, F. H., & Hamblen, J. L. (2004). Standardized self-report measures of civilian trauma and PTSD. In J. P. Wilson & T. M. Keane (Eds.), *Assessing psychological trauma and PTSD* (2nd ed., pp. 63−102). New York, NY: Guilford Press.

Ohan, J. L., Myers, K., & Collett, B. R. (2002). Ten-year review of rating scales. IV: Scales assessing trauma and its effects. *Journal of the Academy of Child and Adolescent Psychiatry, 41*, 1401−1422. doi: 10.1097/00004583-200212000-00012

Ouimette, P., Wade, M., Prins, A., & Schohn, M. (2008). Identifying PTSD in primary care: Comparison of the Primary Care-PTSD Screen (PC-PTSD) and the General Health Questionnaire-12 (GHQ). *Journal of Anxiety Disorders, 22*, 337−343.

Resnick, H. S., Best, C. L., Kilpatrick, D. G., Freedy, J. R., & Falsetti, S. A. (1993). Trauma assessment for adults [Unpublished interview protocol]. Charleston: Medical University of South Carolina.

Saigh, P., Yaski, A. E., Oberfield, R. A., Green, B. L., Halamandaris, P. V., Rubenstein, H., . . . McHugh, M. (2000). The Children's PTSD Inventory: Development and reliability. *Journal of Traumatic Stress, 30*, 369−380. doi: 10.1023/A:1007750021626

Taylor, S., Frueh, B. C., & Asmundson, G. J. G. (2007). Detection and management of malingering in people presenting for treatment of posttraumatic stress disorder: Methods, obstacles, and recommendations. *Journal of Anxiety Disorders, 21*, 22−41. doi: 10.1016/j.janxdis.2006.03.016

Weathers, F. W., Keane, T. M., & Davidson, J. R. (2001). Clinician-administered PTSD scale: A review of the first ten years of research. *Depression and Anxiety, 13*, 132−156. doi: 10.1002/da.1029

Weathers, F., Keane, T., & Foa, E. (2008). Assessment and diagnosis of adults. In E. Foa, T. Keane, M. Friedman, & J. Cohen (Eds.), *Effective treatments for PTSD* (pp. 23−61). New York, NY: Guilford Press.

Weathers, F. W., Litz, B. T., Herman, D. S., Huska, J. A., & Keane, T. M. (1993, October). *The PTSD checklist: Reliability, validity, & diagnostic utility.* Paper presented at the annual meeting of the International Society for Traumatic Stress Studies, San Antonio, Texas.

Weiss, D. S., & Marmar, C. R. (1997). The Impact of Event Scale—Revised. In J. P. Wilson & T. M. Keane (Eds.), *Assessing psychological trauma and PTSD* (pp. 399–411). New York, NY: Guilford Press.

CHAPTER 5

Assessing Comorbid Conditions

The purpose of this chapter is to provide practical, evidence-based suggestions for how to optimally assess for the presence of other psychopathology often associated with posttraumatic stress disorder (PTSD). We begin by discussing the extent of psychiatric comorbidity found with PTSD. Next, we discuss the advantages of, as well as perceived myths about, using structured diagnostic interviews in evaluating individuals for mental disorders. We then discuss details regarding some of the more popular structured diagnostic interviews. Finally, we detail several self-report measures to further narrow a patient's symptoms profile, as a final means of comprehensively evaluating psychopathology.

In the previous chapter, we discussed a top-down approach to assessing psychopathology, which we illustrated with a funnel. At the top of the funnel is the assessment of general psychopathology. Relevant to the present chapter, the most general (widest in the funnel example) would be the assessment of general psychopathology using structured diagnostic interviews and broad-based personality assessments. Subsequently, we advocate for using self-report measures of specific symptom domains found clinically significant from general psychopathology assessment.

PTSD's Comorbidity

In the previous chapter, we discussed methods for evaluating PTSD. However, PTSD seldom presents itself in the absence of other forms of psychopathology. In fact, this issue has been evaluated in the National Comorbidity Survey (NCS), a large-scale, nationally representative study of several thousand United States Residents (Kessler, Sonnega, Bromet, Hughes, & Nelson, 1995). In the NCS data, Kessler et al. found that 44% of women and 59% of men diagnosed with PTSD also met diagnostic criteria for at least *three* additional mental disorders. The most common comorbid disorders with PTSD were major depression and dysthymic disorder, specific and social phobia, agoraphobia, and substance use. Specifically, Kessler et al. found that among those with PTSD, 48% of men and 49% of women had a history of major depression, 52% of men and 28% of women had history of alcohol use disorder, 31% of men and 29% of women had a specific phobia, 28% of both men and women had social phobia, and 21% of men and 23% of women had dysthymia. Other disorders commonly presenting with PTSD in adults include eating disorders (reviewed in Brewerton, 2007), borderline personality disorder (Golier et al., 2003), and cognitive disorders such as mild traumatic brain injury (Stein & McAllister, 2009). In children, PTSD has been found comorbid with additional disorders such as attention deficit hyperactivity disorder (Famularo, Fenton, Kinscherff, & Augustyn, 1996).

PTSD's substantial comorbidity is problematic and important to evaluate for several reasons. First, comorbidity with PTSD may interfere with traditional treatment progress. For example, given PTSD's high comorbidity with alcohol use (Kessler et al., 1995), and because alcohol use is a coping mechanism to suppress painful traumatic memories, empirically supported PTSD exposure therapies may have limited success when the patient is not fully engaged in processing the painful memories because of their alcohol use. Second, empirically supported treatments are usually disorder specific, developed and tested for use with a single, particular mental disorder (Barlow, 2007). Thus, for a patient presenting with PTSD comorbid with another mental disorder, the vast majority of empirically supported treatments have not been developed for treating multiple disorders simultaneously. The clinician therefore must typically choose to focus on treating only one disorder at a time. However, it should be noted that some research demonstrates that treating only one disorder among patients with comorbidity is effective in alleviating symptoms from both disorders (Barlow, Levitt, & Bufka, 1999).

Complicating the issue of PTSD's high comorbidity with other mental disorders is the fact that several PTSD symptoms overlap with other disorders. For example, PTSD's symptoms of difficulty concentrating, difficulty sleeping, and lack of interest in pleasurable activities overlap with major depressive disorder. Additionally, PTSD's symptoms of difficulty sleeping, difficulty concentrating, and irritability overlap with generalized anxiety disorder. So a patient with PTSD is likely to be diagnosed with one or more of these other similar disorders merely by virtue of endorsing some of the overlapping symptoms. Because of the overlap between PTSD and other psychiatric disorders, the practicing clinician may question whether it is appropriate to diagnose the patient with both conditions and fear overpathologizing the patient. However, research has demonstrated that PTSD's symptom overlap with other disorders is not solely responsible for PTSD's high comorbidity (e.g., Elhai, Grubaugh, Kashdan, & Frueh, 2008). With these findings in mind, it may be appropriate to diagnose the patient with PTSD and other psychiatric disorders for which the patient meets criteria, even if symptoms overlap.

We recommend that the clinician carefully assess the timing of onset of psychopathology in order to assist in differential diagnosis, given PTSD's substantial comorbidity. For example, discovering that major depressive disorder preceded trauma exposure and PTSD for a patient could have different treatment implications than if the patient had developed PTSD and depression after traumatic event exposure. Of course, in that scenario, treatment priorities would involve targeting both PTSD and depression, but a premorbid (to the trauma) depressed clinical picture may require more long-term monitoring of depression even after the PTSD symptoms remit.

RECOMMENDATIONS FOR ASSESSING PTSD'S COMORBIDITY

When evaluating trauma victims, we recommend the following strategy in assessing psychiatric disorders in addition to PTSD. First, a structured or semistructured diagnostic interview should be used to assess a full range of Axis I mental disorders. Of course, the specific interview instrument should have a proven track record of being psychometrically sound. Second, based on particular disorders that are diagnosed from the diagnostic interview, focused self-report measures should be used to further probe the frequency and/or intensity of that disorder's symptoms.

We realize that persuading clinicians to use a structured diagnostic interview during an initial evaluation with a patient may be challenging. Many clinicians likely believe that using such interviews is too time intensive, may interfere with establishing rapport, does not allow for the subjective clinical judgment needed in complex cases, and can be costly from a financial standpoint. However, we urge clinicians to consider the following rebuttals to these points. First, some structured diagnostic interviews (i.e., the Mini International Neuropsychiatric Interview [MINI]) have administration times as short as 15 to 20 minutes. Second, most patients, in our experience, appreciate a thorough and standardized diagnostic evaluation and realize that rapport can be established during and immediately after the interview. Third, supplemental, probing questions involving clinical judgment are certainly possible to integrate into such interviews and can further inform the treatment process. Finally, some structured interviews are available at a nominal cost, if not completely free of charge. We therefore recommend that the skeptical clinician keep an open mind about using a structured diagnostic interview and perhaps try one such interview with a client in order to make an informed decision about the cost versus benefit of such practice.

Structured Diagnostic Interviews

In the United States, the most popular structured diagnostic interview for mental disorders in adults is the Structured Clinical Interview for *DSM-IV* Axis I Disorders (SCID-I) (First, Spitzer, Gibbon, & Williams, 1996). The SCID-I is a semistructured interview in that it allows for flexible probes to queries of diagnostic criteria. A version for clinical practice, as well as an expanded version for research purposes, is available. Administration time for the clinical version is roughly 45 to 90 minutes and is available from www.appi.org

For clinicians who are reluctant to dedicate 45 to 90 minutes for an Axis I diagnostic interview, a shorter alternative is the MINI (Sheehan et al., 1998). The MINI was developed as a streamlined alternative to the SCID-I by taking advantage of skip-out rules, taking only 15 to 20 minutes in administration time. It is also less text intensive than the SCID-I; the SCID-I's administration booklet is nearly 100 pages long, compared to roughly 30 pages for the most recent version of the MINI. The MINI has demonstrated adequate reliability and validity when compared to the SCID (Sheehan et al., 1997) and Composite International Diagnostic Interview (CIDI) (Lecrubier et al., 1997). Other structured and semi-structured diagnostic Axis I interviews are also available for adult respondents, including the CIDI and Diagnostic Interview Schedule. These interview measures are discussed elsewhere (Segal & Coolidge, 2003; Summerfeldt & Antony, 2004).

Several structured diagnostic interviews for Axis II (personality) disorders are available (reviewed in Livesley, 2001). For example, the clinician could use the SCID-II (First, Gibbon, Spitzer, Williams, & Benjamin, 1997) or the International Personality Disorder Examination (Loranger, 1999).

Structured diagnostic interviews are also available for children and adolescents. For example, the Diagnostic Interview Schedule for Children (DISC; Shaffer, Fisher, Lucas, Dulcan, & Schwab-Stone, 2000) is highly structured and requires 70 to 120 minutes of administration time. The Diagnostic Interview for Children and Adolescents–Revised (DICA-R; Reich, 2000) is a semistructured interview that takes approximately 2 to 3 hours to administer. For a briefer alternative, a tailored version of the MINI for children and adolescents is available and has been validated (Sheehan et al., 2010). Other similar measures are discussed elsewhere (Hughes & Melson, 2008).

Objective Personality Assessment

Objective personality assessment instruments offer broad assessment of psychopathology through the use of self-report ratings by patients. Some of the more popular instruments in this category include the Minnesota Multiphasic Personality Inventory-2 (MMPI-2, Butcher et al., 2001) and MMPI-A for adolescents (Butcher et al., 1992), and the Personality Assessment Inventory (Morey, 1991). Each of these instruments includes subscales measuring PTSD symptoms. However, these scales do not map onto *DSM-IV*'s PTSD symptom criteria and thus do not offer the precision in evaluating PTSD that PTSD-specific measures offer.

While objective personality assessment instruments such as the MMPI-2 can be useful in the assessment of trauma-related psychopathology, some specific considerations deserve discussion regarding their practical use. One advantage of these instruments is that they include validity scales to measure the respondent's test-taking attitude. And research discussed in Chapter 7 demonstrates that objective personality instruments such as the MMPI-2 are fairly accurate in detecting PTSD symptom overreporting. However, some research has demonstrated that the validity scales on these instruments are problematic with trauma victims and PTSD patients. First, elevations on the MMPI-2's validity scales can be a function of genuine psychopathology that is typical in trauma victims, including PTSD, dissociation, and depression (Klotz Flitter, Elhai, & Gold, 2003). Second, these overreporting scales do not perform as well in discriminating malingered from genuine PTSD as they do in detecting other forms of malingered psychopathology (Rogers, Sewell, Martin, & Vitacco, 2003). Thus, it is quite possible for a genuine PTSD patient to produce an invalid, overreported MMPI-2 profile; in our experiences, this is quite common in patients with extensive trauma histories and multiple comorbidities, despite no tangible incentive to overreport symptoms.

Another challenge in using broad-based personality assessments with trauma victims is the potential for the misidentification of psychotic symptoms. That is, psychopathology that is common to trauma victims, including PTSD, depression, and dissociation, largely accounts for psychotic scale elevations that have been found among trauma survivors on these instruments (Elhai, Frueh, Gold, Hamner, & Gold, 2003; Elhai, Gold, Mateus, & Astaphan, 2001). These scales are probably tapping trauma victims' PTSD-related intrusive memories and negative affect more so than bizarre sensory experience found in the psychotic disorders.

Self-Report Measures

In isolation, when time restraints exist or in combination with one of the more thorough interview measures described earlier, self-report measures of specific forms of psychopathology can further inform the extent and severity of a patient's mental health condition. Fortunately, there are a number of easily accessible self-report measures for almost any psychiatric disorder.

Because roughly half of individuals diagnosed with PTSD also are diagnosed with major depressive disorder (Kessler et al., 1995), depression symptoms are important to evaluate in victims of traumatic events. With regard to depression, two measures in particular deserve discussion: the Beck Depression Inventory-2 (BDI-2, Beck, Steer, & Brown, 1996), which is a fairly brief 21-item measure of depression severity, and the Patient Health Questionnaire-9 (PHQ-9), which is an even shorter screening measure of depression that maps onto the nine *DSM-IV* major depression symptoms (Spitzer, Kroenke, Williams, & Patient Health Questionnaire Primary Care Study Group, 1999). Both are widely used and have sound psychometric properties (Kroenke, Spitzer, & Williams, 2001).

Dissociation is also a common form of psychopathology associated with PTSD. Bernstein and Putnam's (1986) Dissociative Experiences Scale is a 28-item measure of dissociation with adequate psychometric properties (Ijzendoor & Schuengel, 1996). A newer measure of dissociation, the Multiscale Dissociation Inventory (Briere, 2002), is a 30-item multiscale measure with adequate psychometrics (Briere, Weather, & Runtz, 2005).

Anger and aggression are also important, impairing problems in trauma victims. Although lengthy measures of anger are available, such as the State-Trait Anger Expression Inventory-2 (Spielberger, 1999), newer, shorter measures are now available to clinicians, including the Dimensions of Anger Reactions Scale (Forbes et al., 2004). Such measures may be administered especially if the trauma victim endorsed symptoms of anger and irritability when inquiring about PTSD's symptoms.

It is also helpful to evaluate other types of psychopathology often seen in trauma victims. Because of PTSD's previously stated high comorbidity with substance use, using a substance use measure such as the CAGE Questionnaire (Ewing, 1984) and Addiction Severity Index (McLellan et al., 1992) would elucidate substance use problems.

Finally, in addition to measuring specific pathological constructs, it may be helpful to measure physical and mental health quality of life and functional impairment indices in patients. Using measures such as the Quality of Life Inventory (Frisch et al., 2005) and SF-36 (McHorney, Ware, & Raczek, 1993) can assist in this capacity.

CONCLUSION

In sum, after a thorough evaluation of the trauma victim's mental disorders using a structured diagnostic interview, clinicians may also find broad-based personality assessments and more specific self-report measures helpful in uncovering the patient's psychopathology. It should be emphasized, however, that one disadvantage of structured diagnostic interviews is that they typically involve binary "yes"/"no" queries of symptoms that thus do not allow for the dimensionality of responding. However, some objective personality assessments and self-report measures do involve queries of symptoms using a range of response options. These diverse types of measures should be used hand in hand in order to comprehensively evaluate the trauma victim.

REFERENCES

Barlow, D. H. (Ed.). (2007). *Clinical handbook of psychological disorders: A step-by-step treatment manual* (4th ed.). New York, NY: Guilford Press.

Barlow, D. H., Levitt, J. T., & Bufka, L. F. (1999). The dissemination of empirically supported treatments: A view to the future. *Behaviour Research and Therapy, 37*, S147–S162.

Beck, A. T., Steer, R. A., & Brown, G. K. (1996). *Manual for the Beck Depression Inventory-II*. San Antonio, TX: Psychological Corporation.

Bernstein, E. M., & Putnam, F. W. (1986). Development, reliability, and validity of a dissociation scale. *Journal of Nervous and Mental Disease, 174*, 727–735. doi: 10.1097/00005053-198612000-00004

Brewerton, T. D. (2007). Eating disorders, trauma, and comorbidity: Focus on PTSD. *Eating Disorders, 15*, 285–304. doi: 10.1080/10640260701454311

Briere, J. (2002). *Multiscale Dissociation Inventory*. Odessa, FL: Psychological Assessment Resources.

Briere, J., Weather, F. W., & Runtz, M. (2005). Is dissociation a multidimensional construct? Data from the Multiscale Dissociation Inventory. *Journal of Traumatic Stress, 18*, 221–231. doi: 1002/jts.20024

Butcher, J. N., Graham, J. R., Ben-Porath, Y. S., Tellegen, A., Dahlstrom, W. G., & Kaemmer, B. (2001). *MMPI-2 (Minnesota Multiphasic Personality Inventory-2): Manual for administration, scoring, and interpretation* (Revised ed.). Minneapolis: University of Minnesota Press.

Butcher, J. N., Williams, C. L., Graham, J. R., Archer, R. P., Tellegen, A., Ben-Porath, Y. S., & Kaemmer, B. (1992). *MMPI-A manual for administration, scoring, and interpretation*. Odessa, FL: Pearson Assessments.

Elhai, J. D., Frueh, B. C., Gold, P. B., Hamner, M. B., & Gold, S. N. (2003). Posttraumatic stress, depression and dissociation as predictors of MMPI-2 scale 8 scores in combat veterans with PTSD. *Journal of Trauma & Dissociation, 4*(1), 51–64. doi: 10.1300/J229v04n01_04

Elhai, J. D., Gold, S. N., Mateus, L. F., & Astaphan, T. A. (2001). Scale 8 elevations on the MMPI-2 among women survivors of childhood sexual abuse: Evaluating posttraumatic stress, depression, and dissociation as predictors. *Journal of Family Violence, 16*, 47–57. doi: 10.1023/A:1026576425986

Elhai, J. D., Grubaugh, A. L., Kashdan, T. B., & Frueh, B. C. (2008). Empirical examination of a proposed refinement to *DSM-IV* posttraumatic stress disorder symptom criteria using the National Comorbidity Survey Replication data. *Journal of Clinical Psychiatry, 69*, 597–602. doi: 10.4088/JCP.v69n0411

Ewing, J. A. (1984). Detecting alcoholism: The CAGE questionnaire. *JAMA: Journal of the American Medical Association, 252*, 1905–1907. doi: 10.1001/jama.252.14.1905

Famularo, R., Fenton, T., Kinscherff, R., & Augustyn, M. (1996). Psychiatric comorbidity in childhood post traumatic stress disorder. *Child Abuse & Neglect, 20*, 953-961. doi: 10.1016/0145-2134(96)00084-1

First, M. B., Gibbon, M., Spitzer, R. L., Williams, J. B. W., & Benjamin, L. S. (1997). *Structured Clinical Interview for DSM-IV Axis II Personality Disorders (SCID-II)*. Washington, DC: American Psychiatric Press.

First, M. B., Spitzer, R. L., Gibbon, M., & Williams, J. B. (1996). *Structured Clinical Interview for DSM-IV Axis I Disorders, Clinician Version (SCID-CV)*. Washington, DC: American Psychiatric Press.

Forbes, D., Hawthorne, G., Elliott, P., McHugh, T., Biddle, D., & Creamer, M. (2004). A concise measure of anger in combat-related posttraumatic stress disorder. *Journal of Traumatic Stress, 17*, 249–256. doi: 10.1023/B:JOTS.0000029268.22161.bd

Frisch, M. B., Clark, M. P., Rouse, S. V., Rudd, M. D., Paweleck, J. K., Greenstone, A., & Kopplin, D. A. (2005). Predictive and treatment validity of life satisfaction and the quality of life inventory. *Assessment, 12*, 66–78. doi: 10.1177/1073191104268006

Golier, J. A., Yehuda, R., Bierer, L. M., Mitropoulou, V., New, A. S., Schmeidler, J., . . . Siever, L. J. (2003). The relationship of borderline personality disorder to posttraumatic stress disorder and traumatic events. *American Journal of Psychiatry, 160*, 2018–2024. doi: 10.1176/appi.ajp.160.11.2018

Hughes, C. W., & Melson, A. G. (2008). Child and adolescent measures for diagnosis and screening. In A. J. Rush, M. B. First, & D. Blacker (Eds.), *Handbook of psychiatric measures* (2nd ed., pp. 251–308). Arlington, VA: American Psychiatric Publishing.

Ijzendoor, M. H., & Schuengel, C. (1996). The measurement of dissociation in normal and clinical populations: Meta-analytic validation of the Dissociative Experiences Scale (DES). *Clinical Psychology Review, 16*, 365–382. doi: 10.1016/0272-7358(96)00006-2

Kessler, R. C., Sonnega, A., Bromet, E., Hughes, M., & Nelson, C. B. (1995). Posttraumatic stress disorder in the National Comorbidity Survey. *Archives of General Psychiatry, 52,* 1048−1060.

Klotz Flitter, J. M., Elhai, J. D., & Gold, S. N. (2003). MMPI-2 F scale elevations in adult victims of child sexual abuse. *Journal of Traumatic Stress, 16,* 269−274. doi: 10.1023/A:1023700208696

Kroenke, K., Spitzer, R. L., & Williams, J. B. W. (2001). The PHQ-9: Validity of a brief depression severity measure. *Journal of General Internal Medicine, 16,* 606−613. doi: 10.1046/j.1525-1497.2001.016009606.x

Lecrubier, Y., Sheehan, D. V., Weiller, E., Amorim, P., Bonora, I., Sheehan, K. H., . . . Dunbar, G. C. (1997). The Mini International Neuropsychiatric Interview (MINI). A short diagnostic structured interview: Reliability and validity according to the CIDI. *European Psychiatry, 12,* 224−231. doi: 10.1016/ S0924-9338(97)83296-8

Livesley, W. J. (2001). *Handbook of personality disorders: Theory, research, and treatment.* New York, NY: Guilford Press.

Loranger, A. W. (1999). *International Personality Disorder Examination: DSM−IV and ICD-10 Interviews.* Lutz, FL: Psychological Assessment Resources.

McHorney, C. A., Ware, J. E., & Raczek, A. E. (1993). The MOS 36-Item Short-Form Health Survey (SF-36): II. Psychometric and clinical tests of validity in measuring physical and mental health constructs. *Medical Care, 31,* 247−263. doi: 10.1097/00005650-199303000-00006

McLellan, A. T., Kushner, H., Metzger, D., Peters, R., Smith, I., Grissom, G., . . . Argeriou, M. (1992). The fifth edition of the Addiction Severity Index. *Journal of Substance Abuse Treatment, 9,* 199−213. doi: 10.1016/0740-5472(92) 90062-S

Morey, L. C. (1991). *Personality Assessment Inventory: Professional manual.* Lutz, FL: Psychological Assessment Resources.

Reich, W. (2000). Diagnostic Interview for Children and Adolescents (DICA). *Journal of the Academy of Child and Adolescent Psychiatry, 39,* 59−66. doi: 10.1097/ 00004583-200001000-00017

Rogers, R., Sewell, K. W., Martin, M. A., & Vitacco, M. J. (2003). Detection of feigned mental disorders: A meta-analysis of the MMPI-2 and malingering. *Assessment, 10,* 160−177. doi: 10.1177/1073191103010002007

Segal, D. L., & Coolidge, F. L. (2003). Structured interviewing and *DSM* classification. In M. Hersen & S. M. Turner (Eds.), *Adult psychopathology and diagnosis* (4th ed., pp. 72−103). Hoboken, NJ: Wiley.

Shaffer, D., Fisher, P., Lucas, C., Dulcan, M., & Schwab-Stone, M. (2000). NIMH Diagnostic Interview Schedule for Children version IV (NIMH DISC-IV): Description, differences from previous versions, and reliability of some common diagnoses. *Journal of the Academy of Child and Adolescent Psychiatry, 39,* 28−38. doi: 10.1097/00004583-200001000-00014

Sheehan, D. V., Lecrubier, Y., Sheehan, K. H., Amorim, P., Janavs, J., Weiller, E., . . . Dunbar, G. (1998). The Mini-International Neuropsychiatric Interview (MINI): The development and validation of a structured diagnostic psychiatric interview for *DSM-IV* and ICD-10. *Journal of Clinical Psychiatry, 59*(suppl. 20), 22–33.

Sheehan, D. V., Lecrubier, Y., Sheehan, K. H., Janavs, J., Weiller, E., Keskiner, A., . . . Dunbar, G. C. (1997). The validity of the Mini International Neuropsychiatric Interview (MINI) according to the SCID-P and its reliability. *European Psychiatry, 12*, 232–241. doi: 10.1016/S0924-9338(97)83297-X

Sheehan, D. V., Sheehan, K. H., Shytle, R. D., Janavs, J., Bannon, Y., Rogers, J. E., . . . Wilkinson, B. (2010). Reliability and validity of the Mini International Neuropsychiatric Interview for Children and Adolescents (MINI-KID). *Journal of Clinical Psychiatry, 71*, 313–326. doi: 10.4088/JCP.09m05305whi

Spielberger, C. D. (1999). *State-Trait Anger Expression Inventory-2: Professional manual.* Lutz, FL: Psychological Assessment Resources.

Spitzer, R. L., Kroenke, K., Williams, J. B. W., & the Patient Health Questionnaire Primary Care Study Group. (1999). Validation and utility of a self-report version of the PRIME-MD: The PHQ primary care study. *JAMA, 282*, 1737–1744. doi: 10.1001/jama.282.18.1737

Stein, M. B., & McAllister, T. W. (2009). Exploring the convergence of posttraumatic stress disorder and mild traumatic brain injury. *American Journal of Psychiatry, 166*, 768–776. doi: 10.1176/appi.ajp.2009.08101604

Summerfeldt, L. J., & Antony, M. M. (2004). Structured and semistructured diagnostic interviews. In M. M. Antony & D. H. Barlow (Eds.), *Handbook of assessment and treatment planning for psychological disorders* (pp. 3–37). New York, NY: Guilford Press.

CHAPTER 6

Considering Ethnicity, Race, and Culture

Exposure to traumatic stressors and PTSD are epidemic across all ethnoracial groups in the United States and western European countries, as well as globally. The American Psychological Association Division of Trauma Psychology's *Guidelines for Clinicians Regarding the Assessment of Trauma* (Armstrong et al., 2011) describes the range of ethnocultural factors that should be considered in the assessment of trauma history, PTSD, and associated or comorbid disorders, including the clinician's background as well as the client's:

> Clients' responses to traumatic stress should be considered in the context of their gender, ethnic, cultural, and racial identity, socioeconomic status, and sexual orientation, as well as cultural contexts that may help determine both their interpretation of traumatic events and how they express trauma related distress. When the assessor differs from the client on one or more of these identity factors, the potential impact of such differences on the client's reporting style and behavior toward the [assessor] should be considered and . . . addressed (Recommendation #13).

In this chapter, all of these factors will be discussed, beginning with the foundation provided by the thorough research review and cogent recommendations for clinical practice by Pole, Gone, and Kulkarni (2008). Per the APA Guidelines, we address sociodemographic factors, including gender, sexual orientation, and socioeconomic status because they involve (and can create) unique contexts that may affect if, when, how, and with what outcomes people are exposed to traumatic stressors and develop PTSD. We also discuss how socioeconomic status may contribute to ethnocultural differences in PTSD, particularly in relation to actual or possible ethnocultural disparities due to discrimination or stigma. Throughout, we highlight practical implications for clinicians when screening, assessing, planning, and monitoring PTSD treatment progress and outcomes.

ETHNOCULTURAL DIFFERENCES IN TRAUMA EXPOSURE AND TRAUMATIC STRESS DISORDERS

Trauma Exposure

Ethnoracial minority groups historically have experienced higher risk of exposure to traumatic stressors than the majority population, not only in the United States and western European countries but worldwide (Pole et al., 2008). Women (Seedat, Stein, & Carey, 2005) and sexual identity minority groups (Roberts, Austin, Corliss, Vandermorris, & Koenen, 2010) also have been subject to higher risk of exposure to traumatic victimization than men or heterosexuals. Discrimination and stigma based on identity factors such as ethnicity, race, gender, or sexual orientation are key contributors to this elevated risk of trauma exposure, both directly (e.g., slavery, genocide, hate crimes) and indirectly (e.g., barriers leading to disparities in access to socioeconomic resources and health care and law enforcement services).

The preponderance of the evidence suggests that Black and Hispanic individuals are at greater risk for exposure to traumatic stressors than White or other ethnoracial minority persons in the United States. It is apparent that individuals from different ethnoracial backgrounds may have a differential risk for experiencing particular types of traumatic events. However, the variability in findings and an absence of any definitive comparison of adults or children in epidemiological samples in which persons from all major ethnoracial groups were fully represented limit the conclusions that can be made on this topic. Moreover, what appear to be ethnoracial differences in some studies may be better explained by within-group variations (e.g., African American versus Afro-Caribbean Blacks), regional, urban versus rural, socioeconomic, gender, or other differences (Pole et al., 2008).

Traumatic Stress Disorders

Consistent with the findings concerning trauma exposure, Black, Hispanic, American Indian, and other (e.g., Native Hawaiian) ethnoracial minority group membership (except for Asian Americans) has been found to confer increased risk of developing PTSD in some U.S. samples (Pole et al., 2008). However, Roberts, Gilman, Breslau, Breslau, and Koenen (2011) found that Hispanics were less likely than Blacks and no more likely than Whites to develop PTSD. Consistent with the latter result, many studies have failed to find ethnoracial differences in the risk of developing PTSD (Breslau et al., 2006; Pole et al., 2008).

Thus, as Pole et al. (2008) concluded in their research review, results of recent studies examining ethnoracial differences in traumatic stress disorders suggest that ethnoracial minority group members are at risk for PTSD—but in some circumstances they are at no greater risk than Whites, and possibly even more resilient than Whites. Asian Americans in particular seem the most resilient with regard to the development of PTSD, although these findings are largely based on studies of Japanese Americans; other Asian American subgroups have not been studied extensively or have risk factors that place them at greater rather than lesser risk of PTSD (see below).

UTILIZATION OF SERVICES FOR TRAUMATIC STRESS DISORDERS

Several studies on race/ethnic differences in health care utilization patterns following trauma exposure have found that relative to ethnoracial minority group members, Whites are more likely to seek treatment for depression and anxiety (as well as specifically PTSD; Pole et al., 2008). Several reasons have been advanced to explain why, when health care utilization differences are found, Blacks are less likely to seek formal mental health treatment than Whites, including: "shared group perceptions that mental illness is highly stigmatizing . . . ; reluctance to seek help outside the family except in extreme circumstances . . . ; mistrust of physicians (Alim, Charney, & Mellman, 2006, p. 801); perception of racial or ethnic bias in care providers (Pole et al., 2008); and reduced access to general- and mental-health facilities due to residence in poverty areas . . . " (Roberts et al., 2011, p. 79). In addition, Triffleman and Pole (2010) note that a culturally based stigma toward people who seek or appear to need mental health treatment, discrepancies in race and culture between therapists and clients (and potential discomfort on the client's part or discrepancies between the client's and therapist's views of the nature of problems and treatment), the financial costs associated with treatment (including ancillary costs such as transportation, child care, and time off work as well as those due to fees or insurance), and beliefs that professionals and researchers tend to discriminate against ethnoracial minorities (Dovidio et al., 2008) may lead to reluctance to seek professional treatment or to participate in treatment research. A tendency to seek help from traditional healers rather than formal health care providers also has been hypothesized to contribute to ethnoracial differences in health care utilization.

Having stated the above, we concur with Pole et al. (2008), who note that there is sufficient diversity (in norms, beliefs, values, roles, practices, language, and history) *within* categorical ethnocultural groups such as African Americans or Latinos to call into question any sweeping generalizations about their exposure and vulnerability or resilience to psychological trauma. Therefore, in order to meaningfully describe and study racial, ethnic, and cultural differences in exposure to psychological trauma and posttraumatic impairment (resilience or recovery)—let alone to identify individuals in need of treatment or other assistance, or to designate and prescribe certain forms of assessment or treatment as effective for the prevention or amelioration of the adverse effects of exposure to psychological trauma—it is essential to carefully reexamine the categories (and the criteria for assigning people or groups to distinct categories) with which people or groups are classified on race, ethnicity, and culture. Findings from health care utilization studies underscore this point.

Asian Americans consistently report experiencing fewer mental health and medical problems than other ethnocultural groups, including exposure to traumatic stressors and PTSD (Pole et al., 2008). However, there are substantial differences in self-reported health and health care services utilization among culturally and nationally based subgroups of Asian Americans.

THE ROLE OF RACISM AND DISCRIMINATION

The interactive effects of psychological trauma, PTSD, and racism and discrimination are as complex as the effects of racism and discrimination are pernicious (Pole et al., 2008). Racism and discrimination may be (a) a risk factor for exposure to traumatic stressors, (b) a moderator exacerbating the impact of psychological traumas and increasing the risk of PTSD or other posttraumatic disorders, or (c) a direct source of psychological trauma.

Racism and Discrimination as Risk Factors for Trauma Exposure

No studies have directly examined racism as a risk factor for exposure to psychological trauma. However, indirect evidence of this possibility may be found in studies demonstrating that ethnoracial discrimination may play a role in placing military personnel from ethnoracial minority groups at risk for more extensive and severe combat trauma exposure (Pole et al., 2008). This discrepancy in risk of combat exposure may begin well before entry into the military: Personnel entering the military who are of ethnoracial minority backgrounds tend to have less education than Whites, and therefore are less likely to be able to attain the higher rank and specialized duties that are associated with an increased likelihood of serving in less hazardous circumstances.

Discrimination based on homophobia or other prejudices against sexual minorities has been linked to hate crimes and interpersonal violence and harassment and to traumatic victimization. Gay men, lesbians, bisexuals, and heterosexuals with same-sex partners in one study were twice as likely as heterosexual men and women to have PTSD, primarily due to exposure to more extensive violence starting at an earlier age (Roberts et al., 2010).

In addition, several lines of evidence indirectly suggest that racism may contribute to risk of trauma exposure, both in the general community and among individuals in health care settings:

> African-Americans are more likely to be pulled over by law enforcement while driving, and are more likely to perceive being differentially harassed by police. Within mental health treatment settings, African-Americans have been found to receive less comprehensive mental health care and are provided with fewer follow-up services. African-Americans are treated by providers who have less training and fewer resources available to them and they are more likely to report being treated with disrespect by providers. Also, African-Americans come in contact

with the mental health system later in the course of their illness and for different reasons than Caucasians. . . . African-Americans are more likely to be involuntarily committed, put in seclusion or restraint, and treated with high doses of antipsychotic medications than Caucasians. (Cusack et al., 2007, p. 104)

Racism and Risk of PTSD

One study found that self-reported experiences of racial discrimination increased the risk of PTSD among Latino and Black police officers (Pole, Best, Metzler, & Marmar, 2005). As Pole et al. (2008) emphasize, when racism leads to the targeting of ethnoracial minority group members for violence, dispossession, or dislocation, the risk of PTSD increases in proportion to the type and degree of psychological trauma involved.

Racism and Other Forms of Identity-Based Bias as Psychological Trauma

A critical question posed but not yet answered by studies of PTSD and racial discrimination is whether racism or other identity-based biases (e.g., homophobia) constitute a "hidden" or "invisible" form of traumatization (Pole et al., 2008). Waelde et al. (2010) created a measure of exposure to race-related traumatic stressors, which identifies stressors that meet the *DSM-IV* criteria for traumatic stressors, and found that ethnoracial minority group members were more likely than Whites to report experiencing such stressors. In addition, exposure to race-related traumatic stressors was associated with PTSD only for the ethnoracial minority group participants (i.e., Black, Hispanic, and Asian Americans). This study's findings suggest that racism, whether intended or not, can lead to traumatic interpersonal events and posttraumatic stress morbidity for ethnoracial minority group members.

Discrimination may occur on the basis of personal characteristics such as gender and sexual identity as well as race, ethnicity, or culture. The combination of exposure to these forms of discrimination and traumatic stressors may have cumulative effects. For example, torture survivors who reported experiencing ethnoculturally based "identity trauma" had higher levels of PTSD and dissociative symptoms, suicidality, and executive functioning deficits in cognitive processing if they also reported having experienced gender discrimination (Kira, Smith, Lewandowski, & Templin, 2011).

ALTERNATIVE EXPLANATIONS FOR APPARENT ETHNORACIAL DIFFERENCES IN PTSD

It is possible that what appear to be racial or ethnocultural differences in the prevalence of exposure to traumatic stressors or of PTSD may be due to differential exposure to psychological trauma (including prior cultural- or nationality-related traumas that often are not assessed in PTSD clinical or epidemiological studies) or to differences in exposure to other risk or protective factors such as poverty or access to health care and education.

The Interaction of Ethnicity and Gender

Women and girls are more likely than men and boys to be exposed to violence and victimization in intimate relationships (e.g., sexual trauma, domestic violence), and to develop posttraumatic disorders, including eating, sexual, affective, and other anxiety disorders as well as PTSD (Seedat et al., 2005). In addition, gender may moderate the association between ethnoracial background, exposure to traumatic stressors, and the development of PTSD. For example, some studies suggest that Black women may be more vulnerable to trauma exposure but less likely to develop PTSD than White women. A theoretical conceptualization that has been advanced to account for this somewhat paradoxical convergence of risk and resilience for traumatized Black women has been described as the "Strong Black Woman" ideology (Harrington et al., 2010). In this view, Black women with ancestral histories of slavery may be socialized intergenerationally to adopt an implicit belief system that takes stereotypes that have been used to justify such victimization (e.g., Black women are "suited" to slavery because they are exceptionally strong) and turns them into a source of identity and pride (e.g., being strong enough to overcome overwhelming adversity is a quality unique to Black females). Thus, Black women who are exposed to traumatic stressors may believe that they must be strong—or maintain the appearance of being unaffected—in the face of these adversities, and they therefore may either not recognize or not feel able to report posttraumatic distress. This phenomenon of attempting to maintain a stance of relative invulnerability or of transforming trauma into growth (e.g., the colloquial saying, "what doesn't kill you makes you stronger") is not exclusively associated with either gender or any ethnicity, but may play a role in what appears to be a resilient response to traumatic stressors by some individuals including Black women.

The Effect of Disparities in Access to Financial Resources by Ethnoracial Minorities

Ethnoracial minority group members also are disproportionately living in poverty. Poverty is a risk factor for a wide variety of severe medical and psychosocial problems among children and adolescents (Najman et al., 2011) as well as adults (Najman et al., 2010; Waitzman & Smith, 1998). Even when poverty does not appear to play a role in health or health care disparities for ethnoracial minority groups, it is important to consider that this may be an artifact of high rates of poverty in those groups, which can restrict the range and variability of socioeconomic differences compared to nonminority groups (Delgado, Lin, & Coffey, 1995).

The Effect of Disparities in Access to Education by Ethnoracial Minorities

Ethnoracial disparities in access to quality education persist in the United States—and education is a known protective factor mitigating against the risk of PTSD (Brewin, Andrews, & Valentine, 2000) and overall health problems (Wiking, Johansson, & Sundquist, 2004). Racial disparities in access to quality education are due to both direct influences (e.g., lower funding for inner city schools that disproportionately serve ethnoracial minority students) and indirect associations with other racial disparities (e.g., disproportionate juvenile and criminal justice confinement of ethnoracial minority persons). Racial disparities in education have a potentially cumulative adverse effect on vulnerability to PTSD because of its direct relationship to socioeconomic status.

Displacement and Loss of Social Networks

Although ethnoracial subgroups are disproportionately disadvantaged, disparities in access to socioeconomic resources and loss due to displacement from home, community, and national origins have occurred historically to members of many racial and ethnocultural subgroups in the United States as well as in other parts of the world (e.g., massively displaced populations in the Balkans, South America, Asia, and Africa). When primary social ties are cut or diminished as a result of violence and coercion, the challenge extends beyond merely surviving traumatic life-threatening danger to preserving a viable developmental trajectory in the face of life-altering loss.

Barriers Faced by Ethnoracial Minorities in Accessing Health Care

Racial disparities in access to health care result from a variety of factors, including those related to social structures and socioeconomic resources, and others directly and indirectly attributable to racism (Williams & Sternthal, 2010). At least in part as a result of racial disparities in access to health care, ethnoracial minority group members have disparities in health as well, including being at higher risk for a range of medical illnesses and mortality than are Whites in the United States. These disparities may lead some ethnoracial minorities, including Blacks (Hunter & Schmidt, 2010), Hispanics (Marshall, Schell, & Miles, 2009), and Native Americans (Marsella, Friedman, Gerrity, & Scurfield, 1996), to be more aware of and concerned about the risk of chronic health problems than Whites. Such heightened awareness may contribute to Blacks' lesser reporting of anxiety disorder symptoms, due to a belief that physiological components of anxiety symptoms are indications of potentially life-threatening medical conditions (Hunter & Schmidt, 2010).

Social Support and Safety

Independent of major societal-level disparities or disruptions in access to social resources, the individual's access to and conservation of positive social support is a protective factor against the development of posttraumatic stress problems (Brewin et al., 2000). However, distress and strain caused by negative interpersonal interactions is a risk factor for posttraumatic problems (Marra et al., 2009). When factors such as discrimination, displacement, and unequal access to resources undermine the social networks available to ethnoracial minority group members, or reduce their access to otherwise beneficial sources of social support, the resultant decrement in positive social support may result in greater vulnerability to traumatic stressors or to developing PTSD and associated problems.

IMPLICATIONS FOR PTSD ASSESSMENT AND TREATMENT PLANNING

The most crucial take-home point suggested by studies of the role of ethnoracial and sexual identity, and sociocultural characteristics that may interact with those factors (e.g., gender, socioeconomic disparities, discrimination), is that they always must be considered as crucial contextual features when assessing trauma history, PTSD or related symptoms and disorders, and clients' treatment preferences or needs. However, no *a priori* assumptions are warranted about any specific individual based on his or her ethnocultural characteristics. As such, race, ethnicity, and culture should not be used as shorthand labels that obscure actual heterogeneity (Marsella et al., 1996). Indeed, perhaps the best outcome of this research is to alert assessors and treatment providers to their essential responsibility of inquiring rather than assuming how each individual client defines his or her ethnoracial background, support group(s), and identity. And to include other identity factors such as sexual preference, nationality, subculture(s), and peer groups when formulating a clinical impression of the individual and the approach to assessment and treatment that is likely to be most acceptable to, respectful of, and effective for, the individual. Valuable clinical data can be gathered by asking study participants or clinical patients to self-identify their own racial, ethnic, and cultural background (Triffleman & Pole, 2010) rather than assuming that standard forced-choice categorical labels adequately describe any person's ethnocultural heritage.

Beliefs About the Meaning of Trauma Exposure and Posttraumatic Symptoms and Disorders

The variable relationships between ethnocultural background and both risk of trauma exposure and PTSD or posttraumatic symptoms or disorders suggests that race and culture/self-identification may play a role in these domains but probably not in any simple or universal form. What seems clearer is that ethnocultural background is likely to influence the *meaning* attributed to exposure to potentially traumatic events and to experiencing posttraumatic symptoms.

With regard to traumatic event exposure, there is no evidence that race, ethnicity, or any other identity factor (such as sexual preference) makes members of any ethnocultural subgroup more prone to experiencing physical violence or other life-threatening events. However, cultural and social legacies and norms and beliefs may substantially influence whether an event is appraised by an individual as traumatic. Events that are viewed as normative in some circumstances (e.g., community violence or war or sectarian violence) may be viewed as either too common to be considered traumatic even when objectively severe, or so intensely dangerous as to be traumatic even in milder forms. Therefore, rather than assuming that certain ethnocultural groups' members are especially likely to have been exposed to certain types of traumatic stressors, assessors should inquire as carefully as possible about the (often implicit) benchmarks that each individual client uses in interpreting whether certain events are indeed traumatic. When certain types of events are generally considered particularly harmful or unacceptable in a culture or community as a result of significant historical precedents (e.g., mass community violence) or value systems (e.g., religious proscriptions regarding sexuality), it is important for assessors to be respectful of those attributional benchmarks while at the same time not allowing them to lead to overriding the clinical information regarding the specific nature of each event and the biological, psychological, and social impact that the event had on the individual.

In the symptom domain, ethnocultural differences may be expressed in the form of differential sensitivity to certain types of PTSD symptoms or attributions about PTSD symptoms (e.g., based on their increased risk of serious medical problems and concerns about the stigma of mental illness, ethnoracial minority group members may view anxiety or dysphoria symptoms as a medical, not psychological, issue). It also is important to bear in mind that some ethnoracial minority group members may be reluctant to disclose symptoms of emotional distress, or not recognize them as sufficiently significant to merit reporting on questionnaire or interview assessments. The adverse effects of exposure to traumatic stressors thus may be more evident in other types of symptoms or health or behavioral problems than PTSD, for example, in stress-related medical illnesses or health risk behaviors such as smoking or substance misuse. Careful assessment of potential relationships between medical symptoms that have psychological components (e.g., pain, hypertension, gastrointestinal problems) or behavior problems that may result in part from attempts to cope with traumatic stress symptoms (e.g., self-medication with food or substances) is warranted, especially with persons who are culturally predisposed to deny or minimize emotional distress.

Assessing Adversity With Sensitivity to Ethnoracial and Cultural Factors

Although persons of all ethnocultural backgrounds can experience potentially traumatic events and PTSD symptoms, minority groups tend to be more likely than majority groups (e.g., non–Hispanic Whites, heterosexuals) to be subjected to racism and discrimination. As we've discussed, racism and discrimination can lead directly to traumatic victimization (e.g., hate crimes, genocide). In addition, racism and discrimination often result in adversities that are not in and of themselves traumatic (in the technical sense), but that place people at risk for victimization and deplete the personal, social, familial, and community resources that they need in order to cope resiliently with traumatic events (e.g., poverty; property crimes; neighborhood conflict; disparities in access to income, employment, education, and health care). Therefore, especially when assessing PTSD with an individual from an ethnocultural minority group, it is important to expand the focus beyond the formal definition of traumatic stressors and PTSD to consider how the larger range of adversities may have affected the person and his or her ability to cope with traumatic stressors.

Three critical targets for assessment that span the continuum from traumatic stressors to chronic adversities and for which psychometrically validated self-report measures have been developed are race-related stressors (Loo, Fairbank, & Chemtob, 2005; Waelde et al., 2010), identity trauma (Kira et al., 2011), and perceived discrimination (Chae, Lincoln, & Jackson, 2011). In combination with conventional measures assessing exposure to traumatic stressors and PTSD and comorbid or associated symptoms and impairments, these measures provide a basis for understanding the individual's perception of how discrimination and racism or other identity biases have impacted their life.

Assessing and Enhancing Access to Services and Supports

When PTSD or related posttraumatic or behavioral health problems are identified in assessment, treatment planning involves further inquiry and discussion about the wide range of services and sources of support that may be beneficial for and preferred by each individual client. Although evidence-based treatment for PTSD generally is best (see Chapter 2), such treatments and how they are delivered should be flexibly tailored based on the diverse experiences and expectations of clients of varied ethnocultural and sociodemographic backgrounds. To the extent that psychotherapy may be perceived as conferring stigma, it is essential to determine the client's specific concerns and what, if any, adaptations (e.g., by providing choices concerning the characteristics—including but not limited to race, ethnicity, language, and gender—and approach of potential psychotherapists) or protections (e.g., precautions to ensure privacy and confidentiality) could make psychotherapy acceptable to the client as a part of the overall services and supports designed to address PTSD.

It also is important to consider ways to vary assessment and treatment terminology and rationales in order to be maximally responsive to and respectful of each individual's worldview and personal frame of reference. This is equally true for clients of all ethnocultural and identity backgrounds, because the standard introductions to psychological assessment and to psychotherapy tend to discourage the individualization that is necessary in order to establish rapport and maximize client motivation. Ethnoracial or other identity differences simply highlight the importance of this general rule of tailoring the way assessment and treatment are explained and conducted to the individual client.

The possibility that clients from ethnoracial or other minority (e.g., lesbian, gay, bisexual, transgender [LGBT]) backgrounds may have been denied access to health care or other services, or may have encountered stigma, discrimination, or intentional or inadvertent insensitivity to their needs or preferences when seeking or receiving such services, should always be kept in mind when discussing potential approaches to PTSD treatment. Although there are many reasons why patients drop out of treatment prematurely—including having achieved sufficient benefit to warrant stopping before the clinician's or therapy's recommended stopping point—the finding by Lester, Resick, Young-Xu, and Artz (2010) that Black women were twice as likely as White women to drop out of evidence-based PTSD psychotherapy highlights the importance of considering prior experiences with health care services when conducting assessment and treatment planning. Here again, rather than assuming that a person of ethnocultural minority background has had "bad" experiences in prior health care, the recommended approach is to carefully inquire about prior attempts to get services, the nature and satisfactoriness of the services and their outcomes, and instances where services were not sought or were terminated despite experiencing problems.

In addition, members of different ethnocultural groups may prefer to receive help from sources other than formal professional services. Here again there is not a universal link between any ethnocultural background and specific sources of help, and it is important for clinicians not to assume that a given client "must" prefer a certain treatment source because of her or his ethnocultural characteristics. Indeed, other factors such as education, marital status, and illness severity may be more important than race or ethnicity in determining who seeks help from a particular type of provider—and stereotypes are often inaccurate. The key is to learn what sources of help the individual has gone to in the past and with what results (from the person's point of view as well as clinically), and what sources they know about and prefer now. With that information, it is possible to offer options that are consistent with each client's preferences and needs, including ones of which the client may not yet be aware.

CONCLUSION

Ethnoracial and other identity characteristics provide a context for inquiring about and understanding each client's unique trauma history and traumatic stress difficulties. As such, they should never be treated as a given or as an afterthought in PTSD assessment. When assessment helps the client to articulate his or her unique understanding of personal characteristics such as race, ethnicity, nationality, culture, and sexuality, and how these interact with demographics such as gender, age, and socioeconomic status, this foundation can substantially clarify the nature and impact of exposure to traumatic stressors in that individual's life. Of course, it is also important to remember that individual differences tend to be as important as group differences, that people from the same ethnocultural or sociodemographic group often are more different than they are the same, and therefore that it is important to avoid making sweeping assumptions about any one individual based on their ethnocultural or sociodemographic background.

REFERENCES

Alim, T. N., Charney, D. S., & Mellman, T. A. (2006). An overview of posttraumatic stress disorder in African Americans. *Journal of Clinical Psychiatry, 62,* 801–813.

Armstrong, J., Brand, B., Briere, J., Carlson, E., Dalenberg, C., Finn, S., . . . Cole, N. (2011). *Division 56 guidelines for clinicians regarding the assessment of trauma.* Washington, DC: American Psychological Association.

Breslau, J., Aguilar-Gaxiola, S., Kendler, K. S., Su, M., Williams, D., & Kessler, R. C. (2006). Specifying race-ethnic differences in risk for psychiatric disorder in a USA national sample. *Psychological Medicine, 36,* 57–68.

Brewin, C. R., Andrews, B., & Valentine, J. D. (2000). Meta-analysis of risk factors for posttraumatic stress disorder in trauma-exposed adults. *Journal of Consulting Clinical Psychology, 68,* 748–766.

Chae, D. H., Lincoln, K. D., & Jackson, J. S. (2011). Discrimination, attribution, and racial group identification: Implications for psychological distress among Black Americans in the National Survey of American Life (2001–2003). *American Journal of Orthopsychiatry, 81,* 498–506.

Cusack, K. J., Grubaugh, A. L., Yim, E., Knapp, R. G., Robins, C. S., & Frueh, B. C. (2007). Are there racial differences in the experience of harmful or traumatic events within psychiatric settings? *Psychiatric Quarterly, 78*(2), 101–115.

Delgado, D. J., Lin, W. Y., & Coffey, M. (1995). The role of Hispanic race/ethnicity and poverty in breast cancer survival. *Puerto Rico Health Sciences Journal, 14,* 103–116.

Dovidio, J. F., Penner, L. A., Albrecht, T. L., Norton, W. E., Gaertner, S. L., & Shelton, J. N. (2008). Disparities and distrust: The implications of psychological processes for understanding racial disparities in health and health care. *Social Science & Medicine, 67,* 478–486.

Harrington, E. F., Crowther, J. H., & Shipherd, J. C. (2010). Trauma, binge eating, and the "strong Black woman". *Journal of Consulting and Clinical Psychology 78,* 469–79.

Hunter, L. R., & Schmidt, N. B. (2010). Anxiety psychopathology in African American adults: Literature review and development of an empirically informed sociocultural model. *Psychological Bulletin, 136,* 211–235.

Kira, I. A., Smith, I., Lewandowski, L., & Templin, T. (2011). The effects of gender discrimination on refugee torture survivors: a cross-cultural traumatology perspective. *Journal of the American Psychiatric Nurses Association, 16*, 299–306.

Lester, K., Resick, P. A., Young-Xu, Y., & Artz, C. (2010). Impact of race on early treatment termination and outcomes in posttraumatic stress disorder treatment. *Journal of Consulting and Clinical Psychology, 78*, 480–489.

Loo, C. M., Fairbank, J. A., & Chemtob, C. M. (2005). Adverse race-related events as a risk factor for posttraumatic stress disorder in Asian American Vietnam veterans. *Journal of Nervous and Mental Disease, 193*, 455–463.

Marra, J. V., McCarthy, E., Lin, H. J., Ford, J., Rodis, E., & Frisman, L. K. (2009). Effects of social support and conflict on parenting among homeless mothers. *American Journal of Orthopsychiatry, 79*, 348–356.

Marsella, A. J., Friedman, M. J., Gerrity, E. T., & Scurfield, R. M. (Eds). (1996). Ethnocultural aspects of PTSD: Some closing thoughts. In *Ethnocultural aspects of posttraumatic stress disorder: Issues, research, and clinical applications* (pp. 529–538). Washington, DC: American Psychological Association.

Marshall, G. N., Schell, T. L., & Miles, J. N. (2009). Ethnic differences in posttraumatic distress: Hispanics' symptoms differ in kind and degree. *Journal of Consulting and Clinical Psychology, 77*, 1169–1178.

Najman, J. M., Hayatbakhsh, M. R., Clavarino, A., Bor, W., O'Callaghan, M. J., & Williams, G. M. (2010). Family poverty over the early life course and recurrent adolescent and young adult anxiety and depression: A longitudinal study. *American Journal of Public Health, 100*, 1719–1723.

Pole, N., Best, S. R., Metzler, T., & Marmar, C. R. (2005). Why are Hispanics at greater risk for PTSD? *Cultural Diversity and Ethnic Minority Psychology 11*(2), 144–161.

Pole, N., Gone, J. P., & Kulkarni, M. (2008). Posttraumatic stress disorder among ethnoracial minorities in the United States. *Clinical Psychology: Science and Practice, 15*(1), 35–61.

Roberts, A. L., Austin, S. B., Corliss, H. L., Vandermorris, A. K., & Koenen, K. C. (2010). Pervasive trauma exposure among US sexual orientation minority adults and risk of posttraumatic stress disorder. *American Journal of Public Health, 100*, 2433–2441.

Roberts, A. L., Gilman, S. E., Breslau, J., Breslau, N., & Koenen, K. C. (2011). Race/ethnic differences in exposure to traumatic events, development of posttraumatic stress disorder, and treatment-seeking for post-traumatic stress disorder in the United States. *Psychological Medicine, 41*, 71–83.

Seedat, S., Stein, D. J., & Carey, P. (2005). Post-traumatic stress disorder in women: Epidemiological and treatment issues. *CNS Drugs, 19*, 411–427.

Triffleman, E. G., & Pole, N. (2010). Future directions in studies of trauma among ethnoracial and sexual minority samples: Commentary. *Journal of Consulting and Clinical Psychology, 78*, 490–497.

Waelde, L. C., Pennington, D., Mahan, C., Mahan, R., Kabour, M., & Marquett, R. (2010). Psychometric properties of the Race-Related Events Scale. *Psychological Trauma: Theory, Research, Practice, and Policy, 2,* 4—11.

Waitzman, N. J., & Smith, K. R. (1998). Phantom of the area: Poverty-area residence and mortality in the United States. *American Journal of Public Health, 88,* 973—976.

Wiking, E., Johansson, S. E., & Sundquist, J. (2004). Ethnicity, acculturation, and self reported health. A population based study among immigrants from Poland, Turkey, and Iran in Sweden. *Journal of Epidemiology and Community Health, 58,* 574—582.

Williams, D. R., & Sternthal, M. (2010). Understanding racial-ethnic disparities in health: sociological contributions. *Journal of Health and Social Behavior, 51*(Suppl), S15—S27.

CHAPTER 7

Conducting Forensic Evaluations

This chapter discusses the issue of posttraumatic stress disorder (PTSD) within the context of forensic mental health evaluations. More specifically, we focus on important influences and settings in which individuals may demonstrate overreported PTSD, and we review evidence-based psychological assessment methods for detecting overreported PTSD in forensic evaluations.

Symptom overreporting could involve the complete fabrication of psychopathology by an individual who is otherwise symptom free (referred to as *pure malingering*). Overreporting could alternatively involve the exaggeration/amplification of legitimate symptoms by a person who has genuine, but subclinical, levels of psychopathology (referred to as *partial malingering;* Rogers, 2008a). Thus, compelling evidence of symptom overreporting does not necessarily indicate a completely fabricated symptom presentation; but rather it could involve a person in genuine distress and in need of mental health services. As a result of this ambiguity, we view the specific conclusion that someone has malingered PTSD as probabilistic, typically including the categories of *possible, probable,* and *definite* malingering (Slick, Sherman, & Iverson, 1999).

UNPACKING "SECONDARY GAIN": MOTIVES FOR SYMPTOM EXAGGERATION IN PTSD

Several reasons can account for why someone may intentionally overreport PTSD symptoms. These reasons, discussed in detail in this section, primarily involve external financial incentives, inappropriate access to clinical services, avoiding criminal prosecution or reducing criminal penalties, and fraudulently receiving recognition or honor for surviving a traumatic event (Resnick, West, & Payne, 2008; Taylor, Frueh, & Asmundson, 2007).

PTSD can be raised as a legal defense in criminal cases by alleging that the defendant committed a crime as a result of suffering from PTSD. Alternatively (and more commonly), PTSD can be raised as a defense in civil cases, whereby the plaintiff sues a defendant for emotional damages resulting from a traumatic event that led to PTSD. The challenge for the mental health evaluator in such cases is not only to determine whether the individual legitimately satisfied the diagnostic criteria of PTSD (covered in Chapter 4), but also to evaluate whether the individual overreported the severity of his or her PTSD. Because such cases often arise in secondary gain contexts (i.e., those that have potential for the client to gain financial or legal benefits if PTSD is diagnosed or found to impair functioning), the issue of overreported PTSD (in order to reap such secondary benefits) is much more prominent and prevalent than underreported PTSD.

Financial Incentives

The potential for PTSD-related disability compensation due to an inability to function at work because of one's PTSD is one reason why individuals may overreport PTSD symptoms. Social Security Disability Insurance (SSDI) provides such disability compensation to individuals who can provide evidence that a disorder, such as PTSD, is responsible for their inability to work. The Veterans Affairs (VA) system similarly provides disability compensation for veterans who have an impairment (e.g., PTSD) stemming from military service. In both the SSDI and VA contexts, disability benefits can provide annual compensation for many beneficiaries to live comfortably (Frueh et al., 2003), leading to concerns that these programs might provide a disincentive for individuals to return to work and recover from their PTSD (Frueh, Grubaugh, Elhai, & Buckley, 2007). In fact, in the VA setting, PTSD has been noted as one of the most frequent conditions for which veterans apply for disability compensation (Department of Veterans Affairs, Office of Inspector General, 2005).

Another reason individuals might overreport PTSD is worker's compensation. Employees are sometimes exposed to job-related traumatic incidents, such as violent robberies among bank employees, serious injury among construction workers, mass transportation accidents among bus drivers, and others. After such an incident, the employee may file a worker's compensation claim with his or her employer to recover lost wages and/or damages that may have resulted from symptoms associated with the traumatic incident. Given the potential financial benefits in these situations, an employee may have the incentive to overreport his or her PTSD symptoms.

Finally, personal injury lawsuits provide potential incentives for overreporting PTSD symptoms and impairment. In such situations, an individual may allege that he or she suffered damages in a traumatic incident caused by another person or business. For example, a female plaintiff may sue a former boyfriend for PTSD secondary to a domestic assault (Elhai, Sweet, Breting, & Kaloupek, 2012). As another example, a train passenger may sue a railroad company after a train accident that threatened the passenger's life and resulted in the passenger's suffering from PTSD.

Obtaining Treatment

Some individuals overreport PTSD in order to ensure that they receive mental health treatment, especially inpatient hospitalization (e.g., Salloway, Southwick, & Sadowsky, 1990). In many of these cases, the individual patient has some genuine symptoms of PTSD, but in fear of not receiving services, he or she may exaggerate legitimate symptoms in order to increase the likelihood of a hospital admission. To further complicate matters, some such cases involve a patient whose primary intention is to establish a treatment record in order to provide supportive documentation shortly after for a claim of disability compensation, worker's compensation, or a personal injury lawsuit (Taylor et al., 2007).

Avoiding Criminal Penalties

Although far less common, PTSD is sometimes used as part of a defense strategy for deflecting criminal responsibility in a criminal trial, or for mitigating penalty in a trial's sentencing phase (Resnick et al., 2008). Some military veterans in particular, when charged with a serious crime, have attempted to attribute their criminal behavior to PTSD as a defense (Burkett & Whitley, 1998). Resnick et al. (2008) described several ways in which combat PTSD can be successfully used to demonstrate that the defendant did not know that a criminal act was wrong (i.e., the basis of an insanity defense), such as criminally acting during a flashback or to relive the excitement of combat exposure. Nonetheless, it is rare that PTSD has been the basis for an insanity defense, and insanity defenses are rarely successful (Applebaum et al., 1993; Sparr & Pitman, 2007).

Stolen Valor

There is some evidence to suggest that individuals may fabricate a history of traumatic event exposure in order to gain respect and recognition from others. Burkett and Whitley (1998) examined this issue by filing Freedom of Information Act (FOIA) requests to obtain the official military records of individuals claiming to have served in Vietnam combat. They specifically focused on individuals whose claims of war zone service reported in the news media sounded exaggerated or suspicious. Through this process, they discovered a number of examples of individuals who falsely claimed (or exaggerated) combat duty in the Vietnam War, including public figures and celebrities, such as actor Brian Dennehy (Wilonsky, 2007) and Ron Kovic, who was the basis of the 1989 movie, *Born on the Fourth of July*. Worth noting again, however, is the fact that Burkett and Whitley (1998) examined only the records of suspected fraudulent reports of combat; they did not examine the prevalence of false combat reports among a more representative sample of veterans.

Frueh et al. (2005) conducted a more systematic effort to examine the prevalence of false combat exposure claims. In that study, the authors filed FOIA requests for the official military records of 100 veterans consecutively presenting to the Charleston (South Carolina) VA Medical Center's PTSD Clinic. Experienced military records reviewers found that only 68% of those claiming to have experienced combat exposure had documented evidence based on the locations in which these individuals served in Vietnam and the awarding of decorations and medals related to combat. Further, there appeared to be a relatively small subset of untruthful individuals, some of whom served in the military, but did not serve in Vietnam (3%), and some who never served in the military, despite being registered for VA services (2%). At a minimum, this evidence suggests that it is warranted to make an effort to obtain available documentation of military service among individuals claiming military-related traumas. However, obvious difficulties are associated with accurately documenting war zone experiences (both reporting and communicating in the veteran's record) that meet the traumatic stressor criterion for PTSD, given the chaos inherent in frontline of combat (Institute of Medicine of the National Academies, 2006).

Best Methods for Detecting PTSD Symptom Exaggeration

Records-Based Confirmation

It is understandable that a clinician working in a nonforensic setting such as a medical center or private practice might generally accept a patient's report of previous trauma exposure at face value. In such contexts, the incentives for false reporting are not prominent and, as such, there is little need or benefit for the clinician to play the role of a forensic detective. In addition, trust issues are common among individuals who have been exposed to interpersonal trauma, frequently because a family member, caregiver, or significant other betrayed their trust by abusing or assaulting them. Therefore, we discourage therapists in these roles from posing questions that might imply distrust and undermine the therapeutic relationship (Herman, 1992).

Determining whether symptoms of PTSD are legitimate, however, is at the crux of a forensic evaluation because such determinations have the potential to influence criminal penalties or financial compensation for injury or disability. In such a context, the evaluator needs to adopt an empirical, neutral, and skeptical approach. Having concrete evidence is foremost in working with the patient to document his or her traumatic event and symptom presentation. As such, it is extremely important to obtain records that confirm exposure to an index event that is being linked to PTSD and to obtain information that corroborates behaviors that are consistent with a diagnosis of PTSD. Relevant sources often include medical and mental health treatment records, school records, military records, police reports, and employment records. This approach is well suited to the rules of evidence in legal proceedings and will significantly increase the likelihood that the case will withstand direct challenge during cross-examination by opposing counsel.

In addition, records can provide information about other potentially traumatic experiences and reactions that might be relevant to the current symptom presentation. This is broadly important because *DSM-IV* diagnostic rules require that the minimum qualifying set of symptom criteria are satisfied in relation to one specific trauma; meeting some PTSD symptom criteria based on one specific trauma and other symptom criteria based on a different trauma(s) is not permissible (discussed in Elhai et al., 2009; Elhai, Ford, & Naifeh, 2010). This direct link between trauma exposure and emotional problems is particularly relevant to forensic situations in which a specific event is being linked to an individual's PTSD symptoms and disability. Records may help establish a timeline that is either consistent with or contrary to the claim that a PTSD symptom presentation resulted from the traumatic event in question rather than from other traumatic or (nontraumatic) events. Of course, such records would be acquired only with the individual's consent or may be acquired if the records are in the public domain (e.g., police reports, publicly accessible military records).

Overall Assessment Strategies

In Chapter 4, we describe in detail best practices for assessing trauma exposure history and PTSD. In addition, in a forensic context, it is often useful to instruct the individual to elaborate on the index traumatic event in question sequentially and in detail. One aim is to provide opportunity to evaluate credibility. For example, some individuals who were found to have fabricated trauma exposure reported absurd event-related details found only in movies, presumably from where they borrowed aspects of the event (Burkett & Whitley, 1998). Some individuals may present as if the report is being constructed rather than recollected, by the way in which they appear to recollect the details as if they are making up the story as they go. Other fabricated presentations may seem overly rehearsed, perhaps sounding rotely memorized. Suspicion about the validity of reporting may be raised by such behavior, but caution is still warranted and more supporting evidence is needed before arriving at the determination that a report is fabricated or selectively untrue.

Having stated the above, it is important to note that if an individual is questioned about trauma exposure on more than one occasion, discrepancies about the details of the trauma can occur in subsequent interviews (e.g., Southwick, Morgan, Nicolaou, & Charney, 1997; Wessely et al., 2003). Presumably, this can reflect corrupting influences that involve secondary gain, whereby the individual is unable to keep the details of the fabricated trauma consistent over time. However, it is alternatively plausible that individuals with PTSD may recall a traumatic experience in greater detail with later interviews due to factors such as repeated cuing or increases in symptoms that aid retrieval of trauma-related memories. Such a process can often be seen during the treatment of PTSD, which typically involves the frequent recounting or revisiting of the traumatic event.

It also is important to bear in mind that recall of memory generally is subject to change over time and as circumstances change, such that minor insertions, deletions, or modifications in specific events or their timing or sequence are to be expected. Indeed, when an individual's recounting of a past event seems to be exactly verbatim across several tellings, the evaluator should be suspicious that the recollection is not entirely veridical and may be partly or largely fabricated. This should not be confused, however, with a trauma survivor's repetition of the same vivid and emotionally evocative details from a terrible experience, which is consistent with PTSD's intrusive reexperiencing symptoms. Valid PTSD-related recollections tend not to have an artificially "scripted" quality, but may perseveratively repeat a set of distressing details or elements in the trauma memory. In some cases, consistent with PTSD's emotional numbing symptoms, the retelling may be valid despite seeming oddly emotionally detached, given the apparent terrifying or horrifying quality of the events and the person's subsequent problems with disturbing memories, hyperarousal or hypervigilance, dysphoria, or other PTSD symptoms.

In querying the person about PTSD symptoms, using best practices reported earlier in Chapter 4 (i.e., with a structured diagnostic interview for PTSD), the clinical interviewer should not only inquire about symptom frequency and intensity but should also probe the circumstances in which symptoms occur and details of recent episodes. This information can help tease apart credible from noncredible reports of symptoms. Collateral informant interviews are a particularly valuable means for information gathering about PTSD symptoms and their course, especially when an informant has no incentive tied to the outcome of the situation. For example, while we do not discourage using a spouse as a collateral informant in a forensic evaluation, the spouse's report should be viewed with caution because he or she might share the benefit of a financial award as a consequence of a positive PTSD diagnostic determination.

Psychological Testing

An extensive literature exists on detecting exaggerated PTSD symptom reports using psychological testing. Most studies have used multiscale, broadband objective personality assessment instruments such as the Minnesota Multiphasic Personality Inventory-2 (MMPI-2; Butcher et al., 2001), Personality Assessment Inventory (PAI; Morey, 1991), and also a trauma-specific instrument, the Trauma Symptom Inventory (TSI; Briere, 1995). Also reported on is the Structured Interview of Reported Symptoms (SIRS, Rogers, Bagby, & Dickens, 1992). These instruments have validity scales, including "fake bad" or overreporting scales, that assess response patterns including atypical responding about both symptom content and severity, obvious (versus subtle) symptom responding, and inconsistency in symptom presentation (reviewed in Greene, 2008; Rogers, 2008b; Sellbom & Bagby, 2008). A special feature of the SIRS is that it calls for the evaluator to document behavioral indicators of symptom exaggeration. Other types of instruments that have been found ineffective in detecting exaggerated PTSD include projective personality tests and self-report checklists (reviewed in Guriel & Fremouw, 2003).

Interestingly, meta-analytic findings demonstrate that effect sizes for detecting overreported PTSD are generally lower than for detecting other forms of overreported psychopathology (Rogers, Sewell, Martin, & Vitacco, 2003); high scores among genuine PTSD patients may account for the decreased effect sizes when compared to PTSD simulators (Elhai et al., 2010). Most research on overreported PTSD has used the MMPI-2.

Initial studies focused on the F (Infrequency) and F-K (Infrequency minus K Correction) scales of the MMPI-2. The scales were able to individually distinguish between PTSD simulators and genuine patients with roughly 70% to 80% accuracy across men and women based on optimal cutoff scores (e.g., Elhai, Gold, Frueh, & Gold, 2000; Elhai, Gold, Sellers, & Dorfman, 2001). However, the F scale is arguably problematic because it is composed of infrequently endorsed items among healthy individuals, and these items are often endorsed by genuine, mentally ill patients (Arbisi & Ben-Porath, 1995) including those with PTSD (Elhai et al., 2002). Moreover, the F scale is highly correlated with other forms of distress and psychopathology that are relatively common in trauma victims, including depression, dissociation, and PTSD (Klotz Flitter, Elhai, & Gold, 2003). Thus, extreme F scale elevations may not indicate overreporting in trauma-exposed individuals.

Other variations of the MMPI-2's F scale have been developed more recently, aiming to better discriminate genuine from exaggerated psychopathology. Among the most frequently studied in the psychological literature is the Fp (Infrequency Psychopathology) scale, composed of items that were infrequently endorsed among both psychiatric patients and nondisordered individuals. The Fp scale has evidenced adequate discrimination of PTSD simulators from genuine PTSD patients, arguably better than scales from other psychological tests described here, as well as incremental validity over other MMPI-2 fake bad scales. Specifically, based on PTSD simulation studies, Fp has demonstrated detection accuracy in the 80% to 90% range based on a cut score for T between 85 and 100 (Arbisi, Ben-Porath, & McNulty, 2006; Efendov, Sellbom, & Bagby, 2008; Elhai et al., 2001; Marshall & Bagby, 2006). Additionally, the Fptsd (Infrequency PTSD) scale is composed of items infrequently endorsed by combat PTSD patients. Fptsd seems to be more effective in detecting exaggerated PTSD when referenced to military PTSD comparison groups (Arbisi et al., 2006; Elhai et al., 2002) as opposed to civilian PTSD comparison groups (Elhai et al., 2004; Marshall & Bagby, 2006).

The PAI also has been examined in a few studies for overreported PTSD detection; however, the PAI's validity scales have not proven as useful as the MMPI-2's validity scales. Specifically, the NIM (Negative Impression Management) scale and MAL (Malingering Index) have been investigated, achieving no greater than 75% detection rates on average (e.g., Eakin, Weathers, Benson, Anderson, & Funderbunk, 2006; Lange, Sullivan, & Scott, 2010). The TSI has also been investigated for its ability to detect overreported PTSD. The TSI is unique among other measures discussed here because it was specifically developed for assessing trauma-related psychopathology and it is one of the most widely used assessment scales in the traumatic stress field (Elhai, Gray, Kashdan, & Franklin, 2005). Although an early study found accuracy rates in the 80% to 90% range for an optimal T score threshold of 61 on the ATR (Atypical Response) scale (Edens, Otto, & Dwyer, 1998), that promising finding may have been due to the absence of a PTSD patient comparison group. Subsequent research with PTSD patient comparison groups has found less promising results for ATR and a lack of incremental contribution over relevant MMPI-2 scales (e.g., Efendov et al., 2008; Elhai, Gray, Naifeh, et al., 2005; Rogers, Payne, Correa, Gillard, & Ross, 2009). A revised version of the TSI, the TSI-2 (Briere, 2011), was recently published, and one study has used the TSI-2 to compare nonclinical PTSD simulators with nonclinical honest responders screening positive for PTSD, finding an overall correct classification rate of 75%, using a raw score of 7 on the ATR scale (Gray, Elhai, & Briere, 2010).

Finally, the SIRS has been studied via simulation, but without PTSD comparison groups. Freeman, Powell, and Kimbrell (2008) assessed SIRS scores in a sample of veterans presenting for PTSD treatment, and found substantial evidence of symptom exaggeration based on traditional cutoff scores from the SIRS. Another study (Rogers, Kropp, Bagby, & Dickens, 1992) assessed how well SIRS scores could distinguish between simulators feigning PTSD, schizophrenia and mood disorders, and general psychiatric inpatients. They found that SIRS scales distinguished between the disorders and several scales significantly distinguished between patients and PTSD simulators. A revised version of the SIRS, the SIRS-2 (Rogers, Sewell, & Gillard, 2010), is now available; however, studies have not been published testing its validity in detecting simulated PTSD.

Treatment Implications

In a treatment setting, such as a VA Medical Center, clinicians sometimes must deal with patients who are malingering PTSD in order to obtain an external incentive such as disability benefits. If the patient knows that making treatment gains could jeopardize a PTSD disability claim or could reverse a previous successful claim, there is little incentive for the veteran to progress in treatment. Often, clinicians feel frustrated treating such patients because little evidence for positive treatment outcome is apparent, which would be especially surprising and disappointing when the clinician uses state of the art, empirically supported psychological treatments that should be efficacious. Clinicians should be aware of such secondary gain issues and the corresponding disincentive to get better. Given the potential for secondary gain in certain settings such as VA Medical Centers and other forensic settings, clinicians should attempt to aggressively treat the patient, but should anticipate that these external factors may hinder treatment progress.

We would also caution clinicians that focusing too much on an investigation of whether the patient has malingered PTSD can certainly impair the client–therapist relationship. Patients typically enter treatment with the idea that the clinician will be on their side and will believe their story. Doubting the patient's credibility, especially in the context where there is not overwhelming evidence that the patient has malingered PTSD, can damage the therapeutic relationship between a therapist and a potentially bona fide nonmalingering PTSD patient.

Conclusion

Clearly, from this chapter it is apparent that accurately assessing PTSD clinical presentations is challenging in contexts in which there is potential for secondary gain. As we have noted in these contexts, it is often difficult to distinguish a genuine PTSD symptom presentation from a malingered presentation. We have provided some background to elaborate on contextual factors that are relevant to assessing response validity among individuals evaluated for PTSD. We have also offered suggested guidelines and strategies for assessing response validity in such cases.

References

Applebaum, P. S., Jick, R. Z., Grisso, T., Givelber, D., Silver, E., & Steadman, H. J. (1993). Use of posttraumatic stress disorder to support an insanity defense. *American Journal of Psychiatry, 150*, 229–234.

Arbisi, P. A., & Ben-Porath, Y. S. (1995). An MMPI-2 infrequent response scale for use with psychopathological populations: The Infrequency Psychopathology scale, F(p). *Psychological Assessment, 7,* 424–431. doi: 10.1037/1040-3590.7.4.424

Arbisi, P. A., Ben-Porath, Y. S., & McNulty, J. (2006). The ability of the MMPI-2 to detect feigned PTSD within the context of compensation seeking. *Psychological Services, 3,* 249–261. doi: 10.1037/1541-1559.3.4.249

Briere, J. (1995). *Trauma Symptom Inventory professional manual.* Odessa, FL: Psychological Assessment Resources.

Briere, J. (2011). *Trauma Symptom Inventory-2 professional manual.* Odessa, FL: Psychological Assessment Resources.

Burkett, B. G., & Whitley, G. (1998). *Stolen valor: How the Vietnam generation was robbed of its heroes and history.* Dallas, TX: Verity Press.

Butcher, J. N., Graham, J. R., Ben-Porath, Y. S., Tellegen, A., Dahlstrom, W. G., & Kaemmer, B. (2001). *MMPI-2 (Minnesota Multiphasic Personality Inventory-2): Manual for administration, scoring, and interpretation* (Revised ed.). Minneapolis: University of Minnesota Press.

Department of Veterans Affairs, Office of Inspector General. (2005). *Review of state variances in VA disability compensation payments (#05-00765-137).* Washington, DC. Retrieved from www4.va.gov/oig/52/reports/2005/VAOIG-05-00765-137.pdf

Eakin, D. E., Weathers, F. W., Benson, T. B., Anderson, C. F., & Funderbunk, B. (2006). Detection of feigned posttraumatic stress disorder: A comparison of the MMPI-2 and PAI. *Journal of Psychopathology and Behavioral Assessment, 28,* 145–155. doi: 10.1007/s10862-005-9006-5

Edens, J. F., Otto, R. K., & Dwyer, T. J. (1998). Susceptibility of the Trauma Symptom Inventory to malingering. *Journal of Personality Assessment, 71,* 379–392. doi: 10.1207/s15327752jpa7103_7

Efendov, A. A., Sellbom, M., & Bagby, R. M. (2008). The utility and comparative incremental validity of the MMPI-2 and Trauma Symptom Inventory validity scales in the detection of feigned PTSD. *Psychological Assessment, 20,* 317–326. doi: 10.1037/a0013870

Elhai, J. D., Engdahl, R. M., Palmieri, P. A., Naifeh, J. A., Schweinle, A., & Jacobs, G. A. (2009). Assessing posttraumatic stress disorder with or without reference to a single, worst traumatic event: Examining differences in factor structure. *Psychological Assessment, 21,* 629–634. doi: 10.1037/a0016677

Elhai, J. D., Ford, J. D., & Naifeh, J. A. (2010). Assessing trauma exposure and posttraumatic morbidity. In G. M. Rosen & B. C. Frueh (Eds.), *Clinician's guide to posttraumatic stress disorder* (pp. 119–151). Hoboken, NJ: Wiley.

Elhai, J. D., Gold, P. B., Frueh, B. C., & Gold, S. N. (2000). Cross-validation of the MMPI-2 in detecting malingered posttraumatic stress disorder. *Journal of Personality Assessment, 75,* 449–463. doi: 10.1207/S15327752JPA7503_06

Elhai, J. D., Gold, S. N., Sellers, A. H., & Dorfman, W. I. (2001). The detection of malingered posttraumatic stress disorder with MMPI-2 fake bad indices. *Assessment, 8,* 221−236. doi: 10.1177/107319110100800210

Elhai, J. D., Gray, M. J., Kashdan, T. B., & Franklin, C. L. (2005). Which instruments are most commonly used to assess traumatic event exposure and posttraumatic effects? A survey of traumatic stress professionals. *Journal of Traumatic Stress, 18,* 541−545. doi: 10.1002/jts.20062

Elhai, J. D., Gray, M. J., Naifeh, J. A., Butcher, J. J., Davis, J. L., Falsetti, S. A., & Best, C. L. (2005). Utility of the Trauma Symptom Inventory's Atypical Response Scale in detecting malingered post-traumatic stress disorder. *Assessment, 12,* 210−219. doi: 10.1177/1073191105275456

Elhai, J. D., Naifeh, J. A., Zucker, I. S., Gold, S. N., Deitsch, S. E., & Frueh, B. C. (2004). Discriminating malingered from genuine civilian posttraumatic stress disorder: A validation of three MMPI-2 infrequency scales (F, Fp, and Fptsd). *Assessment, 11,* 139−144. doi: 10.1177/1073191104264965

Elhai, J. D., Ruggiero, K. J., Frueh, B. C., Beckham, J. C., Gold, P. B., & Feldman, M. E. (2002). The Infrequency-Posttraumatic Stress Disorder scale (Fptsd) for the MMPI-2: Development and initial validation with veterans presenting with combat-related PTSD. *Journal of Personality Assessment, 79,* 531−549. doi: 10.1207/S15327752JPA7903_08

Elhai, J. D., Sweet, J. J., Breting, L. G., & Kaloupek, D. G. (2012). Assessment in contexts that threaten reporting validity. In J. J. Vasterling, R. A. Bryant & T. M. Keane (Eds.), *PTSD and mild traumatic brain injury* (pp. 174−198). New York: Guilford Press.

Freeman, T., Powell, M., & Kimbrell, T. (2008). Measuring symptom exaggeration in veterans with chronic posttraumatic stress disorder. *Psychiatry Research, 158,* 374−380. doi: 10.1016/j.psychres.2007.04.002

Frueh, B. C., Elhai, J. D., Gold, P. B., Monnier, J., Magruder, K. M., Keane, T. M., & Arana, G. W. (2003). Disability compensation seeking among veterans evaluated for posttraumatic stress disorder. *Psychiatric Services, 54,* 84−91. doi: 10.1176/appi.ps.54.1.84

Frueh, B. C., Elhai, J. D., Grubaugh, A. L., Monnier, J., Kashdan, T. B., Sauvageot, J. A., . . . Arana, G. W. (2005). Documented combat exposure of U.S. veterans seeking treatment for combat-related posttraumatic stress disorder. *British Journal of Psychiatry, 186,* 467−472. doi: 10.1192/bjp.186.6.467

Frueh, B. C., Grubaugh, A. L., Elhai, J. D., & Buckley, T. C. (2007). US Department of Veterans Affairs disability policies for posttraumatic stress disorder: Administrative trends and implications for treatment, rehabilitation, and research. *American Journal of Public Health, 97,* 2143−2145. doi: 10.2105/AJPH.2007.115436

Gray, M. J., Elhai, J. D., & Briere, J. (2010). Evaluation of the Atypical Response Scale of the Trauma Symptom Inventory-2 in detecting simulated posttraumatic stress disorder. *Journal of Anxiety Disorders, 24*, 447–451. doi: 10.1016/j. janxdis.2010.02.011

Greene, R. L. (2008). Malingering and defensiveness on the MMPI-2. In R. Rogers (Ed.), *Clinical assessment of malingering and deception* (3rd ed., pp. 159–181). New York, NY: Guilford Press.

Guriel, J., & Fremouw, W. (2003). Assessing malingered posttraumatic stress disorder: A critical review. *Clinical Psychology Review, 23*, 881–904. doi: 10.1016/j. cpr.2003.07.001

Herman, J. L. (1992). *Trauma and recovery: The aftermath of violence from domestic abuse to political terror.* New York, NY: Basic Books.

Institute of Medicine of the National Academies. (2006). *Posttraumatic stress disorder: Diagnosis and assessment.* Washington, DC: National Academies Press.

Klotz Flitter, J. M., Elhai, J. D., & Gold, S. N. (2003). MMPI-2 F scale elevations in adult victims of child sexual abuse. *Journal of Traumatic Stress, 16*, 269–274. doi: 10.1023/A:1023700208696

Lange, R. T., Sullivan, K. A., & Scott, C. (2010). Comparison of MMPI-2 and PAI validity indicators to detect feigned depression and PTSD symptom reporting. *Psychiatry Research, 176*, 229–235. doi: 10.1016/j.psychres.2009.03.004

Marshall, M. B., & Bagby, R. M. (2006). The incremental validity and clinical utility of the MMPI-2 Infrequency Posttraumatic Stress Disorder Scale. *Assessment, 13*, 417–429. doi: 10.1177/1073191106290842

Morey, L. C. (1991). *Personality Assessment Inventory: Professional manual.* Lutz, FL: Psychological Assessment Resources.

Resnick, P. J., West, S., & Payne, J. W. (2008). Malingering of posttraumatic disorders. In R. Rogers (Ed.), *Clinical assessment of malingering and deception* (3rd ed., pp. 109–127). New York, NY: Guilford Press.

Rogers, R. (2008a). An introduction to response styles. In R. Rogers (Ed.), *Clinical assessment of malingering and deception* (3rd ed., pp. 3–13). New York, NY: Guilford Press.

Rogers, R. (2008b). Structured interviews and dissimulation. In R. Rogers (Ed.), *Clinical assessment of malingering and deception* (3rd ed., pp. 301–322). New York, NY: Guilford Press.

Rogers, R., Bagby, R. M., & Dickens, S. E. (1992). *Structured Interview of Reported Symptoms: Professional manual.* Tampa, FL: Psychological Assessment Resources.

Rogers, R., Kropp, P. R., Bagby, R. M., & Dickens, S. E. (1992). Faking of specific disorders: A study of the Structured Interview of Reported Symptoms (SIRS). *Journal of Clinical Psychology, 48*, 643–648. doi: 10.1002/1097-4679(199209) 48:5<643::AID-JCLP2270480511>3.0.CO;2-2

Rogers, R., Payne, J. W., Correa, A. A., Gillard, N. D., & Ross, C. A. (2009). A study of the SIRS with severely traumatized patients. *Journal of Personality Assessment, 91*, 429–438. doi: 10.1080/00223890903087745

Rogers, R., Sewell, K. W., & Gillard, N. D. (2010). *Structured Interview of Reported Symptoms-2 (SIRS-2) and professional manual.* Odessa, FL: Psychological Assessment Resources.

Rogers, R., Sewell, K. W., Martin, M. A., & Vitacco, M. J. (2003). Detection of feigned mental disorders: A meta-analysis of the MMPI-2 and malingering. *Assessment, 10,* 160−177. doi: 10.1177/1073191103010002007

Salloway, S., Southwick, S., & Sadowsky, M. (1990). Opiate withdrawal presenting as posttraumatic stress disorder. *Hospital and Community Psychiatry, 41,* 666−667.

Sellbom, M., & Bagby, R. M. (2008). Response styles on multiscale inventories. In R. Rogers (Ed.), *Clinical assessment of malingering and deception* (3rd ed., pp. 182−206). New York, NY: Guilford Press.

Slick, D. J., Sherman, E. M., & Iverson, G. L. (1999). Diagnostic criteria for malingered neurocognitive dysfunction: Proposed standards for clinical practice and research. *Clinical Neuropsychologist, 13,* 545−561. doi: 10.1076/1385-4046 (199911)13:04;1-Y;FT545

Southwick, S. M., Morgan, C. A., Nicolaou, A. L., & Charney, D. S. (1997). Consistency of memory for combat-related traumatic events in veterans of Operation Desert Storm. *American Journal of Psychiatry, 154,* 173−177.

Sparr, L. F., & Pitman, R. K. (2007). PTSD and the law. In M. J. Friedman, T. M. Keane & P. Resick (Eds.), *Handbook of PTSD: Science and practice.* New York, NY: Guilford Press.

Taylor, S., Frueh, B. C., & Asmundson, G. J. G. (2007). Detection and management of malingering in people presenting for treatment of posttraumatic stress disorder: Methods, obstacles, and recommendations. *Journal of Anxiety Disorders, 21,* 22−41. doi: 10.1016/j.janxdis.2006.03.016

Wessely, S., Unwin, C., Hotopf, M., Hull, L., Ismail, K., Nicolaou, V., & David, A. (2003). Stability of recall of military hazards over time: Evidence from the Persian Gulf War of 1991. *British Journal of Psychiatry, 183,* 314−322. doi: 10.1192/ bjp.183.4.314

Wilonsky, R. (2007, April 12). Don't tell Glenna Whitley you're a vet if you ain't. Because she knows. We're lookin' at you, Brian Dennehy. *Dallas Observer.* Retrieved from   http://blogs.dallasobserver.com/unfairpark/2007/04/dont_ tell_glenna_whitley_youre.php

CHAPTER 8

Working With Children and Adolescents

CONCEPTUAL AND CLINICAL FOUNDATIONS

E xposure to traumatic stressors unfortunately is not a rare phenomenon, occurring in the lives of 25% (Briggs-Gowan, Ford, Fraleigh, McCarthy, & Carter, 2011; Costello, Erklani, Fairbank, & Angold, 2002; Perkonigg, Kessler, Storz, & Wittchen, 2000) to as many as 50% (Kilpatrick et al., 2000) of children and adolescents in the United States and western European countries. Exposure to potentially traumatic events was more common among South African and Kenyan 10th graders, affecting more than 80% (Seedat, Nyamai, Njenga, Vythilingum & Stein, 2004).

In the United States and western European countries, PTSD is relatively rare among young (ages 0 to 4) children (estimated as about 1 child in every 167) and school-age and adolescent children (about 1 child in every 100) (Scheeringa, Zeanah, & Cohen, 2010). However, these estimates are comparable to those for current (e.g., in the past 6 to 12 months) PTSD prevalence in adults (Kessler, Chiu, Demler, Merikangas, & Walters, 2005). Similar PTSD prevalence estimates have been reported among German adolescents (1% to 2%; Perkonigg et al., 2000), Puerto Rican children (1%; Canino et al., 2004), and Bangaladeshi children (1%; Mullick & Goodman, 2005). Other studies have reported finding PTSD in as few as approximately 1 in 1,000 children and adolescents in Great Britain (T. Ford, Goodman, & Meltzer, 2003) and Brazil (Fleitlich-Bilyk & Goodman, 2004).

Although PTSD is detectable as a diagnostic syndrome relatively infrequently in childhood, it is more common in high-risk groups of children. These include children living in impoverished or violent communities. Children living in slums in Bangaladesh were three times more likely to have PTSD (3% prevalence; Mullick & Goodman, 2005). Adolescents also are more likely than younger children to meet criteria for PTSD. Kilpatrick et al. (2000) found that 5% of a representative national sample of U.S. adolescents met criteria for current (i.e., in the past 6 months) PTSD. An identical prevalence estimate was obtained in a study with Kenyan 10th graders (Seedat et al., 2004). Adolescents in high-risk circumstances are even more likely to develop PTSD. Israeli Jewish children, many of whom have been exposed to societal violence but who have not been displaced from their homes, have been estimated to have a current PTSD prevalence of 8% (Pat-Horenczyk et al., 2007). In contrast, a much higher prevalence (34%) has been estimated for Palestinian children, many of whom become refugees (Khamis, 2005). Abram et al. (2004) found that most (approximately 90%) of the adolescents in an urban juvenile detention center had been exposed to at least one potentially traumatic stressor (on average, the youths reported experiencing 15 separate incidents during their lives), and 11% met criteria for PTSD. More than 25% of a sample of 10th graders in a country fraught with violence (South Africa) met criteria for PTSD (Seedat et al., 2004).

The specific nature of posttraumatic stress symptoms varies for each child, as well as for children living in different socioeconomic and ethnocultural contexts. For example, although the Kenyan youths were less likely than the South African youths to report most PTSD symptoms, they were more likely (50% vs. 30%) to report actively avoiding memories of traumatic experiences. Avoidance of reminders of traumatic experiences can be a positive form of coping, but it also can become a part of a vicious cycle in which avoiding memories provides temporary relief but perpetuates a sense of fearfulness that can become full-blown PTSD if minor stressors build up or new traumas occur in the future. Youths who cope by purposefully avoiding reminders of trauma may fare better in the short run, but for some this involves a continuous state of "survival coping" that is a strain on the body, mind, and emotions.

PTSD is classified by the American Psychiatric Association as an anxiety disorder, yet anxiety is only one of several outcomes for children exposed to traumatic stressors. Among children, PTSD often is accompanied by other anxiety disorders, depression, and behavioral disorders (i.e., comorbidities) and is associated with more severe problems in psychological development, learning and school involvement, peer and family relationships, and (among older children and adolescents; J. D. Ford, Elhai, Ruggiero, & Frueh, 2009) risky and illegal behaviors (D'Andrea, Ford, Stolbach, Spinazzola, & van der Kolk, 2012; Egger & Angold, 2006). The consequences of childhood trauma exposure can extend well beyond PTSD. Moreover, a variety of other clinically significant problems warrant careful assessment with children and adolescents who have been exposed to traumatic stressors. Approximately one in seven children in a community sample in the United States (13%) reported some PTSD symptoms, and those exposed to traumatic stressors also were at risk for depression and anxiety disorders (Copeland, Keeler, Angold, & Costello, 2007). Even very young children may be significantly affected by exposure to traumatic stressors. Approximately 20% of 18- to 36-month-old toddlers in a U.S. urban sample who were exposed to potentially traumatic events were reported by their parents to have dramatically altered functioning following the event, and were described as having higher levels of reexperiencing and arousal symptoms consistent with PTSD (Mongillo, Briggs-Gowan, Ford, & Carter, 2009). In that U.S. urban sample, 2- to 4-year-old toddlers exposed to interpersonal violence had elevated levels of depression, separation anxiety, posttraumatic stress, and conduct problems, and exposure to potentially traumatic noninterpersonal exposure was associated with phobic anxiety (Briggs-Gowan et al., 2011). These associations were not attributable to poverty or parental psychiatric problems, except that parents' anxiety and depression problems mediated the relationship between violence exposure and toddlers' depressive and conduct symptoms (Briggs-Gowan et al., 2011).

SELF-REGULATION AS A FRAMEWORK FOR ASSESSING POSTTRAUMATIC IMPAIRMENT

Exposure to traumatic stressors can lead to fundamental alterations in children's bodies and brains, which are adaptive "survival coping" (J. D. Ford, 2009, p. 33), but which over time can lead children to have serious problems with anger, guilt, shame, grief, dissociation, risky or harmful behavior, damaged or damaging relationships, isolation, and addiction. Perhaps the most harmful effect of persistent posttraumatic survival reactions is failing to develop the abilities necessary for healthy self-regulation. Self-regulation fundamentally involves adaptive engagement in relationships and the ability to utilize and modulate emotions (J. D. Ford, 2010).

The adverse impact of traumatic stressors on the development of self-regulation is illustrated poignantly by a study in which maltreated children were found to be twice as likely (80% vs. 37%) to deal with relationships and emotions in a dysregulated manner (i.e., under-controlled/ambivalent and overcontrolled/unresponsive types), and to have severe problems with depression and anxiety, and it mediated the relationship between maltreatment and depression/anxiety. Physically abused children are reported by independent observers and caregivers (Crittenden, Claussen, & Sugarman, 1994) as well as peers (Salzinger, Feldman, Ng-Mak, Mojica, & Stockhammer, 2001) to be more verbally and physically assaultive than other children. Polyvictimized children and adolescents have been shown to have poorer interpersonal and school functioning (Finkelhor, Turner, Ormrod, & Hamby, 2010; J. D. Ford, Connor, & Hawke, 2009; J. D. Ford, Elhai, Connor, & Frueh, 2010), and an increased likelihood of disruptive behavior problems (Finkelhor et al., 2010; J. D. Ford et al., 2009) and juvenile justice involvement (Finkelhor et al., 2010; J. D. Ford, Grasso, Hawke, & Chapman, 2012) compared to children with more limited or no trauma histories.

Self-regulation and complex posttraumatic dysregulation in childhood and adolescence take many forms that are not fully assessed by any single measure or battery of tests. In addition to pointing to the need for a more comprehensive approach to developing and validating assessment instruments for children's complex traumatic stress reactions, this review raises a further question: Do the existing conceptual and nosological (diagnostic) systems for child psychopathology require revision or expansion to address the full range of complex traumatic stress reactions (D'Andrea et al., 2012). This question is of particular relevance at this time, because the American Psychiatric Association (APA) is considering the nature of and evidence for existing and new psychiatric disorder diagnoses in preparation for a major fifth revision of the *Diagnostic and Statistical Manual of Mental Disorders* (www.DSM5.org).

Diagnosis of PTSD in Children and Adolescents: *DSM-IV* and *DSM-5*

Features of PTSD (e.g., psychological and physiological distress in reaction to reminders of traumatic events, avoidance of such reminders and the associated distress, emotional numbing, hyperarousal) are evident in children's complex traumatic stress reactions. Modification of the diagnostic criteria for children with PTSD has been recommended (Scheeringa, et al., 2010), and as of the writing of this chapter, the APA appears poised to incorporate those changes (www.DSM5.org). Specifically, developmentally appropriate indicators were proposed for several children's PTSD symptoms, including three intrusive reexperiencing symptoms. Unwanted distressing memories of the traumatic event(s) could include "repetitive play . . . in which themes or aspects of the traumatic event(s) are expressed." Nightmares related (in emotional quality or content) to traumatic event(s) could include "frightening dreams without recognizable content." Flashbacks could involve "trauma-specific re-enactment . . . in play." Symptoms of negative emotions and cognitions—the expanded version of what formerly were symptoms of emotional numbing—and of hyperarousal are proposed to have a lower threshold for diagnosis for children (requiring two symptoms present for each of these categories) than for adults (for whom three symptoms must be present in each category to qualify for a diagnosis). The traumatic stressor exposure criterion also may be expanded for children to include the loss of a parent "or other attachment figure." Other developmental indicators have been proposed in order to enable clinicians to adequately identify children's PTSD symptoms (Scheeringa et al., 2010), and as of this writing those modifications were still under consideration for the *DSM-5*.

In addition, a separate PTSD diagnosis for preschool children has been proposed (www.dsm5.org). The traumatic stressor (Criterion A), intrusive reexperiencing (Criterion B), and avoidance of reminders (Criterion C) features of PTSD are largely unchanged in the preschool version, except that young children are not expected to have "repeated or extreme exposure to aversive details of [traumatic] event[s]"—that traumatic stressor is primarily expected to occur to adult war combatants or child welfare or emergency response personnel. A major difference is that the negative emotions feature (Criterion D) for preschool children does not include three symptoms from the adult PTSD criteria, each of which is an internal mental state and therefore difficult to detect reliably in children: psychogenic amnesia, negative beliefs about self, and distorted self-blame. The symptom described as "detachment or estrangement from others" in the core PTSD criteria has been modified to focus on behavioral manifestations in the preschool version (i.e., social withdrawal). As a result of the reduced number of Criterion D symptoms and their close relationship to Criterion C avoidance symptoms, preschool PTSD is proposed to require only one symptom from either Criterion C or D. The final symptom feature, hyperarousal (Criterion E) retains the same five symptoms as in the core PTSD system, but adds "including temper tantrums" to the anger/irritability item.

Although these proposed modifications may increase the developmental sensitivity of the PTSD diagnosis, posttraumatic dysregulation in children does not always take the form of classic PTSD and often involves problems that lead to other comorbid (or alternative) diagnoses—such as reactive attachment disorder (RAD); generalized, phobic, or obsessive compulsive anxiety or panic disorders; bipolar disorder; psychotic or dissociative disorders; disorders of eating, body image, or sexuality; disruptive behavior disorders; or traits of personality disorders (D'Andrea et al., 2012). While childhood exposure to developmentally adverse traumatic stressors may contribute to the onset of these disorders or exacerbate their preexisting symptoms, the most intractable cases (who tend to be children carrying many psychiatric diagnoses) may require treatment addressing traumatic stress reactions in addition to or in lieu of treatment for each of several psychiatric disorders with which they were diagnosed.

For example, J. D. Ford, Connor, and Hawke's (2009) study with psychiatrically impaired children in residential treatment found that, as expected, these children had substantial histories of early life adversity (i.e., documented physical or sexual abuse, impaired parents, multiple out-of-home placements). Cluster analyses revealed distinct subgroups representing different complexities of exposure to these potentially traumatic adversities and showed that the severity of internalizing and externalizing problems could not be fully accounted for by *DSM-IV* psychiatric diagnoses (nor by age or gender). Two subgroups with complex trauma histories were identified that had severe teacher-rated behavior problems and clinician-rated psychosocial impairment independent of substance abuse, developmental disorders, and externalizing behavior disorder diagnoses. Moreover, substance use disorders were unrelated to behavior problems when the effect of complex trauma was included, and externalizing disorders were associated with impulsivity and hyperactivity only after the effect of a core component of complex trauma—multiple out-of-home placements—was accounted for. Multiple out-of-home placements also contributed to the severity of behavior problems beyond the effects of demographics, psychiatric diagnoses, documented abuse, and parental impairment. This is consistent with the presumed etiology of severe attachment problems (e.g., RAD), as well as with evidence that children who lose (or never acquire) stable attachment relationships due to abuse or impaired parenting are at risk for long-lasting (at least into early adulthood) problems with affect regulation, disorganized attachment working models, and dissociation (Lyons-Ruth, Dutra, Schuder, & Bianchi, 2006). Another example is based on findings that physically abused children were observed by adults (Crittenden et al., 1994) and peers (Salzinger et al., 2001) to be more verbally and physically assaultive than other children.

J. D. Ford, Connor, and Hawke's, (2009) results suggest that this aggression may not be due to abuse alone, but to survival adaptations based on experiencing the many potentially traumatic conditions that arise in the context of abuse, including parental impairment and out-of-home placements. Further analyses of the data from that sample of psychiatrically impaired children showed that abuse was associated with reactive (not proactive) aggression (J. D. Ford, Fraleigh, & Connor, 2010) and with a dampened autonomic response to physical pain (J. D. Ford, Fraleigh, Albert, & Connor, 2010). This combination of aggression and reduced physiological responsivity to distress often leads youths to be labeled psychopathic or *callous and unemotional* (CU) and viewed as intractably antisocial. However, studies have shown that some girls (Marsee & Frick, 2007) and boys (Kimonis, Frick, Munoz, & Aucoin, 2008) who endorse CU beliefs may be experiencing emotional dysregulation consistent with traumatic stress reactions rather than being unempathic and intentionally cruel.

Based on these and other relevant findings (D'Andrea et al., 2012), in the past decade a number of therapeutic models have been designed or adapted to address the core self-regulation problems associated with childhood exposure to complex traumatic stressors (see J. D. Ford & Cloitre, 2009). A more parsimonious and trauma-informed approach may be needed to adequately inform treatment planning for children who suffer what Kaffman (2009) has described as an epidemic of neurodevelopmental injury (J. D. Ford & Cloitre, 2009). For example, a new diagnosis, developmental trauma disorder (DTD; van der Kolk, 2005) has been proposed for the *DSM-5*, based on forms of self-dysregulation that are sequelae of childhood traumatic stressors that disrupt (or prevent the formation of) fundamental attachment bonds: emotion, somatic, cognitive, behavioral, relational, and self-identity dysregulation (J. D. Ford, 2005).

Results of a survey of more than 1,300 pediatric mental health, social work, and medical/nursing professionals internationally demonstrated that symptoms from each of those domains of dysregulation were identified as highly important in assessing and treating children with extensive trauma histories, and that developmental trauma symptoms were distinguishable from symptoms of the many other psychiatric disorders with which those children commonly are diagnosed (J. D. Ford, Grasso, Greene, Spinazzola, & van der Kolk 2012). An interview study with several hundred children recruited from mental health and pediatric practices in six U.S. sites (including those with limited or no history of exposure to traumatic stressors or psychopathology as well as those with trauma and psychiatric histories) was designed to test the validity of a DTD interview designed to assess indictors of the six domains of self-dysregulation (see Table 8.1 for sample items; J. D. Ford & the Developmental Trauma Disorder Work Group, 2011).

Regardless of whether the DTD syndrome or a comparable diagnosis is formally codified in the *DSM*, assessment of traumatized children should address deficits in self-regulation that are associated with persistent traumatic stress reactions. We therefore provide a brief overview of tools that clinicians can utilize to assess children's self-regulation (see J. D. Ford, Nader, & Fletcher, in press, for a detailed summary) as well as to assess trauma history, PTSD, and comorbid disorders. First, however, we will discuss basic assessment tactics and strategies with traumatized children.

TABLE 8.1	**DEVELOPMENTAL TRAUMA DISORDER STRUCTURED INTERVIEW (J. D. FORD & THE DEVELOPMENTAL TRAUMA DISORDER WORK GROUP, 2012): PROPOSED STRUCTURE AND SAMPLE ITEMS**

A. Exposure. The child or adolescent has experienced or witnessed multiple or prolonged adverse events beginning in childhood or early adolescence, including:

A.1. Direct experience or witnessing of repeated and severe episodes of interpersonal violence.

A.2. Significant disruptions of protective caregiving due to repeated changes in primary caregiver, repeated separation from the primary caregiver, or severe emotional abuse.

B. Affective and Physiological Dysregulation. The child exhibits impaired normative developmental competencies related to arousal regulation:

B.1. Inability to modulate, tolerate, or recover from extreme affect states (e.g., fear, anger, shame), including prolonged and extreme tantrums, or immobilization.

B.2. Disturbances in regulation in bodily functions (e.g., persistent disturbances in sleeping, eating, and elimination; overreactivity or underreactivity to touch and sounds; disorganization during routine transitions).

B.3. Diminished awareness/dissociation of sensations, emotions, and bodily states.

B.4. Impaired capacity to describe emotions or bodily states

B.1b. Impaired Recovery from Extreme Negative Affect States

Are there times when your child cannot calm down for a long time when upset? Or when s/he gets so upset that s/he shuts down for a long time? Please give a brief example from the past month.

WHEN S/HE COULDN'T CALM DOWN OR STOP BEING TOTALLY SHUT DOWN EMOTIONALLY . . .

(Y) (N) Did s/he yell or scream for a long time?

(Y) (N) Did s/he hit people/animals or hit/break things for a long time?

(Y) (N) Was s/he shut down for a long time?

(Y) (N) Did s/he or anyone else get badly hurt?

(Y) (N) Did s/he or anyone else get into serious trouble such as being arrested, suspended, overdosing, or feeling suicidal?

(Y) (N) Was medical/hospital care necessary?

(Y) (N) Could s/he get along with friends?

(Y) (N) Could s/he get along with your family?

(Y) (N) Could s/he get along with other people in the neighborhood, at school, or at work?

(*continued*)

> (Y) (N) Could s/he still do activities that s/he likes to do, such as sports or clubs or parties?
> (Y) (N) Could s/he watch TV or listen to music?
> (Y) (N) Could s/he go to school and do the work?
> (Y) (N) Could s/he sleep okay at night?
> (Y) (N) Could s/he eat okay?

Yes *in past month* (Continue) No (check Not Present) (P) (PNA) (DNU)

If Yes: How often did this happen in the past month?

☐ Daily or almost every day

☐ 2 or 3 times a week

☐ Once a week or less

If No: Have there ever been any very serious problems with this?

☐ **Not Present** No (or at most developmentally normative) difficulty recovering from episodes of severe distress or emotional shutdown

☐ **Subthreshold** Difficulty in recovering from severe distress or shut down, but able to cope and regain a calm emotional state without harm to self or others or other serious negative consequences

☐ **Threshold** (past month) ☐ **Threshold** *(lifetime)*

Sometimes unable to recover from severe distress or feeling emotional shutdown without this leading to physical harm to self or others, or serious negative consequence such as arrest, school suspension, or acute suicidality, overdose, or other crises

C. **Attentional and Behavioral Dysregulation.** The child exhibits impaired normative developmental competencies related to sustained attention, learning, or coping with stress:

    C.1. Preoccupation with threat, or impaired capacity to perceive threat, including misreading of safety and danger cues.

    C.2. Impaired capacity for self-protection, including extreme risk-taking or thrill seeking.

    C.3. Maladaptive attempts at self-soothing (e.g., rocking and other rhythmical movements, compulsive masturbation).

    C.4. Habitual (intentional or automatic) or reactive self-harm.

    C.5. Inability to initiate or sustain goal-directed behavior.

    C.2. Impaired capacity for self-protection, including extreme risk-taking or thrill seeking.

    C.2a. Are there times your child does dangerous things such as fighting with weapons, driving/riding too fast, running into traffic, or jumping from high places? Or goes to extremely dangerous places, or with dangerous people? Or where people are doing dangerous things, including drinking too much or doing drugs?

WHEN S/HE DID DANGEROUS THINGS OR WAS IN/AROUND DANGEROUS PLACES OR PEOPLE . . .

(Y) (N) Did this involve violent people?

(Y) (N) Did this involve dangerous weapons?

(Y) (N) Did this involve vehicles such as cars or trains, or heavy/sharp equipment or tools?

(Y) (N) Did this involve drinking or drugs?

(Y) (N) Did this involve jumping or falling from high places, including extreme sports?

(Y) (N) Did this involve stealing or other illegal actions such as breaking and entering?

(Y) (N) Or prostitution (sex for money)?

(Y) (N) Or having unprotected sex?

(Y) (N) Did this involve selling drugs?

(Y) (N) Was s/he seriously physically hurt?

(Y) (N) Did s/he seem not to care if s/he got hurt?

(Y) (N) Did s/he try to get seriously hurt?

(Y) (N) Was anyone else badly hurt or killed?

(Y) (N) Did anyone get arrested for doing this?

(Y) (N) Was medical/hospital care necessary?

(Y) (N) Did s/he plan ahead for safety?

(Y) (N) Was the plan realistic and sufficient?

(Y) (N) Did s/he take precautions to avoid getting badly hurt or in trouble (e.g., arrested)?

Or approaches or goes off with people s/he doesn't know? Or doesn't check back with you or other caregivers when in unfamiliar places?

Please give a brief example from the past month.

Yes *in past month* (Continue) No (check Not Present) (P) (PNA) (DNU)

If Yes: How often did this happen in the past month?

☐ Daily or almost every day

☐ 2 or 3 times a week

☐ Once a week or less

If No: Have there ever been any very serious problems with this?

☐ **Not Present** Developmentally normative risks or thrill seeking

☐ **Subthreshold** Persistent or periodic exposure to potential serious injury, but takes precautions that are likely to prevent serious harm

☐ **Threshold** (past month) ☐ **Threshold** (lifetime)

Persistent/ periodic exposure to potential serious injury with insufficient or no precautions, or wish to get seriously hurt

D. Self- and Relational Dysregulation. The child exhibits impaired normative developmental competencies in their sense of personal identity and involvement in relationships, including at least three of the following:

D.1. Intense preoccupation with safety of the caregiver or other loved ones (including precocious caregiving) or difficulty tolerating reunion with them after separation.

D.2. Persistent negative sense of self: self-loathing, helplessness, worthlessness, ineffectiveness, or defectiveness.

D.3. Extreme and persistent distrust, defiance, or lack of reciprocal behavior in close relationships.

D.4. Reactive physical or verbal aggression toward peers, caregivers, or other adults.

D.5. Inappropriate (excessive/promiscuous) attempts to get intimate contact (including but not limited to sexual or physical intimacy) or excessive reliance on peers or adults for safety and reassurance.

D.6. Impaired capacity to regulate empathic arousal as evidenced by lack of empathy for, or intolerance of, or excessive responsiveness to, expressions of distress by others.

D.6b. Are there times when your child feels just as bad, or even worse, than someone else who is upset? Or times s/he seems to feel responsible for making other people feel upset, or for helping them feel better? Please give a brief example from the past month.

WHEN YOUR CHILD FEELS BAD BECAUSE SOMEONE IS UPSET OR WORRIES ABOUT SOMEONE BEING UPSET . . .

(Y) (N) Did s/he offer emotional support?

(Y) (N) Did s/he feel better if s/he tried to help?

(Y) (N) Did s/he wish s/he could help but not feel guilty if s/he couldn't make things better?

(Y) (N) Did s/he think it's too bad they're hurt or need help and hope they would be okay?

(Y) (N) Did s/he feel so bad for them that s/he broke down and sobbed or cried?

(continued)

(Y) (N) Did s/he feel so worried about them that s/he couldn't think about anything else?

(Y) (N) Did s/he feel so mad that s/he wanted to attack the people hurting them (see D4)?

(Y) (N) Was s/he willing to take risks or make sacrifices to help them recover or feel better?

(Y) (N) When s/he felt bad for them was s/he able to stay calm or to calm down before long?

(Y) (N) Could s/he still get along with family, friends, and other people (such as at school)?

(Y) (N) Could s/he still do activities s/he usually does, such as sports or clubs or parties?

(Y) (N) Could s/he sleep okay at night?

(Y) (N) Could s/he eat okay?

Yes *in past month* (Continue) No (check Not Present) (P) (PNA) (DNU)
If Yes: How often did this happen in the past month?

☐ Daily or almost every day

☐ 2 or 3 times a week

☐ Once a week or less

If No: Have there ever been any very serious problems with this?

☐ **Not Present** Developmentally normative sympathy/compassion

☐ **Subthreshold** Intense and developmentally immature sympathetic distress, but consistently able to regain emotional balance/calm and function with at most moderate impairment

☐ **Threshold** (past month) ☐ **Threshold** *(lifetime)*

Intense and developmentally immature sympathetic distress that is expressed in emotionally dysregulated intentions or actions and seriously impairs functioning

G. Functional Impairment. Symptoms cause clinically significant distress or impairment:

- Scholastic
- Familial
- Peer Group
- Legal
- Health
- Vocational (if seeking or referred for employment, volunteer work, or job training)

CLINICAL CONSIDERATIONS IN CONDUCTING ASSESSMENT WITH TRAUMATIZED CHILDREN

A thorough summary of key clinical considerations in trauma history and traumatic stress can be found in Nader's (2008) text (pp. 217–227). Safety and privacy are critical to the welfare of both the child and caregiver, as well as to their willingness to openly and honestly disclose about sensitive topics. Clearly explaining the purpose of the assessment in terms relevant to the goals of the child and the caregiver also is essential for both informed consent and engagement. The language used in open-ended discussion and structured assessment instruments should be appropriate to the age and developmental level (which often are not the same) of the child, as well as to the education and literacy levels of the child and caregiver.

Assessment of trauma history and posttraumatic symptomatology and functioning most often are done clinically via interview with, or self-report questionnaires or ratings from, youths, parents, other caregivers, teachers, or other knowledgeable informants. For school-age and older children and adolescents, self-report generally can provide a meaningful assessment of trauma history, PTSD, externalizing (e.g., aggression, attention and conduct problems, hyperactivity, substance abuse) and internalizing (anxiety, depression, somatization, dissociation, withdrawal, psychosis, eating and body image) problems and several domains of self-regulation and social competence (e.g., learning problems, daily activities, adaptability, functional communication, leadership, social skills, study skills). However, including the perspective of adult informants and collecting archival data (e.g., school, medical, legal, and child protective services records) is considered best practice because of memory, recognition, and response bias (e.g., under- or overreporting) problems that may limit or distort the information provided by youth self-report. It is important to remember that adult informants also are subject to the same potential sources of inaccuracy of reporting, and archival records may be incomplete or inaccurate. Thus, it always is necessary to triangulate the data from each pair of sources and develop hypotheses about the most likely findings rather than assuming that any single source is the gold standard.

For preadolescents and adolescents, it is particularly important to assess risk factors for trauma exposure, exacerbation of symptoms, and serious academic, relational, medical, and legal problems and crises (e.g., suicidality, self-harm, substance use problems, criminal involvement). It is essential to assess age-relevant competences (e.g., impulse control, altruism, consideration, empathy, and responsibility in relation to others, psychological mindedness, executive functions, self-efficacy, and optimism). It is vital to assess these youths' social and physical environment to identify ecological risk (e.g., community or domestic violence, deviant peer group affiliations, modeling of conduct problems by family members) and protective (e.g., parental monitoring, responsivity, collaborativeness, and fostering of autonomy; prosocial peers and activities; adult mentoring) factors. While these risk and protective factors are of particular relevance with older children and adolescents, they should be considered with children of all ages, especially when the child may be in danger of, or actually experiencing, serious physical or psychological harm. In addition to parent/caregiver rating measures, for toddlers and preschoolers, direct observation in home, day care, or clinical settings of parent–child interaction can provide valuable information about the caregiver's and child's strengths and difficulties in self-regulation and relatedness.

In special settings, such as psychiatric inpatient, residential, or day treatment programs; special education classrooms or programs; or the juvenile justice system, assessment measures must have been adapted and normed and validated for the youth in those distinct subpopulations (Ko et al., 2008). Ecologically valid assessment of children's trauma history, PTSD, and related self-dysregulation is increasingly recognized as the standard of care in intensive psychiatric settings (J. D. Ford, Connor, & Hawke 2009). However, other service systems are only beginning to define and attempt to develop trauma-informed programs. For example, the juvenile justice system has custodial, school, treatment, and rehabilitative programs where screening for trauma history and posttraumatic symptoms and impairment is vital because of the elevated prevalence of these problems in this subpopulation (J. D. Ford, Chapman, Connor, & Cruise, 2012).

Several practical, therapeutic, and ethical considerations are essential when clinicians use evidence-based, evidence-informed assessment with traumatized children (J. D. Ford & Cloitre, 2009).

First Priority: Identify and Address Imminent Threats to the Child's or Family's Safety and Stability

The ethical principles of *primum non nocere* (first do no harm) and *parens patriae* (temporary guardianship) provide a framework for assessment and treatment of traumatized children, and their often secondarily (or directly) traumatized families. Potential threats to safety include: (a) self-harm and suicidality; (b) ongoing family violence, abuse, neglect, substance abuse, or psychopathology; or (c) behavior that places the child or youth at risk for sexual victimization, community violence (e.g., physical assault, gang conflicts), abduction or kidnapping, life-threatening accidents, life-threatening illness (e.g., sexually or needle-transmitted diseases), or legal problems and incarceration. With ongoing or imminent threats to safety, assessment should concentrate on delineating their acuity and severity and monitoring this as treatment proceeds. Optimally, treatment reduces safety risks or harm by enhancing the child's/youth's and caregivers' competences, such that the child and caregiver can attribute improvements in safety to their own actions (and thereby internalize an increased sense of self-efficacy and personal responsibility), rather than viewing themselves as helpless and dependent on powerful others (including the therapist) to protect or rescue them.

Therapeutic Relationship and Alliance

The importance of engaging clients from the start of treatment in a therapeutic relationship and working alliance is particularly important in PTSD psychotherapy because this provides an experiential basis for clients to observe and learn self-regulation skills (J. D. Ford, 2012). In addition, traumatized children are still developing (in early childhood) or capable of fundamentally revising (in later childhood and adolescence) what Bowlby (1969) described as secure "working models" of responsive, helpful, and trustworthy primary relationships. In addition, traumatized children's caregivers, often traumatized in their own lives (as well as secondarily or vicariously due to their child's traumatization), may have difficulty in establishing or maintaining a secure attachment bond with their child. The therapeutic relationship in treating traumatized children therefore should be viewed as triadic rather than dyadic: linking the child, caregiver, and therapist affectively to each other such that the therapist provides coregulation for the child and caregiver, while empowering the caregiver to assume this role with the child while secure in the therapist's unconditional, nonintrusive, noncompetitive empathy and guidance (J. D. Ford & Cloitre, 2009). With young children, dyadic parent–child psychotherapies provide a model for this triadic therapeutic alliance (Van Horn & Lieberman, 2008). A relational therapeutic model also has been shown to enable older delinquent girls to achieve therapeutic engagement and recover from PTSD (J. D. Ford, Steinberg, Hawke, Levine, & Zhang, 2012).

Diagnosis, treatment planning, and outcome monitoring with traumatized children and their caregivers are always built on a relational foundation. The child's and parent's goals, needs, and resources *as they perceive them* are just as important to assess and monitor as the more objective circumstances and diagnostic and therapeutic indicators. Assessment should focus on both short-term (e.g., reduced day-to-day problems) and long-term (e.g., remission from PTSD) goals in order to maximize child and parent motivation to participate in therapy and to make changes. In so doing, the assessor can establish two complementary roles in the therapeutic relationship, both as an objective collector of information and as a collaborative partner with the child and parent in deciding how best to select and use the assessment findings therapeutically. For example, rather than assuming that a traumatized child or his/her caregiver will automatically agree that reducing avoidance of reminders of past trauma experiences is a desirable treatment goal, the therapeutic alliance can be strengthened if the clinician focuses assessment on the child's and parent's day-to-day goals (e.g., reducing nightmares, increasing school attendance) in order to determine how reduced PTSD avoidance symptoms could help them achieve their personal goals. While this motivational enhancement perspective may seem intuitively obvious, it is easily forgotten when clinicians become so preoccupied with symptoms, diagnoses, and administering evidence-based interventions (all of which are important) that they overlook ways to harness client motivation.

Strengths-Based Approach to Assessment

Existing or former strengths, resources, and resilience are the best predictors of children's recovery from PTSD and associated disorders. It can be difficult to discern meaningful strengths or competences with youths who seem detached, despondent, anxious, and dissociative, or impulsive, oppositional, and hostile. Their parents or caregivers may seem to be reactive, dejected, resigned, confused, of defensive and in denial—all of which are understandable in light of the frustration, loss, worry, helplessness, or guilt and self-blame that they may be feeling in spite of their best efforts to protect and nurture their child. Thus, it is important for both the child and the caregiver(s) to learn in treatment that some (or many) of the child's abilities and positive characteristics remain intact or are attenuated but not completely lost, despite the traumatic exposure and posttraumatic symptoms and impairments. Adding a self-regulation perspective to the traumatic stress paradigm provides a systematic basis for assessors to survey the youth's potential capabilities and strengths, because traumatic stress symptoms tend to alter, retard the development, or reduce the recognizability of self-regulatory capacities but does not destroy them or prevent their formation. The challenge for the assessor is to find evidence of self-regulatory capacities that have been preserved despite the dysregulation caused by coping with traumatic stressors and posttraumatic symptoms (J. D. Ford & Cloitre, 2009).

For example, this requires a rigorous and disciplined focus by the assessor on identifying the capabilities that have made it possible for the child and caregiver(s) to continue to seek help (even if they seem to be rejecting or sabotaging that very help) and to pursue their personal goals (even if the goals seem to be primarily dysfunctional), beginning from the first therapeutic encounter and continuing in each subsequent assessment and treatment session.

With traumatized young children, strengths-based assessment includes learning how the child handles play, interactions with caregiver(s) or peers, and preparing for and rehearsing daily activities (e.g., meals, bedtime, self-care, problem solving). With school-age and preadolescent children, assessment should include a survey of evidence of autonomy, relatedness, creativity, persistence, achievement, and impulse control. With adolescents, strengths-based assessment should address the youth's age-appropriate capacities to act in accord with core values and a coherent and realistic sense of self, to initiate as well as cooperate with others in goal-directed behavior, to maintain intimate relationships with safe yet flexible boundaries, and to recognize and make decisions to protect self and others from risky behavior and situations. An integrative psychological strength that warrants assessment across all developmental stages beginning in early childhood is the ability to reflectively "mentalize" (i.e., to observe and constructively utilize one's own and others' thought processes; Allen, Fonagy, & Bateman, 2008).

Assessing Dissociation

Posttraumatic dissociation involves not just colloquially familiar features such as "spacing out" or freezing "like a deer in the headlights," but moreover a fundamentally fragmented internal experience of self (DePrince & Freyd, 2007; Putnam, 2009). Pathological dissociation is considered an associated feature of PTSD and an integral component of complex variants of childhood PTSD such as DTD (D'Andrea et al., 2012). No structured interview has been developed to assess children's dissociation or dissociative disorders, and, as we shall describe in the next chapter only one parent/adult informant measure of dissociation for children and a few self-report measures for adolescents have been developed.

The International Society for the Study of Trauma and Dissociation developed a set of guidelines for clinical assessment and treatment of childhood dissociation (Silberg et al., 2004). The guidelines recommend caution by assessors in order to avoid suggesting to the child or caregiver that the child is experiencing dissociation or has experienced the kinds of traumatic victimization that are known to be associated with vulnerability to pathological dissociation (e.g., most notably sexual abuse, but also a range of types of maltreatment or violence; Putnam, 2009). They also emphasize that normal manifestations of dissociation should be distinguished from clinically significant dissociative symptoms, which tend to be repetitive and prolonged (rather than transient) and to be experienced by the child as "dramatic, uncontrollable, and puzzling" (Silberg et al., 2004, p. 131). Dissociative symptoms that warrant assessment include trance states, psychogenic amnesia (which also is a symptom of PTSD), fantasy (e.g., imaginary playmates), derealization and depersonalization, somatoform dissociation (i.e., breakdown in body functions, unusual sensory experiences, or analgesia or extreme pain sensitivity that cannot be accounted for or treated medically), or flashbacks (another PTSD symptom).

Severe forms of childhood or adolescent dissociative disorders such as dissociative identity disorder (DID) are rare. DID involves identity alteration characterized by "difficulty in the integration of affect, consciousness and identity" such as "sudden regression, rageful behavior, apparent loss of consciousness, or suddenly talking about oneself in the third person or with a new name," Silberg, 2000, p. 131). A review of published reports since 1980 found only 255 cases of childhood DID reported as individual case studies or in aggregate in empirical studies (Boysen, 2011). Almost two thirds of the cases were reported by four research groups in the United States, and more than 90% of the cases involved children in treatment—yet most (77%) of the children were in treatment for problems other than multiple personalities. The reviewer notes that hypnosis, structured interviews, and multiple raters were rarely used in obtaining the diagnoses (Boysen, 2011). These findings suggest that assessors must be careful to avoid two key mistakes when assessing dissociative symptoms with children. The first error is to fail to consider that dissociative symptoms, especially those that are rarest and most severe, may be contributing to the impairments experienced by a traumatized child or adolescent. This is particularly important when assessing a youth who exhibits extreme emotion states or behavior (e.g., substance abuse, sexual promiscuity or offending, self-injury; Silberg, 2000). The second error is to overinterpret normative dissociative experiences that occur for most children and adolescents—or that are better explained by situational stressors or symptoms of other disorders (e.g., severe depression involving problems with memory, social withdrawal, and mood-related somatic complaints)—as pathological dissociation. The latter mistake is of particular relevance when considering a severe diagnosis such as DID with a child or adolescent, given its rarity and the normal developmental discontinuities in children's sense of self and identity while they are developing that very self.

Identifying Somatic Manifestations of Posttraumatic Symptoms

Somatic conditions require a systemic approach to assessment and treatment, with collaboration among medical (e.g., pediatric, family practice, emergency medicine), psychiatric/psychopharmacology, social work, education, and psychotherapy professionals (Saxe, Ellis, & Kaplow, 2007). Somatic expressions of anxiety, dysphoria, grief, anger, and shame often are observed clinically with traumatized children, especially in early childhood and adolescence (D'Andrea et al., 2012). Once medical explanations are ruled out and a temporal association is established between onset or worsening of somatic problems and the occurrence of traumatic event(s), the challenge for assessors is to distinguish between developmentally normative somatic complaints versus clinically significant ones. An algorithm has been developed based on using clinical data and the Child Behavior Checklist (CBCL) Somatization subscale (Postilnik, Eisman, Price, & Fogel, 2006) and empirically validated (Eisman, Fogel, Lazarovich, & Postilnik, 2007) for defining and identifying somatization in children.

Determining With Whom, When, and How to Address Traumatic Memories

The core goal for the assessment and treatment of traumatized children and adolescents is to enable them to recall traumatic events and to cope with reminders of those memories in a regulated manner. Thus, the answer to the first question—*with whom should traumatic memories be addressed in assessment and therapy?*—is: with *every* traumatized child or adolescent who is experiencing psychosocial impairment due to PTSD or related symptoms (Cohen, Deblinger, & Mannarino, 2005; Saxe et al., 2007). However, the second question—*when?*—is crucial because it is not a given that inquiring about trauma history or traumatic stress symptoms is clinically indicated or safe simply because an assessment is requested (whether the request comes from the parent, a school or health care professional, or a legal agency such as child welfare or juvenile justice authorities).

The timing of doing a trauma history and traumatic stress assessment depends upon the answer to the third question—*how?* Before assessing such sensitive areas, it is important to provide psychoeducation about stress reactions to enhance clients' understanding of and ability to manage trauma-related stress reactions and self-dysregulation. This is crucial when (a) a history of exposure to specific psychologically traumatic event(s) has been confirmed or is probable based on credible (preferably multiple independent) sources, including archival (e.g., child protective services, legal, school) or clinical records, and child and caregiver self-reports; (b) the child's living arrangements and social support network are unstable, unpredictable, invalidating, or violent (e.g., when there is no intact family system or permanent residence, or when primary caregivers are likely to be impaired or potentially are maltreating the child).

Given these considerations, criteria for undertaking trauma-focused assessment should include (a) a stable physically and psychologically available permanent primary caregiver who is willing and able to help the child work through traumatic memories; (b) a child with adequate core self-regulation capacities and environmental supports (in daily life settings and via a therapeutic safety net) to be able to manage episodically intense distress and stress reactions without becoming sufficiently affectively, dissociatively, or behaviorally destabilized to pose an immediate or chronic threat to the child's psychological health or safety (e.g., suicidality; psychotic or dissociative identity decompensation; severe self-injury, substance dependence, or reactive aggression); and (c) a therapist with expertise in conducting trauma history assessment with children of this age and developmental epoch, who has access to psychiatric and crisis backup (e.g., pharmacotherapy, acute crisis evaluation and hospitalization, case management wraparound resources, pediatric care) to be able to identify, prevent, or rapidly resolve treatment-related or unrelated crises.

Preventing and Managing Relational Discontinuities and Psychosocial Crises

Exposure to a traumatic stressor can turn any child's world upside down. Unfortunately, some traumatized children and adolescents also have to cope with chronic and often unpredictable discontinuities in their primary relationships and social support systems: losses due to deaths, out-of-home placements, institutionalization, family abandonment, and serial treatment providers (Faust & Katchen, 2004); neglect and abuse due to parental and familial psychopathology, substance use disorders, violent or antisocial lifestyles, or severe socioeconomic adversities. They often have come to associate caring and facilitative adults or prosocial and accepting peers or peer-group activities (e.g., school, recreational, or social) as transient and likely to lead to disappointment or rejection—thus, even apparently positive events (e.g., birthdays; holidays; field trips; family visits; recognition for accomplishments in school, sports, or arts; graduation ceremonies; new residence or school) may elicit stress-related dysregulation. This may be misinterpreted in pathologizing terms as self-sabotage, oppositional-defiance or incorrigibility, an inability to tolerate delay of gratification or any deviation from the familiar, dependency, immaturity, or relational "splitting" consistent with borderline personality disorder. The result may be increased restrictiveness and intensity of supervision and treatment emphasizing crisis deescalation or a decision that the child cannot tolerate (or even benefit from) treatment.

An alternative and more therapeutic approach is to plan on preventing or managing relational discontinuity-related crises or deterioration with these children and their caregivers by taking a systemic approach of coordinating carefully with health care, educational, judicial/legal, and mental health professionals and social/human service program staff to anticipate and address the predictable stress reactions and dysregulation that may occur in the course of assessment due to the triggering nature of the topics discussed or for completely unrelated reasons. This involves understanding how stress reactions are adaptive; for example, attempting to protect against additional distress and demoralization, and communicating the importance of relational continuity to responsible adults. And it involves engaging the child and caregiver(s) as active collaborators in learning and using self-regulation skills if they feel distressed or shut down.

When crises occur despite best efforts to prevent them, a similar approach focused on restoring a sense of relational continuity and self-regulation provides a framework for helping to deescalate and stabilize the traumatized child or adolescent. This is an adaptation or special case of generic models of crisis intervention, which prescribe activating two palliative factors: (1) social support to reduce extreme spikes in the intensity of anxiety, dysphoria, anger, confusion, or detachment; and (2) active problem solving in order to increase the sense of control, efficacy, and optimism. Beyond the generic approaches to providing reassurance, immediate safety, structure, and limits (e.g., verbal deescalation tactics, time out), crisis deescalation with traumatized children may include some focal interventions: "grounding" strategies to counteract detachment, dissociation, and impulsivity; affective engagement strategies to reestablish an immediate sense of emotional connection with self and others; and sensorimotor strategies to increase bodily awareness and arousal modulation (J. D. Ford & Cloitre, 2009). In the aftermath of crises, if therapeutic processing includes discussion of how these self-regulation skills were used by the child in order to restabilize, more than a generic review of the "lessons learned," the result may be reaffirmation of the child's commitment to responsible behavior and self-care. Every crisis is an opportunity to highlight and enhance the traumatized child's competence and sense of efficacy in her or his self-regulation skills and trust in relational continuity.

CONCLUSION

Psychosocial assessment with traumatized children and adolescents involves clinical complexities that require careful attention in order for the clinician to safely and effectively implement evidence-based interview, questionnaire, and clinical observational measures. Therefore, in the following chapter, we turn to a description of the assessment instruments that have been developed and empirically validated for use with traumatized children.

REFERENCES

Abram, K. M., Teplin, L. A., Charles, D. R., Longworth, S. L., McClelland, G. M., & Dulcan, M. K. (2004). Posttraumatic stress disorder and trauma in youth in juvenile detention. *Archives of General Psychiatry, 61*(4), 403–410.

Allen, J. G., Fonagy, P., & Bateman, A. (2008). *Mentalizing in clinical practice.* Washington, DC: American Psychiatric Press.

Bowlby, J. (1969). *Attachment and loss* (Vol. 1). London, UK: Hogarth.

Boysen, G. A. (2011). The scientific status of childhood dissociative identity disorder: A review of published research. *Psychotherapy and Psychosomatics, 80*, 329–334.

Briggs-Gowan, M. J., Ford, J. D., Fraleigh, L., McCarthy, K., & Carter, A. S. (2011). Prevalence of exposure to potentially traumatic events in a healthy birth cohort of very young children in the northeastern United States. *Journal of Traumatic Stress, 23*, 725–733.

Canino, G., Shrout, P. E., Rubio-Stipec, M., Bird, H. R., Bravo, M., Ramirez, R., . . . Martinez-Taboas, A. (2004). The *DSM-IV* rates of child and adolescent disorders in Puerto Rico: Prevalence, correlates, service use, and the effects of impairment. *Archives of General Psychiatry, 61*, 85–93.

Cohen, J. A., Deblinger, E., & Mannarino, A. P. (2005). Trauma-focused cognitive–behavioral therapy for sexually abused children. In E. D. Hibbs & P. S.

Jensen (Eds.), *Psychosocial treatments for child and adolescent disorders: Empirically based strategies for clinical practice* (2nd ed., pp. 743–765). Washington, DC: American Psychological Association.

Copeland, W. E., Keeler, G., Angold, A., & Costello, E. J. (2007). Traumatic events and posttraumatic stress in childhood. *Archives of General Psychiatry, 64*, 577–584.

Costello, E. J., Erkanli, A., Fairbank, J. A., & Angold, A. (2002). The prevalence of potentially traumatic events in childhood and adolescence. *Journal of Traumatic Stress, 15*, 99–112.

Crittenden, P. M., Claussen, A. H., & Sugarman, D. P. (1994). Physical and psychological maltreatment in middle childhood and adolescence. *Development & Psychopathology, 6*, 145–164.

D'Andrea, W., Ford, J. D., Stolbach, B., Spinazzola, J., & van der Kolk, B. (2012). Phenomenology of symptoms following interpersonal trauma exposure in children: An empirically-based rationale for enhancing diagnostic parsimony. *American Journal of Orthopsychiatry, 82*, 187–200.

DePrince, A. P., & Freyd, J. J. (2007). Trauma-induced dissociation. In M. J. Friedman, T. M. Keane, & P. A. Resick (Eds.), *Handbook of PTSD: Science and practice* (pp. 135–150). New York, NY: Guilford Press.

Egger, H. L., & Angold, A. (2006). Common emotional and behavioral disorders in preschool children: presentation, nosology, and epidemiology. *Journal of Child Psychology and Psychiatry, 47*(3–4), 313–337.

Eisman, H. D., Fogel, J., Lazarovich, R., & Postilnik, I. (2007). Empirical testing of an algorithm for defining somatization in children. *Journal of the Canadian Academy of Child and Adolescent Psychiatry, 16*, 124–131.

Faust, J., & Katchen, L. (2004). Treatment of children with complicated posttraumatic stress reactions. *Psychotherapy: Theory, Research, Practice, Training, 41*(4), 426–437.

Finkelhor, D., Turner, H., Ormrod, R., & Hamby, S. L. (2010). Trends in childhood violence and abuse exposure: Evidence from 2 national surveys. *Archives of Pediatric and Adolescent Medicine, 164*(3), 238–242.

Fleitlich-Bilyk, B., & Goodman, R. (2004). Prevalence of child and adolescent psychiatric disorders in southeast Brazil. *Journal of the American Academy of Child and Adolescent Psychiatry, 43*(6), 727–734.

Ford, J. D. (2005). Treatment implications of altered neurobiology, affect regulation and information processing following child maltreatment. *Psychiatric Annals, 35*, 410–419.

Ford, J. D. (2009). Neurobiological and developmental research: Clinical implications. In C. Courtois & J. D. Ford (Eds.), *Treating complex traumatic stress disorders: An evidence-based guide* (pp. 31–58). New York, NY: Guilford Press.

Ford, J. D. (2010). Complex adult sequelae of early life exposure to psychological trauma. In R. A. Lanius, E. Vermetten, & C. Pain (Eds.), *The hidden epidemic: The impact of early life trauma on health and disease* (pp. 69–76). New York, NY: Cambridge University Press.

Ford, J. D. (2011). *Developmental Trauma Disorder Structured Interview.* Farmington: University of Connecticut.

Ford, J. D. (2012). Enhancing affect regulation in psychotherapy with complex trauma survivors. In D. Murphy, S. Joseph, & B. Harris (Eds.), *Trauma, recovery, and the therapeutic relationship.* London, UK: Oxford University Press.

Ford, J. D., Chapman, J., Connor, D. F., & Cruise, K. C. (2012). Complex trauma and aggression in secure juvenile justice settings. *Criminal Justice & Behavior. 39,* 695–724.

Ford, J. D., & Cloitre, M. (2009). Best practices in psychotherapy for children and adolescents. In C. Courtois & J. D. Ford (Eds.), *Treating complex traumatic stress disorders: An evidence-based guide* (pp. 59–81). New York, NY: Guilford Press.

Ford, J. D., Connor, D. F., & Hawke, J. (2009). Complex trauma among psychiatrically impaired children. *Journal of Clinical Psychiatry, 70,* 1155–1163.

Ford, J. D., Connor, D. F., & Hawke, J. (2009). Complex trauma among psychiatrically impaired children: A cross-sectional, chart-review study. *Journal of Clinical Psychiatry, 8,* 1155–1163.

Ford, J. D., & The Developmental Trauma Disorder Work Group (2012). *Developmental trauma disorder structured interview.* Farmington: University of Connecticut.

Ford, J. D., Elhai, J. D., Connor, D. F., & Frueh, B. C. (2010). Poly-victimization and risk of posttraumatic, depressive, and substance use disorders and involvement in delinquency in a national sample of adolescents. *Journal of Adolescent Health, 46,* 545–552.

Ford, J. D., Elhai, J. D., Ruggiero, K. J., & Frueh, B. C. (2009). Refining posttraumatic stress disorder diagnosis: Evaluation of symptom criteria with the National Survey of Adolescents. *Journal of Clinical Psychiatry, 70,* 748–755.

Ford, J. D., Fraleigh, L. A., Albert, D. B., & Connor, D. F. (2010). Child abuse and autonomic nervous system hyporesponsivity among psychiatrically impaired children. *Child Abuse & Neglect, 34,* 507–515.

Ford, J. D., Fraleigh, L. A., & Connor, D. F. (2010). Child abuse and aggression among psychiatrically impaired children. *Journal of Clinical Child and Adolescent Psychology, 39,* 25–34.

Ford, J. D., Grasso, D., Greene, C., Spinazzola, J., & van der Kolk, B. (2012). *Developmental trauma disorder field trial clinician survey.* Farmington: University of Connecticut.

Ford, J. D., Grasso, D., Hawke, J., & Chapman, J. (2012). *Poly-victimization among juvenile justice-involved youths.* Farmington: University of Connecticut.

Ford, J. D., Nader, K., & Fletcher, K. (in press). Assessment guidelines and instruments. In J. D. Ford & C. A. Courtois (Eds.), *Treating complex traumatic stress disorders in children and adolescents: An evidence-based guide.* New York, NY: Guilford Press.

Ford, J. D., Steinberg, K., Hawke, J., Levine, J., & Zhang, W. (2012). Randomized trial comparison of emotion regulation and relational psychotherapies for PTSD with girls involved in delinquency. *Journal of Clinical Child and Adolescent Psychology, 41,* 1–12.

Ford, T., Goodman, R., & Meltzer, H. (2003). The British Child and Adolescent Mental Health Survey 1999: The prevalence of *DSM-IV* disorders. *Journal of the American Academy of Child and Adolescent Psychiatry, 42,* 1203–1211.

Kaffman, A. (2009). The silent epidemic of neurodevelopmental injuries. *Biological Psychiatry, 66*(7), 624–626.

Kessler, R. C., Chiu, W. T., Demler, O., Merikangas, K. R., & Walters, E. E. (2005). Prevalence, severity, and comorbidity of 12-month *DSM-IV* disorders in the National Comorbidity Survey Replication. *Archives of General Psychiatry, 62*(6), 617–627.

Khamis, V. (2005). Post-traumatic stress disorder among school age Palestinian children. *Child Abuse and Neglect, 29,* 81–95.

Kilpatrick, D. G., Acierno, R., Saunders, B., Resnick, H. S., Best, C. L., & Schnurr, P. P. (2000). Risk factors for adolescent substance abuse and dependence: Data from a national sample. *Journal of Consulting and Clinical Psychology, 68,* 19–30.

Kimonis, E. R., Frick, P. J., Munoz, L. C., & Aucoin, K. J. (2008). Callous-unemotional traits and the emotional processing of distress cues in detained boys: testing the moderating role of aggression, exposure to community violence, and histories of abuse. *Development and Psychopathology, 20*(2), 569–589.

Ko, S., Ford, J. D., Kassam-Adams, N., Berkowitz, S., Saunders, B., Smith, D., . . . Layne, C. (2008). Creating trauma-informed child-serving systems. *Professional Psychology, 39,* 396–404.

Lyons-Ruth, K., Dutra, L., Schuder, M. R., & Bianchi, I. (2006). From infant attachment disorganization to adult dissociation: Relational adaptations or traumatic experiences? *Psychiatric Clinics of North America, 29*(1), 63–86.

Marsee, M. A., & Frick, P. J. (2007). Exploring the cognitive and emotional correlates to proactive and reactive aggression in a sample of detained girls. *Journal of Abnormal Child Psychology, 35*(6), 969–981.

Mongillo, E. A., Briggs-Gowan, M., Ford, J. D., & Carter, A. S. (2009). Impact of traumatic life events in a community sample of toddlers. *Journal of Abnormal Child Psychology, 37,* 455–468.

Mullick, M. S., & Goodman, R. (2005). The prevalence of psychiatric disorders among 5–10 year olds in rural, urban and slum areas in Bangladesh: An exploratory study. *Social Psychiatry and Psychiatric Epidemiology, 40,* 663–671.

Nader, K. (2008). *Understanding and assessing trauma in children and adolescents: Measures, methods, and youth in context.* New York, NY: Routledge.

Pat-Horenczyk, R., Abramovitz, R., Peled, O., Brom, D., Daie, A., & Chemtob, C. M. (2007). Adolescent exposure to recurrent terrorism in Israel: posttraumatic distress and functional impairment. *American Journal of Orthopsychiatry, 77,* 76–85.

Perkonigg, A., Kessler, R. C., Storz, S., & Wittchen, H. U. (2000). Traumatic events and post-traumatic stress disorder in the community: Prevalence, risk factors and comorbidity. *Acta Psychiatrica Scandinavica, 101,* 46–59.

Postilnik, I., Eisman, H. D., Price, R., & Fogel, J. (2006). An algorithm for defining somatization in children. *Journal of the Canadian Academy of Child and Adolescent Psychiatry, 15*, 64–74.

Putnam, F. W. (2009). Taking the measure of dissociation. *Journal of Trauma and Dissociation, 10*, 233–236.

Salzinger, S., Feldman, R. S., Ng-Mak, D. S., Mojica, E., & Stockhammer, T. F. (2001). The effect of physical abuse on children's social and affective status: A model of cognitive and behavioral processes explaining the association. *Development & Psychopathology, 13*(4), 805–825.

Saxe, G. N., Ellis, B. H., & Kaplow, J. B. (2007). *Collaborative treatment of traumatized children and teens.* New York, NY: Guilford Press.

Scheeringa, M. S., Zeanah, C. H., & Cohen, J. A. (2010). PTSD in children and adolescents: Toward an empirically based algorithm. *Depression and Anxiety, 28*, 770–782.

Seedat, S., Nyamai, C., Njenga, F., Vythilingum, B., & Stein, D. J. (2004). Trauma exposure and post-traumatic stress symptoms in urban African schools: Survey in CapeTown and Nairobi. *British Journal of Psychiatry, 184*, 169–175.

Silberg, J. L. (2000). Fifteen years of dissociation in maltreated children: Where do we go from here? *Child Maltreatment, 5*(2), 119–136.

Silberg, J. L., Waters, F., Nemzer, E., McIntee, J., Wieland, S., Grimminck, E., . . . Emsond, E. (2004). *Guidelines for the evaluation and treatment of dissociative symptoms in children and adolescents.* Northbrook, IL: International Society for the Study of Trauma and Dissociation.

van der Kolk, B. A. (2005). Developmental trauma disorder: Toward a rational diagnosis for children with complex trauma histories. *Psychiatric Annals, 35*(5), 401–408.

Van Horn, P., & Lieberman, A. (2008). Using dyadic therapies to treat traumatized children. In D. Brom, R. Pat-Horenzcyk, & J. D. Ford (Eds.), *Treating traumatized children* (pp. 210–224). London, UK: Routledge.

CHAPTER 9

Assessing Children and Adolescents

EVIDENCE-BASED ASSESSMENT INSTRUMENTS

I n the past two decades there has been a rapid expansion of the available empirically validated assessment instruments for clinical (and research) studies of traumatized children and adolescents. Measures have been developed and validated for a wide range of child and adolescent community (e.g., schools, juvenile justice, postdisaster) and clinical (e.g., emergency, outpatient, residential, and inpatient treatment settings for mental health, addictions, and pediatric medicine) populations. While the selection of specific measures must be done on an individualized basis in order to use instruments that have been validated—and if possible, normed to provide results that can be interpreted in relation to benchmark groups representative of the clinical or research population being assessed—clinicians need a large menu of potential assessment measures in order to acquire a complete understanding of each youth's often complex trauma history, posttraumatic symptoms, associated behavioral and physical health problems, and strengths as well as impairments.

In this chapter we provide an overview of validated assessment instruments that clinicians can use in order to identify potentially applicable measures, with information about published or publicly or commercially available sources that the interested clinician can consult to obtain the instruments. The sources cited for each measure provide evidence that clinicians need in order to evaluate its reliability, validity, and representativeness for youth of different ages, genders, ethnicities, involvement in child-serving systems, and family and community backgrounds.

CHILD AND ADOLESCENT TRAUMA HISTORY ASSESSMENT

Several interview and questionnaire measures have been developed to assess children's history of exposure to potentially traumatic events (Nader, 2008). Five measures will be briefly described to illustrate the types of psychometrically validated instruments that have been developed for clinicians and clinical researchers to assess children's and adolescents' trauma histories. These include questionnaires and interviews that survey a wide range of potentially traumatic events that may happen to children or adolescents, as well as others that assess a more limited set of potentially traumatic interpersonal stressors including physical, sexual, or emotional victimization or violence. Instruments designed exclusively to determine children's and adolescents' histories of exposure to potentially traumatic events for epidemiologic research studies (e.g., see Finkelhor, Ormrod, Turner, & Hamby, 2005; Finkelhor, Turner, Ormrod, & Hamby, 2010, for examples) are not discussed in this book.

The UCLA PTSD Index (Steinberg, Brymer, Decker, & Pynoos, 2004) is a self-report questionnaire that has both child (ages 7 to 12 years old) and adolescent (ages 13 to 17 years old) as well as parent/adult caregiver versions. The measure has 13 questions to assess exposure to potentially traumatic events (i.e., accidents, disasters, violence, abuse, loss of a caregiver, or painful/frightening medical procedures) and 13 follow-up items assessing severity of objective danger/harm and subjective distress (corresponding to *DSM-IV* Criteria A1 and A2 for traumatic stressors). The UCLA scale is available from the National Center for Child Traumatic Stress (www.nctsnet.org).

The Traumatic Events Screening Inventory (TESI; Daviss et al., 2000; Ford et al., 2000; see Table 9.1 for sample items) is a semistructured interview designed to be administered by clinically trained assessors with children ages 8 to 17 years old (TESI-C) or with the parents or caregivers of children ages 0 to 18 years old (TESI-PRR). A self-report version was designed for children ages 10 and older and adolescents (TESI-C/SR;

TABLE 9.1	**TRAUMATIC EVENTS SCREENING INVENTORY (TESI) SAMPLE ITEMS**

TESI-C: Have you ever *been in* a really bad accident, like a car accident, a fall, or a fire? How old were you when this happened? Were you hurt? [What was the hurt?] Did you go to the doctor or hospital? Was someone else really hurt in the accident? [Who? What was the hurt? Did they go to the doctor or the hospital?]

Clinician appraisal of objective physical threat [*DSM-IV* Criterion A1]: Interviewer: In your clinical judgment, was each incident life threatening? Was or could the child or another person have been killed/severely injured?

Child's appraisal of fear/helplessness/horror [*DSM-IV* Criterion A2]: When [the event] was happening, did you feel as scared as you'd ever been, like this was one of the scariest things that EVER happened to you? [If no, ask:] When [the event] happened, did you feel really confused or mixed up? [If no, ask:] Did [the event] make you feel sick or disgusted?

TESI-PRR: Has your child ever been in a serious accident like a car accident, a fall, or a fire? What happened? How old was your child when this happened? Was your child hurt? If so, what were the injuries? Was an ambulance/paramedic called? Did your child go to the doctor or hospital? Was someone else in the accident? If so, were they seriously injured or killed?

Parent's appraisal of event [*DSM-IV* Criterion A1]: Was or could someone have been killed or seriously physically injured in the accident?

Parent's appraisal of child's fear, helplessness, or horror [*DSM-IV* Criterion A2]: Did your child feel extremely scared or afraid? Did your child feel sick/disgusted? Did your child appear to be really confused or mixed up?

Parent's appraisal of own fear, helplessness, or horror: Did YOU feel extremely scared or afraid? Did YOU feel helpless? Did YOU feel sick/disgusted or horrified?

TESI-C-SR: Have you ever had a time in your life when *you did not have the right care*—like not having enough to eat or drink, being homeless, being left alone when you were too young to care for yourself, or being left with someone using drugs? Or have you ever been left in charge of your younger brothers or sisters for long periods of time, sometimes for several days?

☐ Yes

☐ No

☐ Pass

IF YES How old were you?

The first time:_____

The last time:_____

The worst time:_____

Self-appraisal of fear/helplessness/horror [*DSM-IV* Criterion A2]:

Did you feel really bad, upset, scared, sad, or mixed up the worst time this happened?

☐ Yes

☐ No

☐ Pass

Ford, Hartman, Hawke, & Chapman, 2008). The TESI is available at no charge from Dr. Julian Ford (jford@uchc.edu). Each TESI version provides behaviorally specific questions about the type, number of episodes, and developmental/ chronological index (i.e., before age 6, before age 18, age 18 or later, in the past year) of experiences fulfilling the *DSM-IV-TR* criteria for Criterion A1 (life threat, severe injury, or violation of personal integrity, witnessed or directly experienced) and Criterion A2 (fear, helplessness, horror). Fifteen to 26 questions inquire at a fifth-grade reading level about children's direct exposure to and witnessing of potentially traumatic accidents, illness, loss or separation, family violence, community violence, physical assault, and sexual assault or abuse. Follow-up probes provide qualitative information about other persons involved (as victims or perpetrators) and the specific nature of the events.

The Conflict Tactics Scale—Revised (CTS-R; Straus, Hamby, Boney-McCoy, & Sugarman, 1996) is a 39-item questionnaire with five empirically derived subscales (physical assault, psychological aggression, injury, sexual coercion, and negotiation) that assesses intimate partner or family violence victimization and perpetration. Behaviorally specific questions assess whether potentially traumatic interpersonal violence events have occurred by or to the individual, and the frequency of occurrence in the past year. A short form has been validated for brief screening (Straus & Douglas, 2004). A 28-item version has been developed and validated for the assessment of violence by parents toward their child, the Parent—Child CTS (CTSPC; Straus, Hamby, Finkelhor, Moore, & Runyan, 1998), which has subscales for psychological aggression, corporal punishment, physical maltreatment, and severe physical maltreatment, neglect, and sexual maltreatment. The CTS-R and CTSPC also each has a subscale for nonviolent conflict resolution (i.e., negotiation and nonviolent discipline, respectively). The CTS-R also has been used as a screening instrument to identify adolescents in an urban hospital emergency department who are experiencing dating violence (Carroll, Raj, Noel, & Bauchner, 2011). The CTS can be purchased from Western Psychological Services (www.wpspublish.com).

The Childhood Trauma Questionnaire (CTQ; Bernstein, Ahluvalia, Pogge, & Handelsman, 1997) is a 70-item measure with five empirically derived subscales (emotional abuse, emotional neglect, sexual abuse, physical abuse, physical neglect) that has been validated with 12- to

17-year-old adolescents in psychiatric treatment. A briefer version, the 28-item CTQ-SF also was found to yield similar subscales with 12- to 17-year-old adolescents in psychiatric treatment. Both versions of the CTQ include validity questions to identify potential under- or over-reporting or other response biases. The CTQ can be purchased from the Psychological Corporation, www.harcourtasessment.com

A large study of adults in a health maintenance organization demonstrated that those who recalled having experienced 10 forms of adversity in childhood were more likely to develop not only anxiety and affective disorders, but a range of psychological and medical health problems in adulthood (Anda, Butchart, Felitti, & Brown, 2010). This Adverse Childhood Experiences (ACE) study has led to the development of a brief screen for potentially traumatic events that children (or their caregivers) can complete as well as adults (see Table 9.2).

ASSESSMENT MEASURES FOR CHILD AND ADOLESCENT PTSD

Several specialized PTSD diagnostic interviews have been developed for use with children and adolescents or their parents and caregivers (Nader, 2008). For elementary school age and older children, the Children's PTSD Inventory (CPTSDI) inquires about typical traumatic events and assesses PTSD symptoms with dichotomous (present versus absent) items (Saigh et al., 2000; available for purchase from the Psychological Corporation, www.PsychCorp.com). For adolescents, the National Survey of Adolescents (www.nsa.org) PTSD Interview Module surveys potentially traumatic events and the 17 *DSM-IV* symptoms of PTSD (Kilpatrick et al., 2000).

The Clinician Administered PTSD Scale for Children and Adolescents (CAPS-CA; Nader, 2008) also inquires about potentially traumatic events and assesses the intensity (0 = none to 4 = extreme distress) and frequency (0 = never to 4 = daily or almost every day) of the 17 *DSM-IV* PTSD symptoms. The CAPS-CA is available at no charge from the National Center for PTSD (www.ncptsd.gov). The CAPS-CA also assesses eight "associated features" that are a subset of the DTD symptoms, including guilt, shame, dissociation, and trauma-related fears.

The most widely used and best researched structured interviews for psychiatric diagnosis of children have PTSD modules with screening

TABLE 9.2	**ADVERSE CHILDHOOD EXPERIENCES SCALE**

While you were growing up, during your first 18 years of life:

1. Did a parent or other adult in the household **often or very often** . . .
   Swear at you, insult you, put you down, or humiliate you? **or**
   Act in a way that made you afraid that you might be physically hurt?
2. Did a parent or other adult in the household **often or very often** . . .
   Push, grab, slap, or throw something at you? **or**
   Ever hit you so hard that you had marks or were injured?
3. Did an adult or person at least 5 years older than you **ever** . . .
   Touch or fondle you or have you touch their body in a sexual way? **or**
   Attempt or actually have oral, anal, or vaginal intercourse with you?
4. Did you **often or very often** feel that . . .
   No one in your family loved you or thought you were important or special? **or**
   Your family didn't look out for each other, feel close to each other, or support each other?
5. Did you **often or very often** feel that . . .
   You didn't have enough to eat, had to wear dirty clothes, and had no one to protect you? **or**
   Your parents were too drunk or high to take care of you or take you to the doctor if you needed?
6. Were your parents **ever** separated or divorced?
7. Was your mother or stepmother:
   Often or very often pushed, grabbed, slapped, or had something thrown at her? **or**
   Sometimes, often, or very often kicked, bitten, hit with a fist, or hit with something hard? **or**
   Ever repeatedly hit at least a few minutes or threatened with a gun or knife?
8. Did you live with anyone who was a problem drinker or alcoholic or who used street drugs?
9. Was a household member depressed or mentally ill, or ever attempted suicide?
10. Did a household member go to prison?

Accessed 12/14/11 from www.acestudy.org

---

questions for history of exposure to potentially traumatic events and symptom questions based on the *DSM-IV.* The Diagnostic Interview for Children and Adolescents—Revised (DICA-R; Reich, 2000) is a semistructured interview for clinically trained interviewers that is available for purchase in an electronic delivery format from Mental Health Resources (www.mhs.com). The Kiddie-Schedule of Affective Disorders and Schizophrenia (K-SADS; McLeer, Deblinger, Henry, & Orvaschel, 1992) is a semistructured instrument for clinically trained interviewers and is available at no charge for not-for-profit uses (or with permission for other uses) from the University of Pittsburgh Department of Psychiatry (www .wpic.pitt.edu/ksads). The Child and Adolescent Psychiatric Assessment (CAPA; Angold et al., 1995) is a semistructured instrument for clinically trained interviewers (who must receive specialized training in using this measure) and is available at no charge by permission of the Duke University Developmental Epidemiology Center (http://devepi.duhs.duke .edu/capa.html). The Diagnostic Interview Schedule for Children (DISC; Shaffer, Fisher, Lucas, Dulcan, & Schwab-Stone, 2000) is highly structured to be appropriate for interviewers who do not have clinical training, and is available in a computerized version from the Columbia DISC Development Group (www.promotementalhealth.org/downloads/DISC%20 Brochure.pdf).

Questionnaires assessing self-reported or parent/caregiver reported PTSD symptoms also have been developed and validated for children. The UCLA PTSD Index (Steinberg et al., 2004) assesses the *DSM-IV* PTSD symptoms in 21-item versions for children or parents and a 22-item adolescent version. Some of the symptoms are assessed with two items in order to capture the different aspects of the symptom (e.g., emotional numbing may take the form of difficulty in feeling either positive emotions such as happiness or love, or negative emotions such as sadness or anger). Three items on the adolescent version assess "associated features" (i.e., guilt; fear of revictimization; hopelessness), and the latter two associated features are assessed on the child version. All of the symptom items are rated for their frequency of occurrence (from 0 = none of the time to 4 = most of the time) in the past month.

The Child PTSD Symptom Scale (Foa, Johnson, Feeny, & Treadwell, 2001; Rachamim, Helpman, Foa, Aderka, & Gilboa-Schechtman, 2011) is a self-report questionnaire for children and adolescents ages 8 to 17 years old, which begins with two questions about potentially traumatic events and then surveys the 17 *DSM-IV* PTSD symptoms, with one item for each symptom. Each symptom item is rated for its frequency of occurrence in the past 2 weeks (from 0 = not at all or only at one time to 3 = five or more times a week/almost always). An additional seven questions ask whether the symptoms have interfered with functioning at home, in school, with peers, in activities, in prayer, or in overall happiness.

The measure may be obtained at no cost from Dr. Edna Foa (foa@mail. med.upenn.edu).

The PTSD Checklist for Children/Parent Report (PCL-C/PR; Ford et al., 2000) assesses the 17 *DSM-IV* PTSD symptoms by asking a parent or caregiver of a child or adolescent to describe the extent to which the youth was bothered by each symptom in the past month (from 1 = not at all to 5 = extremely). Although functional impairment is not directly assessed as in the CPSS, the scoring instructions for the PCL-C/PR define higher severity ratings based not only on the youth's subjective distress but also whether the youth was able to cope with the symptom without experiencing difficulty engaging in activities, getting along with others, or following rules, or seeming to be different than her/his usual self. The PCL-C/PR may be obtained from Dr. Julian Ford at no cost (jford@uchc.edu).

The Trauma Symptom Checklist for Children (TSCC) is a 54-item scale and was developed for 8- to 16-year-olds, with minor normative adjustments for 17-year-olds (Wolpaw, Ford, Newman, Davis, & Briere, 2005). The TSCC has two validity scales (Underresponse and Hyperresponse) and six clinical scales: Anxiety, Depression, Anger, Posttraumatic Stress, Sexual Concerns (with two subscales), and Dissociation (with two subscales). An alternate form (the TSCC-A) excludes items about sexuality. The Trauma Symptom Checklist for Young Children (TSCYC) is a 90-item scale developed for 3- to 12-year-olds (Briere, 2005) that has two validity scales (Response Level and Atypical Response) and nine clinical scales: Posttraumatic Stress—Intrusion, Posttraumatic Stress—Avoidance, Posttraumatic Stress—Arousal, Posttraumatic Stress—Total, Sexual Concerns, Anxiety, Depression, Dissociation, and Anger/Aggression. The TSCC and TSCYC can be purchased from Psychological Assessment Resources (www.parinc.com).

The Los Angeles Symptom Checklist (LASC) is another wide-ranging measure of posttraumatic symptomatology that has been validated with high-risk adolescents as well as with adults (Foy, Wood, King, King, & Resnick, 1997). The 43-item questionnaire includes a 17-item PTSD Index with each *DSM-IV* PTSD symptom and empirically based subscales for Criteria B, C, and D. Each item is rated for the severity of problems that it is perceived to be causing, on a 5-point scale from "not a problem" to "an extreme problem." The LASC also assesses problems with alcohol/

substance use, eating, relationships, and negative emotions. The LASC may be obtained from Dr. David Foy (dfoy@pepperdine.edu).

The Child Sexual Behavior Inventory (CSBI; Friedrich et al., 2001) is a 38-item measure designed to be completed by an adult caregiver for children ages 2 to 12 years old who have been, or are suspected of having been, sexually abused. Each item is rated for its frequency of occurrence in the past 6 months (from 0 = never to 3 = at least once a week). In addition to a total score and scores for developmentally related and sexual abuse–related behavior, the CSBI has nine subscales: (1) Boundary Problems, (2) Exhibitionism, (3) Gender Role Behavior, (4) Self-Stimulation, (5) Sexual Anxiety, (6) Sexual Interest, (7) Sexual Intrusiveness, (8) Sexual Knowledge, and (9) Voyeuristic Behavior. The CSBI may be purchased from Psychological Assessment Resources (www.parinc.com).

Measures of Posttraumatic Dysregulation

The TSCC, LASC, and CSBI, as well as several omnibus questionnaire measures for children and adolescents (see Ford, 2011, for a summary), identify symptomatic and behavioral problems that may be downstream results of the impairments in self-regulation that often are sequelae of complex adverse childhood experiences such as polyvictimization or developmentally adverse interpersonal trauma. We will provide a brief overview of measures tapping the aspects of dysregulation identified in the complex PTSD (developmental trauma disorder) construct, beginning with emotion dysregulation.

The empirically based Negative Intensity and Negative Reactivity subscales of the 27-item Affect Intensity and Reactivity Measure for Youth (AIR-Y; Jones, Leen-Feldner, Olatunji, Reardon, & Hawks, 2009) provide brief questionnaire measures of two aspects of *emotion dysregulation* in adolescence. The 92-item Dysregulation Inventory and the briefer (30-item) Abbreviated Dysregulation Inventory (ADI) is a questionnaire validated for children and adolescents ages 10 to 22 years old, which has an empirically based affect dysregulation subscale (Mezzich, Tarter, Giancola, & Kirisci, 2001). The ADI has parent- and teacher-report versions as well as a version for youth self-report. The affect dysregulation subscale has items tapping difficulty with anger (e.g., "I fly off the handle for no good reason"), anxiety (e.g., "I lose sleep because I worry"), hyperarousal (e.g., "There are days when I'm on edge all the time"), mood lability (e.g., "My mood goes up and down without reason"), and loss of control (e.g., "Often, I am afraid I will lose control of my feelings"). The affect dysregulation subscale may be particularly useful with oppositional or defiant youth because it has been shown to be distinct from the callous and unemotional traits associated with psychopathy (Pardini, Lochman, & Frick, 2003).

Three emotion dysregulation measures developed primarily for adults may be used with older adolescents. The Inventory of Altered Self-Capacities (IASC; Briere & Rickards, 2007) is a questionnaire that has subscales for affect dysregulation and tension reduction. The Generalized Expectancies for Negative Mood Regulation (NMR; Catanzaro & Mearns, 1990) is a 30-item questionnaire assessing emotion modulation and distress tolerance that is appropriate for youth with reading levels at or above fifth-grade level. The Difficulties with Emotion Regulation Scale (DERS; Gratz & Roemer, 2004) is a 36-item questionnaire with a particularly nuanced set of subscales, which has been validated with college students. The DERS subscales include unawareness of emotions; alexithymia; nonacceptance of emotions; difficulty engaging in goal-directed behavior or with impulse control when emotionally upset; unawareness of emotions; and difficulty recovering from emotional distress.

Neuropsychological tests of executive functions provide sophisticated assessments of youths' *cognitive self-regulation* capacities and problems, including attentional focusing/shifting, working memory, verbal/declarative and procedural memory, narrative memory, and higher order conceptual thinking/problem solving. When neuropsychological testing is not feasible, the ADI cognitive dysregulation scale (Mezzich et al., 2001) can screen for cognitive dysregulation. The ADI subscale provides 10 positively worded items that tap competence (or deficits therein) in proactive consequence-based planning (e.g., "I develop a plan for all my important goals"; "I think about the future consequences of my actions"), error monitoring and course correction (e.g., "As soon as I see things are not working, I do something about it"), and perseverance ("Failure at a task or in school makes me work harder"; "I stick to a task until it is finished").

Behavioral and relational self-regulation may be assessed by subscales from omnibus measures of child and adolescent personality and psychopathology (see Ford, Nader, & Fletcher, in press, for a summary). In addition, the TSCC and TSYCC have subscales for behavioral dysregulation associated with exposure to sexual trauma (Sexual Concerns) and violence or physical abuse (Anger/Aggression). Several CSBI domain scores refer to dysregulated sexual behavior (e.g., intrusiveness, voyeurism, exhibitionism, self-stimulation; Friedrich et al., 2001). The third ADI subscale ("behavioral dysregulation") assesses hyperactivity (e.g., "I have difficulty remaining seated at school or at home during dinner"), argumentativeness ("I get into arguments when people disagree with me"), boredom ("I get bored easily"), and impulsivity ("I spend money without thinking about it first") (Mezzich et al., 2001). The Perceived Competence Scales for Children (PCSC; Harter & Whitesell, 2003) assess behavioral, peer, and physical competence in early childhood (i.e., ages 4 to 7) with questions asking the child to identify which of several pictures is most self-descriptive. The PCSC for latency-age children and adolescents assesses athletic, scholastic, behavioral, friendship, romantic relationship, and job competence.

Posttraumatic somatic dysregulation has not been systematically operationalized in any measures or theoretical measurement models. The TSCC and omnibus psychopathology or personality questionnaires for children and adolescents provide empirically based subscales for somatic complaints that may serve as indirect indices of somatic dysregulation (Ford et al., in press). Self-report questionnaires have been developed for or used with school-age children and adolescents to assess fatigue and somatic complaints (Jellesma, Rieffe, & Terwogt, 2007; Walker, Beck, Garber, & Lambert, 2009), and the associated problem of alexithymia (van de Putte, Engelbert, Kuis, Kimpen, & Uiterwaal, 2007).

Finally, dysregulation of self-perception in childhood or adolescence may be assessed with questionnaires such as the Hopelessness Scale for Children (Kazdin, Rodgers, & Colbus, 1986; Spirito, Williams, Stark, & Hart, 1988), the Beck Depression Inventory for Youth (BDI-Y; Stapleton, Sander, & Stark, 2007), or the Children's Depression Inventory (CDI; Cole & Martin, 2005). These measures do not, however, clearly distinguish between affective dysphoria, a negative view of the world and other people, and specific negative perceptions of or beliefs about self. For example, in a sample of 9- to 13-year-old girls, Stapleton et al. (2007) found that the BDI-Y item designed to measure worthlessness, unlovability, self-blame, and self-hatred were not strongly interrelated once their relationship to a general depression factor was accounted for. However, the self-hatred item was uniquely related to an item tapping the wish for death, and items reflecting self-perceived incompetence and isolation were less strongly related to the general depression factor than other items. Also, a study with the CDI found evidence of a distinct self-deprecation factor (Garcia, Aluja, & Del Barrio, 2008). These findings point the way to a more refined approach to assessing negative self-perceptions separate from the more general emotional state of dysphoria or hopelessness.

TREATMENT STRATEGIES

Practice guidelines for the assessment and treatment of children and adolescents with PTSD were first developed by an expert panel convened more than a decade ago by the American Academy of Child and Adolescent Psychiatry (Cohen & AACAP, 1998). More recently, authoritative reviews of treatments for children and adolescents with PTSD have been published (Saxe, MacDonald, & Ellis, 2007; Vickerman & Margolin, 2007), including several in the second edition of the International Society for Traumatic Stress Studies (ISTSS) Practice Guidelines, *Effective Treatments for PTSD* (Foa, Keane, Friedman, & Cohen, 2009). These include eye movement desensitization and reprocessing (EMDR; Spates, Koch, Cusack, Pagoto, & Waller, 2009), school-based cognitive behavior therapies (Jaycox, Stein, & Amaya-Jackson, 2009), psychodynamic therapies (Lieberman, Ghosh Ippen, & Marans, 2009), creative arts therapies (Goodman, Chapman, & Gantt, 2009), and psychopharmacotherapy (treatment with therapeutic medications; Donnelly, 2009). Family systems therapies were included in the ISTSS Practice Guidelines only for adults, but promising approaches for family therapy with children with PTSD have been developed (Ford & Saltzman, 2009). Psychotherapies that focus on affective and interpersonal self-regulation also have been identified as promising for children with PTSD by the National Child Traumatic Stress Network (see Ford & Cloitre, 2009).

The key elements in psychotherapy for children with PTSD are summarized by the acronym PRACTICE (Cohen, Deblinger, & Mannarino,

2005): **P**arenting skills and **P**sychoeducation, **R**elaxation skills, **A**ffect modulation (helping the child and caregivers manage emotional distress), **C**ognitive coping skills, **T**rauma narrative reconstruction, *In vivo* application of skills (practicing skills and confronting reminders of traumatic experiences in daily life), **C**onjoint parent—child sessions (treatment sessions with the parent and child together), and **E**nsuring safety and posttherapy adjustment. Each approach to therapy provides these forms of assistance in different ways.

For traumatized toddlers and preschoolers, Van Horn and Lieberman (2008) developed and validated a parent—child dyadic model (Child— Parent Psychotherapy [CPP]) in which the therapist educates and guides the parent in understanding how traumatic stress is affecting their child and developing skills for responsively and nurturingly assisting the child in coping with and recovering from traumatic stress reactions in the context of play and tasks of daily living. CPP has been found to not only reduce children's PTSD symptoms and problem behaviors but also to enhance attachment security. Other approaches to dyadic family psychotherapy with traumatized young children and their parent(s) include a more behavioral approach that has shown promise in field trials including with formerly abusive parents (Parent—Child Interaction Therapy; Urquiza & Timmer, 2012), a psychodynamic model that helps parents understand their child's emotions and motivation (Watch, Wait, and Wonder; Cohen et al., 1999), and a dyadic model in which parents view videotapes of interactions with their child in order to use their observations to develop ways of interacting that elicit prosocial behavior (Interaction Guidance; McDonough, 2000).

For victimized children from preschool age through adolescence the best validated psychotherapy approach for sexually or physically abused or traumatically bereaved children with PTSD is Trauma-Focused Cognitive Behavior Therapy (TF-CBT; Cohen et al., 2005; Cohen, Mannarino, & Iyengar, 2011). For traumatized toddlers and preschoolers, adaptations of TF-CBT have shown promise and evidence that trauma memory work (exposure) and relaxation skill training are feasible as long as the protocol is developmentally appropriate and parents are able to manage their anxiety sufficiently to be able to help the child with each step of the process (Scheeringa, Zeanah, & Cohen, 2010).

TF-CBT was developed to decrease symptoms of PTSD and depression by providing a combination of cognitive–behavioral skill building and gradual therapeutic exposure to trauma memories in which the youth constructs a narrative story of specific traumatic events and then shares the narrative with the parent. TF-CBT follows a three-phase approach comparable to that in PTSD therapy with adults, typically for at least 12 to 16 90-minute sessions—often with longer duration and shorter session length in community (versus research) settings (Cohen et al., 2011). Phase One includes educating the child and parents separately about PTSD symptoms and skills that include relaxation, labeling specific emotion states, and cognitive coping for the child and supportive listening, positive reinforcement, and consistent monitoring and limit setting for the parent(s). In Phase Two, the therapist assists the child in constructing a story-like description of a specific traumatic event that has been identified as most troubling currently for the child. The child often will not be able to recall every aspect, and details that were not recalled originally often emerge spontaneously. Phase Two memory-telling should never be a "fishing expedition" or an attempt to retrieve or recover "lost" or "repressed" memories. The purpose is to enable the child to purposefully describe—in words and pictures—a troubling experience in a manner that shows both the child and the parent(s) that they can cope successfully with recalling the memory. In Phase Three, the child and parent apply the new confidence and skills they have learned to deal with other troubling memories or stressful or problematic current situations in their lives.

For adolescents, Trauma Affect Regulation: Guide for Education and Therapy (TARGET; Ford & Hawke, 2012; Ford, Steinberg, Hawke, Levine, & Zhang, 2012; Marrow, Knudsen, Olafson, & Becker, in press) intervention has been shown to be effective, as well as with women in substance abuse treatment and low-income women with PTSD who are parenting young children (Ford, Steinberg, & Zhang, 2011). TARGET is a 4- to 12-session manualized individual or group therapy intervention that provides psychoeducation about the impact of psychological trauma on the brain and a skill set of seven sequential self-regulation steps organized by the acronym FREEDOM: **F**ocusing to interrupt stress-related reactivity or impulsivity, **R**ecognizing stress/trauma triggers, **E**motion recognition,

Evaluating thoughts, Defining personal goals, choosing Options to achieve goals, and Making a contribution in others' lives. Woven into the intervention is a "lifeline" in which youths create a multimedia creative arts representation of their lives, identifying how they can use the FREEDOM skills to recover from traumatic stress.

Seeking Safety (Najavits, Gallop, & Weiss, 2006) is a 25-session structured psychoeducational model that has been adapted for traumatized girls who are abusing substances. Seeking Safety provides psychoeducation about PTSD and substance abuse as well as cognitive–behavioral skills for coping with addictive thinking and behavior as well as with PTSD avoidance and hyperarousal symptoms. Similar to TARGET, Seeking Safety does not require the trauma memory processing that is done in TF-CBT, EMDR, and Cognitive Behavioral Intervention for Trauma in Schools (CBITS), but focuses on helping adolescents to gain skills and confidence in their ability to handle trauma reminders and addictive urges adaptively.

CONCLUSION

Clinical assessment with traumatized children and adolescents can prepare the child and adult caregivers (including parents, teachers, case managers, mentors, child welfare workers, juvenile justice and court professionals, and other support persons) as well as the clinician to plan an approach to therapy for PTSD and related symptoms. Thorough assessment takes into account not only the child's trauma history and symptoms but also the alterations in the child's self-regulation capabilities that are crucial both to impairment and to recovery. The focus of the assessment is on traumatic stress but not merely as past events or current symptoms. When traumatic stress is understood developmentally, the goal of assessment (and treatment) is the restoration or building of self-regulation competences that were blocked or altered by trauma and that can provide the child with a basis for recovering from traumatic stress symptoms.

REFERENCES

Anda, R. F., Butchart, A., Felitti, V. J., & Brown, D. W. (2010). Building a framework for global surveillance of the public health implications of adverse childhood experiences. *American Journal of Preventive Medicine, 39*(1), 93–98.

Angold, A., Prendergast, M., Cox, A., Harrington, R., Simonoff, E., & Rutter, M. (1995). The Child and Adolescent Psychiatric Assessment (CAPA). *Psychological Medicine, 25,* 739–753.

Bernstein, D. P., Ahluvalia, T., Pogge, D., & Handelsman, L. (1997). Validity of the Childhood Trauma Questionnaire in an adolescent psychiatric population. *Journal of the American Academy of Child and Adolescent Psychiatry, 36,* 340–348.

Briere, J. (2005). *Trauma symptom checklist for young children (TSCYC): Professional manual.* Odessa, FL: Psychological Assessment Resources.

Briere, J., & Rickards, S. (2007). Self-awareness, affect regulation, and relatedness: Differential sequels of childhood versus adult victimization experiences. *Journal of Nervous and Mental Disease, 195,* 497–503.

Carroll, B. C., Raj, A., Noel, S. E., & Bauchner, H. (2011). Dating violence among adolescents presenting to a pediatric emergency department. *Archives of Pediatric and Adolescent Medicine, 165,* 1101–1106.

Catanzaro, S. J., & Mearns, J. (1990). Measuring generalized expectancies for negative mood regulation: Initial scale development and implications. *Journal of Personality Assessment, 54,* 546–563.

Cohen, J. A., & American Academy of Child and Adolescent Psychiatry. (1998). Practice parameters for the assessment and treatment of children and adolescents with conduct disorder. *Journal of the American Academy of Child & Adolescent Psychiatry, 37*(10 Suppl), 4S–26S.

Cohen, J. A., Deblinger, E., & Mannarino, A. P. (2005). Trauma-focused cognitive–behavioral therapy for sexually abused children. In E. D. Hibbs & P. S. Jensen (Eds.), *Psychosocial treatments for child and adolescent disorders: Empirically based strategies for clinical practice* (2nd ed., pp. 743–765). Washington, DC: American Psychological Association.

Cohen, J. A., Mannarino, A. P., & Iyengar, S. (2011). Community treatment of post-traumatic stress disorder for children exposed to intimate partner violence: A randomized controlled trial. *Archives of Pediatric and Adolescent Medicine, 165,* 16–21.

Cohen, N. J., Muir, E., Lojkasek, M., Muir, R., Parker, C. J., Barwick, M., & Brown, M. (1999). Watch, wait, and wonder: Testing the effectiveness of a new approach to mother-infant psychotherapy. *Infant Mental Health Journal, 20*(4), 429–451.

Cole, D. A., & Martin, N. C. (2005). The longitudinal structure of the Children's Depression Inventory: Testing a latent trait-state model. *Psychological Assessment, 17,* 144–155.

Daviss, W. B., Mooney, D., Racusin, R., Ford, J. D., Fleischer, A., & McHugo, G. (2000). Predicting post-traumatic stress after hospitalization for pediatric injury. *Journal of the American Academy of Child and Adolescent Psychiatry, 39,* 576–583.

Donnelly, C. L. (2009). Psychopharmacotherapy for children and adolescents. In E. B. Foa, T. M. Keane, M. J. Friedman, & J. A. Cohen (Eds.), *Effective treatments for PTSD* (2nd ed., pp. 269–278). New York, NY: Guilford Press.

Finkelhor, D., Ormrod, R. K., Turner, H. A., & Hamby, S. L. (2005). Measuring poly-victimization using the Juvenile Victimization Questionnaire. *Child Abuse and Neglect, 29,* 1297–1312.

Finkelhor, D., Turner, H., Ormrod, R., & Hamby, S. L. (2010). Trends in childhood violence and abuse exposure: evidence from 2 national surveys. *Archives of Pediatric and Adolescent Medicine, 164*(3), 238–242.

Foa, E. B., Johnson, K. M., Feeny, N. C., & Treadwell, K. R. H. (2001). The Child PTSD Symptom Scale: A preliminary examination of its psychometric properties. *Journal of Clinical Child Psychology, 30,* 376–384.

Foa, E. B., Keane, T. M., Friedman, M. J., & Cohen, J. A. (Eds.). (2009). *Effective treatments for PTSD* (2nd ed.). New York, NY: Guilford Press.

Ford, J. D. (2011). Assessing child and adolescent complex traumatic stress reactions. *Journal of Child and Adolescent Trauma, 4*(3), 217–232.

Ford, J. D., & Cloitre, M. (2009). Chapter 3. Best practices in psychotherapy for children and adolescents. In C. Courtois & J. D. Ford (Eds.), *Treating complex traumatic stress disorders: An evidence-based guide* (pp. 59–81). New York, NY: Guilford Press.

Ford, J. D., Hartman, J. K., Hawke, J., & Chapman, J. (2008). Traumatic victimization, posttraumatic stress disorder, suicidal ideation, and substance abuse risk among juvenile justice-involved youths. *Journal of Child and Adolescent Trauma, 1,* 75–92.

Ford, J. D., & Hawke, J. (2012). Trauma affect regulation psychoeducation group and milieu intervention outcomes in juvenile detention facilities. *Journal of Aggression, Maltreatment & Trauma, 21,* 365–384.

Ford, J. D., Nader, K., & Fletcher, K. (in press). Assessment guidelines and instruments. In J. D. Ford & C. A. Courtois (Eds.), *Treating complex traumatic stress disorders in children and adolescents: An evidence-based guide.* New York, NY: Guilford Press.

Ford, J. D., Racusin, R., Ellis, C., Daviss, W. B., Reiser, J., Fleischer, A., & Thomas, J. (2000). Child maltreatment, other trauma exposure, and posttraumatic symptomatology among children with oppositional defiant and attention deficit hyperactivity disorders. *Child Maltreatment, 5,* 205–217.

Ford, J. D., & Saltzman, W. (2009). Family therapy. In C. Courtois & J. D. Ford (Eds.), *Treating complex traumatic stress disorders: An evidence-based guide* (pp. 391–414). New York, NY: Guilford Press.

Ford, J. D., Steinberg, K., Hawke, J., Levine, J., & Zhang, W. (2012). Randomized trial comparison of emotion regulation and relational psychotherapies for PTSD with girls involved in delinquency. *Journal of Clinical Child and Adolescent Psychology, 41,* 1–12.

Ford, J. D., Steinberg, K., & Zhang, W. (2011). A randomized clinical trial comparing affect regulation and social problem-solving psychotherapies for mothers with victimization-related PTSD. *Behavior Therapy, 42,* 561–578.

Foy, D. W., Wood, J. L., King, D. W., King, L. A., & Resnick, H. S. (1997). Los Angeles Symptom Checklist: Psychometric evidence with an adolescent sample. *Assessment, 3,* 377−384.

Friedrich, W. N., Fisher, J. L., Dittner, C. A., Acton, R., Berliner, L., Butler, J., . . . Wright, J. (2001). Child Sexual Behavior Inventory: Normative, psychiatric, and sexual abuse comparisons. *Child Maltreatment, 6,* 37−49.

Garcia, L. F., Aluja, A., & Del Barrio, V. (2008). Testing the hierarchical structure of the Children's Depression Inventory: A multigroup analysis. *Assessment, 15,* 153−164.

Goodman, R., Chapman, L., & Gantt, L. (2009). Creative arts therapies for children. In E. B. Foa, T. M. Keane, M. J. Friedman, & J. A. Cohen (Eds.), *Effective treatments for PTSD* (2nd ed., pp. 491−507). New York, NY: Guilford Press.

Gratz, K. L., & Roemer, L. (2004). Multidimensional assessment of emotion regulation and dysregulation: Development, factor structure, and initial validation of the Difficulties in Emotion Regulation Scale. *Journal of Psychopathology and Behavioral Assessment, 26,* 41−54.

Harter, S., & Whitesell, N. R. (2003). Beyond the debate: Why some adolescents report stable self-worth over time and situation, whereas others report changes in self-worth. *Journal of Personality, 71,* 1027−1058.

Jaycox, L. H., Stein, B. D., & Amaya-Jackson, L. (2009). School-based treatment for children and adolescents. In E. B. Foa, T. M. Keane, M. J. Friedman, & J. A. Cohen (Eds.), *Effective Treatments for PTSD* (2nd ed., pp. 327−345). New York, NY: Guilford Press.

Jellesma, F. C., Rieffe, C., & Terwogt, M. M. (2007). The Somatic Complaint List: Validation of a self-report questionnaire assessing somatic complaints in children. *Journal of Psychosomatic Research, 63,* 399−401.

Jones, R. E., Leen-Feldner, E. W., Olatunji, B. O., Reardon, L. E., & Hawks, E. (2009). Psychometric properties of the Affect Intensity and Reactivity Measure adapted for Youth (AIR-Y). *Psychological Assessment, 21,* 162−175.

Kazdin, A. E., Rodgers, A., & Colbus, D. (1986). The hopelessness scale for children: Psychometric characteristics and concurrent validity. *Journal of Consulting and Clinical Psychology, 54*(2), 241−245.

Kilpatrick, D. G., Acierno, R., Saunders, B., Resnick, H. S., Best, C. L., & Schnurr, P. P. (2000). Risk factors for adolescent substance abuse and dependence: Data from a national sample. *Journal of Consulting and Clinical Psychology, 68,* 19−30.

Lieberman, A. L., Ghosh Ippen, C., & Marans, S. (2009). Psychodynamic therapy for child trauma. In E. B. Foa, T. M. Keane, M. Friedman, & J. A. Cohen (Eds.), *Effective treatments for PTSD* (pp. 370−387). New York, NY: Guilford Press.

Marrow, M., Knudsen, K., Olafson, E., & Becker, S. (in press). Pilot of a trauma-focused intervention in a juvenile justice setting. *Journal of Child and Adolescent Trauma.*

McDonough, S. C. (2000). Interaction guidance: An approach for difficult-to-engage families. In C. H. Zeanah, Jr. (Ed.), *Handbook of infant mental health* (2nd ed., pp. 485−493). New York, NY: Guilford Press.

McLeer, S. V., Deblinger, E., Henry, D., & Orvaschel, H. (1992). Sexually abused children at high risk for post-traumatic stress disorder. *Journal of the American Academy of Child and Adolescent Psychiatry, 31*(5), 875−879.

Mezzich, A., Tarter, R., Giancola, P., & Kirisci, L. (2001). The Dysregulation Inventory. *Journal of Child and Adolescent Substance Abuse, 10*, 35−43.

Nader, K. (2008). *Understanding and assessing trauma in children and adolescents: Measures, methods, and youth in context.* New York, NY: Routledge.

Najavits, L. M., Gallop, R. J., & Weiss, R. D. (2006). Seeking safety therapy for adolescent girls with PTSD and substance use disorder: A randomized controlled trial. *Journal of Behavioral Health Services & Research, 33*(4), 453−463.

Pardini, D. A., Lochman, J. E., & Frick, P. J. (2003). Callous/unemotional traits and social−cognitive processes in adjudicated youths. *Journal of the American Academy of Child and Adolescent Psychiatry, 42*, 364−371.

Rachamim, L., Helpman, L., Foa, E. B., Aderka, I. M., & Gilboa-Schechtman, E. (2011). Validation of the Child Posttraumatic Symptom Scale in a sample of treatment-seeking Israeli youth. *Journal of Traumatic Stress, 24*, 356−360.

Reich, W. (2000). Diagnostic Interview for Children and Adolescents (DICA). *Journal of the American Academy of Child & Adolescent Psychiatry, 39*(1), 59−66.

Saigh, P. A., Yasik, A. E., Oberfield, R. A., Green, B. L., Halamandaris, P. V., Rubenstein, H., . . . McHugh, M. (2000). The children's PTSD Inventory: Development and reliability. *Journal of Traumatic Stress, 13*(3), 369−380.

Saxe, G., MacDonald, H., & Ellis, H. (2007). Psychosocial approaches for children with PTSD. In E. B. Foa, M. J. Friedman, T. M. Keane, & P. Resick (Eds.), *Handbook of PTSD: Science and practice* (pp. 359−375). New York, NY: Guilford Press.

Scheeringa, M. S., Zeanah, C. H., & Cohen, J. A. (2010). PTSD in children and adolescents: Toward an empirically based algorithm. *Depression and Anxiety, 28*, 770−782.

Shaffer, D., Fisher, P., Lucas, C. P., Dulcan, M. K., & Schwab-Stone, M. E. (2000). NIMH Diagnostic Interview Schedule for Children Version IV (NIMH DISC-IV): Description, differences from previous versions, and reliability of some common diagnoses. *Journal of the American Academy of Child & Adolescent Psychiatry, 39*(1), 28−38.

Spates, C. R., Koch, E., Cusack, K. J., Pagoto, S., & Waller, S. (2009). Eye movement desensitization and reprocessing. In E. B. Foa, T. M. Keane, M. J. Friedman, & J. A. Cohen (Eds.), *Effective treatments for PTSD* (2nd ed., pp. 279−305). New York, NY: Guilford Press.

Spirito, A., Williams, C. A., Stark, L. J., & Hart, K. J. (1988). The Hopelessness Scale for Children: Psychometric properties with normal and emotionally disturbed adolescents. *Journal of Abnormal Child Psychology, 16*, 445−458.

Stapleton, L. M., Sander, J., & Stark, K. (2007). Psychometric properties of the Beck Depression Inventory for Youth in a sample of girls. *Psychological Assessment, 19,* 230–235.

Steinberg, A. M., Brymer, M. J., Decker, K. B., & Pynoos, R. S. (2004). The University of California at Los Angeles Post-traumatic Stress Disorder Reaction Index. *Current Psychiatry Reports, 6*(2), 96–100.

Straus, M. A., & Douglas, E. M. (2004). A short form of the Revised Conflict Tactics Scales, and typologies for severity and mutuality. *Violence and Victomology, 19,* 507–520.

Straus, M. A., Hamby, S. L., Boney-McCoy, S., & Sugarman, D. B. (1996). The revised Conflict Tactics Scales (CTS2): Development and preliminary psychometric data. *Journal of Family Issues, 17,* 283–316.

Straus, M. A., Hamby, S. L., Finkelhor, D., Moore, D. W., & Runyan, D. (1998). Identification of child maltreatment with the Parent–Child Conflict Tactics Scales: Development and psychometric data for a national sample of American parents. *Child Abuse and Neglect, 22,* 249–270.

Urquiza, A., & Timmer, S. (2012). Parent–child interaction therapy for traumatized children. In J. D. Ford & C. A. Courtois (Eds.), *Treating complex traumatic stress disorders in children and adolescents: An evidence-based guide.* New York, NY: Guilford Press.

van de Putte, E. M., Engelbert, R. H., Kuis, W., Kimpen, J. L., & Uiterwaal, C. S. (2007). Alexithymia in adolescents with chronic fatigue syndrome. *Journal of Psychosomatic Research, 63*(4), 377–380.

Van Horn, P., & Lieberman, A. (2008). Using dyadic therapies to treat traumatized children. In D. Brom, R. Pat-Horenzcyk, & J. D. Ford (Eds.), *Treating traumatized children* (pp. 210–224). London: Routledge.

Vickerman, K. A., & Margolin, G. (2007). Posttraumatic stress in children and adolescents exposed to family violence: II. Treatment. *Professional Psychology: Research and Practice, 38*(6), 620–628.

Walker, L. S., Beck, J. E., Garber, J., & Lambert, W. (2009). Children's Somatization Inventory: Psychometric properties of the revised form (CSI-24). *Journal of Pediatric Psychology, 34*(4), 430–440.

Wolpaw, J. M., Ford, J. D., Newman, E., Davis, J. L., & Briere, J. (2005). Trauma Symptom Checklist for Children. In T. Grisso, G. Vincent, & D. Seagrave (Eds.), *Mental health screening and assessment in juvenile justice.* (pp. 152–165). New York, NY: Guilford Press.

CHAPTER 10

Working With Veterans

Recent wars in Iraq and Afghanistan, along with the more general "Global War on Terror," have starkly increased the number of military veterans with mental illnesses in society, including combat-related PTSD and other related behavioral health problems, such as suicidality, depression, addictions, and violence. In terms of the immediate pain and suffering, broken families, lost wages, impaired health status, medical services, and criminal justice involvement, the cost to individuals, families, and society is enormous. Mental health clinicians must play a critical role in helping to mitigate these costs by working with traumatized veterans and their families. Indeed, the U.S. Department of Veterans Affairs (VA) has increased the number of mental health practitioners employed by about 300% since 2006. Thus, military veterans currently make up one of the largest, if not the largest, groups currently receiving mental health care services in the United States and many other Western countries. Moreover, given the recent historical course of combat-related PTSD, they are likely to remain one of the largest groups in need for decades to come.

In this chapter, we review prevalence, PTSD onset and course, sociopolitical and cultural factors, compensation and pension evaluations, clinical assessment, and treatment planning implications pertaining to military veterans. This will include discussion of unique factors associated with combat and military service, detection and management of malingering and symptom overreporting, and working within the VA health care system.

PREVALENCE

There is a large body of literature on the prevalence of combat-related PTSD among military personnel and veterans dating back to the Vietnam War and including all U.S. wars since. Contrary to popular perception, only a small percentage of combat veterans actually develop PTSD. Across studies, the point prevalence of combat-related PTSD in U.S. military veterans ranges from about 2% to 17% (reviewed in Richardson, Frueh, & Acierno, 2010). The most recent sophisticated study of Vietnam War veterans puts the prevalence of PTSD at 9.1% (Dohrenwend et al., 2006). Recent studies suggest that combat-related PTSD afflicts between 4.7% and 17.1% of U.S. Iraq War veterans, but only 3% to 6% of returning U.K. Iraq War veterans (Richardson et al., 2010). A large recent study, which is perhaps the most rigorous epidemiological study of U.S. forces, estimated the prevalence of PTSD at about 8% (with slight variations by branch and rank; Smith et al., 2008), which is quite consistent with the prevalence estimate for Vietnam War veterans.

Variability in prevalence is likely due to differences in sampling strategies; measurement strategies; inclusion and measurement of the *Diagnostic and Statistical Manual of Mental Disorders, Fourth Edition* (*DSM-IV*) clinically significant impairment criterion; timing and latency of assessment and potential for recall bias; and combat experiences. Prevalence rates are also likely affected by issues related to PTSD course, chronicity, and comorbidity; symptom overlap with other psychiatric disorders; and sociopolitical and cultural factors that may vary over time and by nation. Even with prevalence estimates under 10%, the disorder of PTSD represents a significant and costly illness to veterans, their families, and society as a whole.

PTSD ONSET AND COURSE

As noted in the preceding section, it is important to be mindful that the vast majority (e.g., > 90%) of combat veterans do not have PTSD. Moreover, studies that estimate both lifetime and current prevalence of PTSD typically find that roughly half of the veterans who had PTSD at some point in the past do not meet diagnostic criteria for current PTSD (Centers for Disease Control and Prevention [CDC], 1988; Dohrenwend et al., 2006).

However, retrospective studies in samples of Holocaust survivors (Yehuda et al., 2006), Korean war veterans (Ikin et al., 2007), and World War II veterans (Bramsen & van de Ploeg, 1999; Schnurr, Spiro, Vielhauer, Findler, & Hamblen, 2002) indicate that the duration of "chronic PTSD" can span an entire adult lifetime, up to 50 years after combat exposure (Schnurr, Lunney, Sengupta, & Waelde, 2003). The phenomenon of "delayed-onset" PTSD, that is, PTSD that develops suddenly years after the war, remains somewhat controversial. While there is some limited empirical evidence to support the phenomenon (Gray, Bolton, & Litz, 2004), a recent review of delayed-onset PTSD found the phenomenon in the absence of prior symptoms was rare (see review by Andrews, Brewin, Philpott, & Stewart, 2007). In fact, one recent study found that delayed-onset PTSD was extremely rare among veterans more than 1 year after combat exposure, and there was no evidence of PTSD symptom onset 6 or more years after combat (Frueh, Grubaugh, Yeager, & Magruder, 2009). Thus, the notion of the veteran suffering a sudden onset of PTSD 25 years after combat service is an unlikely phenomenon. Consider the following case study:

P.N. was a World War II veteran in his late 70s when evaluated some years ago. He was seen in a VA outpatient clinic, accompanied by his wife of about 50 years. During the war he had been based in the United Kingdom, where he served on a flight crew conducting bombing runs over German-occupied territory. After many missions, his aircraft had been shot down and he was able to survive by bailing out and parachuting to a safe landing on the ground, where he was picked up by the German Army and placed in a prisoner-of-war camp. While in this camp he described experiencing 18 months of hardship, deprivation, cold, hunger, fear, and extended periods of boredom. After the war, he returned home, got married, had a long career as a low-level executive for a large manufacturing firm, and was a well-respected member of his church and community for many years. Along the way he had several children and grandchildren, and his marriage by both his and his wife's account was a loving and happy one. Although he had never been diagnosed with or treated for any type of psychiatric disorder, he reported that he thought perhaps he might have PTSD (which he had heard about through newspapers and talking with other veterans at meetings of different service organizations). Upon structured interview, he described a history of irritability, anger control problems, emotionality when the subject of the war arose, sleep disturbance, and moodiness; he denied suicidality, symptoms of major depression, substance abuse, violence, nightmares, cued reactivity, flashbacks of any sort, and all Cluster C symptoms. His wife agreed with much of his report, but noted that while he denied nightmares, he often "thrashed around and cried out" in his sleep. She also added that he exhibited restricted range of affect and interpersonal detachment. Thus, her report suggested he had long met criteria for Cluster C of PTSD. Both patient and wife agreed that his symptoms had not interfered with his ability to work and provide financially for his family, or have a positive, loving relationship with his children and other family members—and both agreed that the reported symptoms of irritability and anger, which had been present since the war, had improved significantly in the past 5 years.

So, what do we make of this patient and his symptom picture? Did P.N. have PTSD? Did he have delayed-onset PTSD? The answers are not clear and simple. Certainly, he appears to have had a history of irritability, sleep disturbance, and emotionality to war cues dating over 50 years back to the war. However, to a certain extent, the emotionality to the images of death and destruction that he experienced during the war is a normal response, not necessarily indicative of psychopathology. Altogether, the psychiatric difficulties he described did not meet criteria for past or current PTSD because he did not endorse Cluster C symptoms, although his wife's report suggested a slightly different picture. Thus, a diagnosis of PTSD was hard to make, unless one gave more weight to his wife's report as a collateral informant.

Another important facet of P.N.'s clinical presentation to consider is that of functional impairment. It appears that the quality of his life (and his wife's) may have been affected by the irritability and sleep disturbance; however, the impact of this appears to have been mild to moderate, at most, as he reported a stable and successful marriage and career over the preceding 50 years. This, in combination with his symptom report, suggests that his PTSD symptoms have been subthreshold for many years. And the fact that he is only now seeking evaluation and treatment is ultimately not an indicator of "delayed onset," but rather of delayed treatment seeking. In fact, after about six sessions of cognitive–behavioral treatment for irritability, anger, and sleep disturbance, P.N. decided that he did not need any further treatment at this time. He conceded part of the reason he sought the evaluation in the first place was that he was hearing so much about "PTSD" and wanted to be reassured that he did not have it and that the symptoms he did have were not likely to grow dramatically worse in the future.

SOCIOPOLITICAL AND CULTURAL FACTORS

Historical, Contextual, and Socioeconomic Factors

Recall, as we discussed in Chapter 1, that the diagnosis of PTSD, first added to the *DSM* in 1980, was largely the result of attempts to account for the challenging impairment that was presented by Vietnam veterans at the time of homecoming and in the aftermath of the war (Shephard, 2001; Wessely, 2005). In the immediate post-Vietnam era, compensation for significant functional impairment was difficult to obtain other than for easily observable physical injuries, and access to VA medical services were possible only via a "war-related" disorder (Wessely & Jones, 2004). Thus, the development of the clinical conceptualization of PTSD has been heavily influenced by socioeconomic and political factors. In recent years, there has been concern that health care systems and disability policies may encourage psychiatric illness or lead to self-fulfilling prophecies. In fact, some argue that the U.S. VA health care system has failed to benefit from the lessons of 20th-century military psychiatry regarding social expectations and incentives (Burkett & Whitley, 1998; Jones & Wessely, 2007; Mossman, 1996; Summerfield, 2001; Wessely, 2005). Supporting this concern are recent administrative trends regarding PTSD disability claims that show steeply rising rates of claims among younger generations of veterans. Among the relatively small subset of veterans seeking mental health treatment in VA clinics, most (over 90%) also concurrently apply for PTSD disability benefits (Frueh et al., 2003). Also, the number of veterans receiving VA disability payments for PTSD increased 79.5% from 1999 to 2004, while all other disabilities within the VA increased only 12.2% during that same period (Department of Veterans Affairs Office of Inspector General [DVAOIG], 2005).

A particular concern, backed by a wealth of empirical data, is that veterans' disability-seeking status may influence their clinical presentation in health care settings. Some veterans seeking evaluation in U.S. VA medical centers may exaggerate or falsify their combat experiences (Frueh, Grubaugh, Elhai, & Buckley, 2007; McNally, 2003; McNally & Frueh, in press). Not surprisingly, there have been documented cases of combat exaggeration or misrepresentation by some veterans, and even some in which military service itself was fictitious (Burkett & Whitley, 1998; Frueh et al., 2005). Studies also show that veterans evaluated for PTSD in VA clinical settings may malinger or exaggerate psychiatric symptoms when disability compensation is at stake (Freeman, Powell, & Kimbrell, 2008; Frueh, Hamner, Cahill, Gold, & Hamlin, 2000; Jones & Wessely, 2007). For example, in one study that used a structured instrument to evaluate malingering (Structured Interview for Reported Symptoms [SIRS]), Freeman et al. (2008) found that just over half of those veterans in a PTSD treatment-seeking clinical sample appeared to exhibit malingering psychopathology. For a thoughtful review of the effects of government disability pensions and benefits on veterans' psychiatric functioning, see Jones and Wessely (2007).

The effect of disability seeking for subjective ailments like PTSD on the behavior of claimants remains a significant issue in research and clinical practice with veterans, and a matter of discussion among a number of U.S. policy agencies (DVAOIG, 2005; Institute of Medicine and National Research Council, 2007; United States Government Accountability Office, 2007). As such, researchers conducting clinical trials with veteran populations have been encouraged to control for or exclude compensation-seeking veterans from clinical research (Charney et al., 1998; Freeman et al., 2008; Frueh et al., 2005). However, the extent to which secondary gain may influence prevalence rates is unclear, as is the impact on any given individual veteran seeking evaluation and treatment.

It is important to be mindful of meaningful differences between clinical, forensic, and community samples, and that conclusions generated from one do not necessarily generalize to the other (McNally, 2007). Also, while certain VA system policies or incentives may have an influence on treatment-seeking veterans (a small subset of all veterans), they may have relatively little impact on the larger veteran population represented in community samples and on veterans evaluated outside of the VA. Thus, it is difficult to estimate how health care or other government policies might shape larger attitudes and reporting styles related to PTSD in community samples by influencing social attitudes and expectations. Clinicians working with veterans are advised (as they are with patients of all types!) to be mindful of context, setting, and incentives when evaluating the clinical needs of patients and families.

Media and Popular Culture Influences

We also have good reason to believe that the media and other cultural forces have an effect on how veterans—and their spouses and families— view and understand their own behaviors. Media stories and societal expectations are likely to influence psychiatric symptom reporting and effect the validity of any retrospectively determined relationship between the trauma and psychiatric symptoms (Ikin et al., 2004; Wessely et al., 2003). We know that research into significant historical events and memory recall has consistently demonstrated that frequently repeated media-based narratives may reinforce inaccurate memories and beliefs about an event (Hotopf & Wessely, 2005). Memory is certainly fallible, and while we generally take patients at their word, we also need to be mindful of the limitations associated with memory.

Mainstream media publicity and films surrounding the Vietnam and later wars may affect how veterans (and society) view their combat experiences and interpret their reactions, symptoms, and behaviors afterward. The wide-scale portrayal of Vietnam veterans as a psychologically impaired victim-hero is found in virtually every Hollywood movie produced about the Vietnam War, from *Coming Home* (1978) to *Born on the Fourth of July* (1989; Lembke, 2000). Media commentator James Bowman (2006) speculates that "when Hollywood glamorizes the conscience-stricken vet, is it not reasonable to suppose that the numbers of conscience-stricken vets will increase?" Wessely and Jones (2004) have discussed how the Vietnam War is an example of how the public's changing opinion surrounding the war likely influenced "a gradual 'inflation' of traumatic memories to fit with the changing views (p. 12)." See also Burkett and Whitley (1998), Shephard (2001), Jones and Wessely (2007), and Satel and Frueh (2009) for further discussion of this topic. Again, this is not at all to say that all or most posttraumatic reactions to combat experiences reported by veterans are invalid or flawed in some way, but rather that clinicians should be mindful of this historical and sociopolitical context of combat-related PTSD.

COMPENSATION AND PENSION EVALUATIONS AND TREATMENT PLANNING IMPLICATIONS

The information presented in the preceding sections of this chapter carry a number of important implications for clinical evaluation and treatment planning with combat veterans. As we noted earlier (see Chapters 1 and 7), for the past 30 years, PTSD has been one of the psychiatric diagnoses that is most commonly invoked in forensic situations across all populations (Taylor, Frueh, & Asmundson, 2007). This is, in part, due to the fact that it is virtually the only psychiatric disorder with a specific external cause (i.e., the traumatic event), which makes it relevant as the basis for a wide range of disability and legal claims. Among other forensic uses, it is potentially a basis for worker's compensation and other disability claims, civil lawsuits, and legal defense of felony charges.

From an economic perspective, perhaps the most important forensic context of PTSD is its use in U.S. VA disability claims by veterans seeking financial compensation for psychiatric disability caused by their military service. The VA provides significant lifetime psychiatric disability compensation for veterans diagnosed with combat-related PTSD (typically over $35,000 tax free for a veteran with a 100% service-connected rating). Over the course of the lifetime of all veterans currently receiving such disability, the VA will pay out billions of dollars in disability compensation. This is a well-intentioned safety net for veterans who suffer because of the sacrifices they made for their country. In this and many other ways, the financial cost of this disorder to the government and society is quite large. Given that a large percentage of the clinical research on PTSD has been conducted in the VA system, disability incentives are obviously an important contextual factor to consider on how veterans present their symptoms and respond to treatment—and therefore influences our ability to study and understand this condition.

Mental health clinicians working with veterans in any clinical setting should be aware of and consider the following:

- The VA has experienced rapidly increased rates of disability claims and payments due to combat-related PTSD, including a 149% increase in payments from 1999 to 2004, whereas all other disability awards increased by only 42% (DVAOIG, 2005).

- Recent analyses by a team of labor economists clearly show that the dramatic rise in PTSD disability claims largely comes from veterans whose limited vocational skills reduce their ability to earn a decent living (Angrist, Chen, & Frandsen, 2010).

- An audit by the Office of Inspector General found that 25% of recent disability award files lacked compelling evidence of combat exposure, putting the monetary risk of potential fraud at about $20 billion over the lifetime of veterans with current PTSD disability (DVAOIG, 2005).

- Most veterans' self-reported symptoms of PTSD become steadily worse over time until they reach the 100% disability level, at which point there is an 82% *drop* in use of VA mental health services, but *no change* in other VA medical health service use (DVAOIG, 2005).

- Treatment outcome studies of PTSD in veterans show markedly less robust treatment effects than similar studies conducted with other PTSD populations (e.g., survivors of sexual assault; Bradley, Greene, Russ, Dutra, & Westen, 2005; Frueh et al., 2007), and the VA has never disseminated any administrative data showing that veterans recover from PTSD (Frueh et al., 2007).

- Virtually all veterans seeking PTSD treatment at VA medical centers also apply for VA disability for the disorder, and there is some evidence of symptom overreporting among these veterans (Frueh et al., 2000) as well as cases of outright malingering (Freeman et al., 2008) and exaggeration/misrepresentation of combat experiences, as shown by review of military personnel records (Frueh et al., 2005).

- A recent survey found that virtually no clinicians who evaluate veterans for service-connected disability pensions use the full range of recommended best practices to assess for PTSD diagnostic status and functional impairment (Jackson et al., 2011).

Compounding these concerns is that recent legislative changes have been made to the VA's consideration of Criterion A, namely, that they have liberalized the evidentiary standard for establishing the required in-service stressor (Department of Veterans Affairs, 2010). This amendment eliminates the requirement for corroborating that the claimed in-service stressor occurred if a stressor claimed by a veteran is related to the veteran's fear of hostile military or terrorist activity, and appears to mean that merely serving in hazardous areas (e.g., military bases in theater) is itself now categorized as a "traumatic event." Although on its face this does not seem consistent with *DSM-IV* definition of "trauma," the VA claims that it is. It is very possible this legislative change will be even more problematic with the implementation of *DSM-5*, which is expected to include a narrower and more specific definition of traumatic event exposure (see Chapter 12).

Taken together, the VA's PTSD disability policies and incentives represent an important contextual foundation that clinicians should be mindful of. Although some practitioners and policy makers are reluctant to acknowledge it, malingering and overreporting of PTSD symptoms is a very real concern in a variety of health care and forensic settings and requires additional attention in the *DSM*, including with veterans in both clinical and forensic practice (Taylor et al., 2007; Rosen & Taylor, 2007). We remind clinicians of the wording in *DSM-IV*, which counsels that "Malingering should be ruled out in those situations in which financial remuneration, benefit eligibility, and forensic determinations play a role (p. 427)." Although most clinicians know this, consideration of malingering and symptom exaggeration is typically ignored in most clinical settings (Jackson et al., 2011) where it should be appropriately ruled out. In fact, there is anecdotal evidence that in some places the VA system actively discourages the use of validity and forensic assessment strategies out of concern that it does not provide the veteran with the benefit of the doubt (Poyner, 2010). This is an odd perspective given the clinical and financial purpose of such evaluations!

CLINICAL ASSESSMENT WITH VETERANS

Veterans are typically evaluated in a variety of clinical settings, including primary care, general mental health, PTSD specialty, and more rural community-based outpatient clinics. These clinics may or may not have specialty mental health care services available onsite. The VA system conducts separate forensic evaluations to assess (or consider) veterans' applications for compensation and additional benefits for psychiatric disabilities related to their military service (also known as compensation and pension or C&P evaluations). All evaluations conducted within the VA system—and often those conducted outside of it—carry important implications for disability applications and treatment planning. This is because most veterans seeking PTSD treatment within the VA apply for VA disability, and clinical records make up an important part of the documentation that is used in adjudicating disability claims. Thus, every diagnostic report and clinical treatment progress note entered into the VA's electronic medical record becomes part of the available legal documentation that may be considered in the adjudication process.

The Basics of Assessment

In many respects, clinical assessment with veterans is not fundamentally different from assessment of people from any other potentially traumatized group. Most of the basics, including the information provided in Chapters 1 through 6 of this book, still apply. You should take a sensitive and caring approach, be mindful of relevant cultural and contextual factors, use the best psychometrically valid measures available (include a mix of self-report and diagnostic interview strategies), assess for problems and strengths in a variety of different domains, pay special attention to interpersonal role functioning, include family and relevant collateral reports where appropriate, and thoughtfully develop multicomponent written reports and treatment plans that include the patient in a respectful and collaborative manner. For an excellent and thorough article on this, see Worthen and Moering (in press).

You should use instruments developed specifically for veterans wherever appropriate. These may include measures to evaluate military and combat experiences and symptom scales that have been adapted for and normed with military or veteran populations. You should also consult military discharge papers (e.g., the DD214) or other relevant military personnel records to corroborate descriptions of combat experiences. Robert

Moering (in press) has written an excellent article that provides practical guidance on how to review, interpret, and understand these types of records.

Unique Factors Associated With Combat and Military Service

There are many aspects of a veteran's military service that are quite unique from the experiences of civilians with and without trauma exposure or PTSD. These aspects include (but are not limited to) military training experiences, which are often quite hazardous and include the use of firearms; a warrior culture, which values accomplishment of a mission through the use of arms and force; a unique vocabulary, with a mixture of both slang and technical terms; a macho sexual culture; a sense of pride in remaining strong and resolute in the face of adversity; specific deployment stressors that are unique to each war zone and type of duty specialty; deployment stressors on marriage and family relationships; potential for strong feelings of guilt and loss that result from combat activities; the adaptive role of anger and violence in the military, which is far less adaptive once the veterans are back in civilian life; and a wide range of perceptions on society, government, and religion after war zone deployment.

We have found that a common initial question that many veterans ask of their clinicians is whether the clinician has served in the military. It is important that the clinician communicate an honest and nondefensive answer to this question, while also making it clear that they would like to learn from the veteran what it is they need to know about. In other words, acknowledge that the veteran is the expert on his or her military experiences, and that you, as the clinician, are a willing and interested student. Over time, you will learn and absorb the necessary terms and specialty knowledge for the various wars represented among your patients. It is also worthwhile to seek out authoritative historical sources of information so that you can understand various aspects of the wars relevant to your clinical work. Consider the three contrasting war zone experiences briefly presented here:

J.H. was a 62-year-old Vietnam veteran who had served a 1-year tour of duty in the Army infantry conducting long-range patrols that took him deep into potentially hostile territory for days and weeks at a time. Typically, he had to carry a 60+-pound pack that included food, ammunition (bullets and mortar rounds), gear, and medicines, along with an M-16 rifle. His missions were ones of walking with a platoon into uncertain territory (largely rainforest jungle), always alert for the possibility of an enemy ambush. On four separate occasions he and his unit engaged in intense small-arms firefights with other small units. J.H. believes he killed several enemy combatants, and he saw several of his comrades killed in these fights. He suffered a minor shrapnel wound in his leg. During his tour, his communication with family members back home was almost entirely via handwritten letters and care packages. When his 1-year tour was over, he returned to the United States on a plane with several other soldiers whom he did not know. Less than 48 hours after leaving his unit in the jungle, he was sitting at his mother's kitchen table. After the war, he was proud of his service and did not hesitate to let other people know he had served. Several times in the years immediately after his return, he was berated and reviled by other people in the United States for his service in the Vietnam War.

R.T. was a 64-year-old Vietnam War Army veteran who had served a 1-year tour of duty as a clerk stationed at a large airbase near Saigon. His working environment was in a partially air-conditioned office, where he had a desk and spent most of his day using a typewriter. He never came under direct fire during the war, but he spent much of the year being anxious and fearful that the airbase would come under attack. After the war, he came home and did not talk about his service. He never experienced anyone criticizing or berating him individually for his service in the war.

L.W. was a 24-year-old Army infantryman who had served two tours in the Iraq War. He performed a variety of combat duties, including convoy escort and patrols, where a primary danger was the possibility of stepping on or driving over an improvised explosive device (IED). On two occasions the unit he was with fell prey to IEDs, which killed and wounded several soldiers on each occasion. He also came under small-arms fire on several occasions from concealed enemy fighters. Several times he returned fire but does not believe that he hit anyone. Much of his service time in Iraq was spent in relatively comfortable quarters, with Internet access, movies, air conditioning, and videoconferencing for communicating with his family at home. At one point he became embroiled in near daily conferences with his wife, who was coping with a sick child, mounting medical bills, unemployment, and severe financial problems. During this period he experienced a great deal of stress (sleep disturbance, rumination, worry) and was frustrated that he was unable to help his wife more directly. When he returned home after his second tour, he remained in the Army for 2 more years, stationed at various stateside bases.

What are we to make of the different experiences faced by each of these soldiers? Obviously, different wars meant that they served in different parts of the world and experienced different geographical and climate-related hardships. They also had different missions, faced different types of enemies, used different technology—both to fight and to communicate back home, and they received different reactions from the society they returned to. Even the experiences of the two Vietnam veterans were extremely different, based on where they were stationed and their different military occupational duties. However, these men also experienced tremendous similarities. They served far from home and in hostile territory. They experienced periods of boredom and great danger, and each had known or seen comrades killed in action. They all made great personal sacrifices for their country, and though they had received somewhat different reactions from the society they returned to, they each felt isolated and detached from that society. In our clinical and personal experience, veterans from different wars and different eras often quickly find themselves recognizing a common bond—and many will tell you that they and their experiences are more similar than different.

Unique Clinical Needs of Veterans

Not only are there unique military experiences faced by combat veterans, but there are often also unique behavioral problems and clinical needs faced by veterans and their families. In fact, there is some evidence for military context having a unique influence on the expression of PTSD symptoms. One example of this is PTSD-related compulsive checking behaviors among veterans of Operation Iraqi Freedom/Operation Enduring Freedom (OIF/OEF) who were exposed to the dangers of IEDs—where constant vigilance and checking were crucial to survival (Tuerk, Grubaugh, Hamner, & Foa, 2009). Other examples of military experiences influencing clinical needs include (but are not limited to) extreme hypervigilance to danger cues; cued reactivity to loud, sudden noises or helicopters; anger management problems that are often complicated by combat training and access to firearms; substance abuse and reliance on prescription medications, many of which were started by the military during war zone deployment (especially in the case of OIF/OEF veterans); psychiatric comorbidities that may have been exacerbated by trauma occurring in early adulthood; injuries and medical illnesses associated with military training and service; marital and family stressors, often with their roots in extended deployments away from home; and the various challenges of navigating within the VA system to obtain access to benefits and services, including disability compensation. In fact, necessary engagement with the VA system, which is frequently confusing, fragmented, rule driven, and even adversarial in nature, can be a major source of ongoing frustration and stress for many veterans.

Let's compare the reported symptoms of the three soldiers described in the preceding section, in order of their presentation, which match the military context of their war experiences. J.H.'s symptoms appeared to be classic PTSD—nightmares, flashbacks, cued reactivity, avoidance, social detachment, emotional numbing, sleep disturbance, anger, and so on—which he had suffered chronically since returning home from the war. R.T. was diagnosed not with PTSD, but with GAD that was relatively moderate and well controlled using medication and cognitive–behavioral therapy. L.W. was diagnosed with PTSD and alcohol abuse, and his PTSD symptoms were characterized by prominent compulsive checking behaviors, similar to those often seen in people diagnosed with obsessive–compulsive disorder. Obviously, these were cherry-picked cases, but they demonstrate the point that veterans from different wars and different eras may have very different types of military experiences, and may accordingly experience the clinical syndrome of PTSD differently—or they may not have PTSD at all, but appear to have other variants of posttraumatic reactions.

Detection and Management of Malingering and Symptom Overreporting

Clinicians should be alert to the possibility that veterans may overreport symptoms or invent them. Since many veterans present for treatment to support claims for compensation, clinicians should incorporate appropriate instruments and assessment strategies into their routine practice that are sensitive to the possibility of malingering (see Chapter 7). This carries with it a number of practical and theoretical implications (for review and discussion of these issues, see also Taylor et al., 2007; Worthen & Moering, in press).

Clinicians are advised to take the "funnel" approach to assessment of malingering and symptom overreporting (just as we recommended this same approach for assessment more broadly in Chapter 4). This means including some very general measures of validity and effort (such as those included in the MMPI-2 or Personality Assessment Inventory) and remaining alert for unlikely symptoms or patterns of symptoms, inconsistencies in descriptions of daily role functioning (e.g., a veteran who reports a complete inability to relate to others or experience pleasure who is later observed talking and laughing with other people while standing in front of the hospital), and inconsistencies or anachronisms in historical reports. If you note cues to potential malingering or symptom overreporting, then the next evaluation procedures can be implemented more specifically and include self-report measures (e.g., the M-FAST), structured interviews for malingering (e.g., the SIRS), psychophysiological measures, or review of military personnel records and other historical documents (as well as other instruments and strategies described in Chapter 7).

It is challenging to detect malingering with a high degree of certainty. Unless there is clear documentation in military personnel records of gross factual inconsistencies, videotaped surveillance, or an actual confession, the detection of malingering remains merely probabilistic. No single clinical instrument or variable can definitively prove malingering. Therefore, while caution is always warranted, give every patient the benefit of the doubt. Each relevant bit of information is a "clue," and the more clues accumulate in the course of assessment, the greater the odds that the veteran is malingering. However, you should be wary of a number of potential false leads in this process. Two of the most common false leads are multiple symptoms and symptom inconsistency. To be sure, each of these are often noted in patients who malinger. Yet, due to the high degree of psychiatric comorbidity associated with PTSD, as well as the sensitivity of symptoms to stressors and cues, they are also commonly seen in patients who actually have the disorder. Even modest inconsistencies in trauma memories can be potential false leads. Remember, memory for events is not static. It often changes over time, fluctuates with mood (i.e., can be state dependent), and can be susceptible to change over the course of treatment (or even as a result of treatment).

Other considerations come into play at this point. When the clinician suspects malingering, the therapeutic alliance between clinician and patient may be threatened. This can manifest in a number of ways. From the clinicians' point of view, they risk becoming cynical or skeptical of the motivations of *all* of their patients. In fact, some data suggest that clinicians working with veterans do indeed express doubts about the symptom validity of most veterans evaluated for PTSD (Burkett & Whitley, 1998; Mossman, 1996) and have a more negative view of the "treatment engagement" of veterans who are seeking disability than they do of those not seeking disability (Sayer & Thuras, 2002). Ironically, clinicians who rigorously assess for potential malingering may actually be less cynical because they have more confidence in those patients who are not identified as malingering or symptom exaggerators.

From the individual patient's point of view, concerns about malingering may lead to confrontations, anger, and mistrust that affect their care—especially where red flags or assessment data strongly support the presence of malingering. This is especially important because patients, influenced by secondary gain factors, may malinger specific symptoms of PTSD, and yet still struggle with very serious psychiatric and medical problems that require care. In clinical practice it is not uncommon for clinicians to face reactions of anger and frustration from veterans diagnosed with serious Axis I and II disorders, yet denied the PTSD diagnosis. Rigorous assessment may reduce this concern by providing the clinician with specific data that can be presented to patients to explain why and how diagnostic decisions were made.

Given the special threat to the therapeutic alliance, it is usually preferable for malingering assessments to be conducted by an independent practitioner (Greenberg & Shuman, 1997), who can remove a potential source of conflict by separating the "forensic" role from the "therapeutic" role. However, the VA system does not typically allow for assessment and treatment to be provided by different clinicians. Moreover, in the absence of malingering (which is the majority of the time), it can actually be quite useful for the treating clinician to have been heavily involved in the clinical assessment. A good collaborative assessment sets the stage for treatment, helps establish rapport and trust, and essentially functions as an early stage of treatment itself.

But what is the compassionate clinician to do with a veteran suspected of malingering? Two of the more common responses are to confront and terminate treatment (LoPiccolo, Goodkin, & Baldewicz, 1999), which may be expedient for busy clinicians but not necessarily in the patient's best interest, especially if other serious Axis I or II diagnoses are present. An alternative approach is for clinicians to "tactfully and nonjudgmentally present inconsistencies to the patient and offer a face-saving way out of the interaction" (Adetunji et al., 2006, p. 61). This may allow for exploring of alternative explanations for the inconsistencies or reconfiguring treatment priorities to address problems that are more authentic.

Remember, the goal here is not to play "gotcha" with patients, but instead to convey accurate diagnoses to them (e.g., that they do not have PTSD) and, wherever possible, to address the actual difficulties that they face—which may include factors that contribute to their perceived need to malinger PTSD. In a review on the detection and management of malingering of PTSD, Taylor et al. (2007, p. 36) offer examples of potentially useful things that clinicians can say to their patients. Here is an adapted example, revised specifically for use with veterans:

> I've now completed a comprehensive mental health evaluation, which includes information from the self-report symptom measures you completed, our structured diagnostic interviews with you, symptom validity scales, and a review of your military personnel records. The good news is that you don't appear to have the disorder of PTSD at this time. You appear to have some other sort of problem, although at this stage it's difficult to say precisely what it is. I think it is possible that you are struggling with [*insert actual diagnostic decision if there is one*]. The reason for our uncertainty is that disability claims that are pending adjudication may cloud the diagnostic process. This is very common, and it's understandable. Applying for disability has various effects, and does not affect everyone the same way. For some veterans it is quite stressful, it is perceived to be a very adversarial process, and it therefore causes or worsens their problems. For other veterans, applying for disability may provide

incentives to exaggerate symptoms or interpersonal problems relating to other people. Regardless of the precise effects of litigation, it is often easier to diagnose and treat the veteran's problems once their claim has been settled. Although I do not think you currently have PTSD, I am concerned that instead you may have [*insert actual diagnostic decision if there is one*]. Therefore, I would like to propose that we further explore that possibility, and begin to develop a treatment plan for it if necessary. What do you think about that?

Working With the Veterans Affairs System

As a form of epilogue to this chapter, we remind clinicians that the U.S. Veterans Affairs system, a health care and benefits agency designed to serve military veterans, is a large federal organization. Its chief is a member of the cabinet (secretary of the VA), appointed by the U.S. president, and the U.S. Congress appropriates its budget. Therefore, national politics and interest groups (e.g., veterans service organizations) strongly influence legislation regarding funding, policies, and administration of the VA system. And, as is the case with any large bureaucratic organization, it may be fragmented from within with competing priorities and agendas. Thus, VA clinicians, much like the patients they serve, are often treading on shifting sands. They must balance the need to provide services that are rooted in evidence-based practices, while satisfying their patients, political masters, and other constituent groups.

How might this play out in practical terms? The answer is a number of ways—and on a regular basis. The VA may have rules and procedures that conflict with some clinical practice standards. Examples of this abound. The legislative changes to the evidentiary standard for defining and assessing traumatic event exposure that were enacted in July 2010 (Department of Veterans Affairs, 2010) appear to many to obviate the *DSM-IV* criteria (Frueh, Elhai, & Acierno, 2010). There also is evidence that forensic psychologists have been sanctioned for or discouraged from using routine measures of effort, malingering, or symptom overreporting out of concern that it does not give the veterans the "benefit of the doubt" (Poyner, 2010). Sometimes the VA is quite heavy handed, even canceling contracts with private examiners if their evaluations are too rigorous (Poyner, 2010).

In some instances, researchers have been pressured by veteran interest groups to withhold data on veterans seeking treatment for PTSD in fear that the data might hurt congressional funding of PTSD research and treatment services for veterans. One study (Frueh et al., 2005) came under quite a bit of national scrutiny and criticism while it was still under journal review, with one critic expressing concern that it could have an adverse effect on congressional funding of veterans' programs. It was subsequently published in the *British Journal of Psychiatry*, one of the top psychiatry journals. Although it has been widely cited and much discussed in academic and lay circles, it does not appear to have had any adverse affect on congressional funding of VA services or research for PTSD. To the contrary, this funding has essentially quadrupled since 2006.

Clinicians should also be mindful of the historical reality that through the years the VA's funding priorities, procedures, and eligibility criteria for receipt of services and benefits has been subject to constant change, both nationally and regionally. This means that veterans have good cause to approach the VA with a degree of suspicion and doubt, which is naturally transferred, at least initially, toward the VA's representatives they need to interact with—including even the most well intentioned clinicians! Finally, because the VA is a system of political patronage, dissatisfied patients may be quick to appeal to patient representatives, hospital directors, congressmen, and veterans' service organizations. This is certainly often the case for veterans who are denied diagnoses of PTSD or disability for the disorder, and leads many VA clinicians to be extremely risk averse in their diagnostic patterns and report writing.

CONCLUSION

Despite the forensic challenges described in this chapter, on balance the VA is a successful and modern health care organization that provides essential health care services to a deserving group of people who have, often at tremendous sacrifice, served their nation dutifully. It is generally very well run, with excellent resources and support for clinical activities. We recommend that clinicians focus their attention on "doing the right thing" with regard to their professional duties, and the other aspects we discuss in this section will usually take care of themselves. This means clinicians should do what they should always do: maintain an appropriate scope of practice, rely on evidence-based practices in both assessment and treatment approaches, respect all relevant professional discipline boundaries and ethics, implement standard risk-management strategies (e.g., thorough documentation), and strive always to remain compassionate and thoughtful in their work.

REFERENCES

Adetunji, B. A., Basil, B., Mathews, M., Williams, A., Osinowo, T., & Oladinni, O. (2006). Detection and management of malingering in a clinical setting. *Primary Psychiatry, 13*, 61–69.

Andrews, B., Brewin, C. R., Philpott, R., & Stewart, L. (2007). Delayed-onset posttraumatic stress disorder: A systemic review of the evidence. *American Journal of Psychiatry, 164*, 1319–1326.

Angrist, J. D., Chen, S. H., & Frandsen, B. R. (2010). Did Vietnam veterans get sicker in the 1990s? The complicated effects of military service on self-reported health. *Journal of Public Economics, 94*, 824–837.

Bradley, R., Greene, J., Russ, E., Dutra L., & Westen, D. (2005). A multidimensional meta-analysis of psychotherapy for PTSD. *American Journal of Psychiatry, 162*, 214–227.

Bramsen, I., & van de Ploeg, H. M. (1999). Use of medical and mental health care by World War II survivors in the Netherlands. *Journal of Traumatic Stress, 12*, 243–261.

Bowman, J. (2006). Spielberg stress disorder. *American Spectator, 39*, 64–66.

Burkett, B. G., & Whitley, G. (1998). *Stolen valor: How the Vietnam generation was robbed of its heroes and history.* Dallas, TX: Verity Press.

Centers for Disease Control and Prevention. (1988). Vietnam Experience Study: Health status of Vietnam veterans: Psychosocial characteristics. *Journal of American Medical Association, 259*, 2701–2707.

Charney, D. S., Davidson, J. R. T., Friedman, M. J., Judge, R., Keane, T. M., McFarlane, A. C., . . . Zohar, J. (1998). A consensus meeting on effective research practice in PTSD. *CNS Spectrums, 3*, 7–10.

Department of Veterans Affairs. (2010). Stressor determinants for posttraumatic stress disorder (38 CFR Part 3). *Federal Register, 75*, 39843–39852.

Department of Veterans Affairs Office of Inspector General. (2005). *Review of state variances in VA disability compensation payments* (#05-00765-137). Washington, DC: Author.

Dohrenwend, B. P., Turner, J. B., Turse, N., Adams, B. G., Koenan, K. C., & Marshall, R. (2006). The psychological risks of Vietnam for U.S. veterans: A revisit with new data and methods. *Science, 313*, 979–982.

Freeman, T., Powell, M., & Kimbrell, T. A. (2008). Measuring symptom exaggeration in veterans with chronic posttraumatic stress disorder. *Psychiatry Research, 158*, 374–380.

Frueh, B. C., Elhai, J. D., & Acierno, R. (2010). The future of posttraumatic stress disorder in the DSM. *Psychological Injury and Law, 3*, 260–270.

Frueh, B. C., Elhai, J. D., Gold, P. B., Monnier, J., Magruder, K. M., Keane, T. M., & Arana, G. W. (2003). Disability compensation seeking among veterans evaluated for posttraumatic stress disorder. *Psychiatric Services, 54*, 84–91.

Frueh, B. C., Elhai, J. D., Grubaugh, A. L., Monnier, J., Kashdan, T. B., Sauvageot, J. A., . . . Arana, G. W. (2005). Documented combat exposure of US veterans seeking treatment for combat-related post-traumatic stress disorder. *British Journal of Psychiatry, 186*, 467–472.

Frueh, B. C., Grubaugh, A. L., Elhai, J. D., & Buckley, T. C. (2007). U.S. Department of Veterans Affairs disability policies for PTSD: Administrative trends and implications for treatment, rehabilitation, and research. *American Journal of Public Health, 97*, 2143–2145.

Frueh, B. C., Grubaugh, A. L., Yeager, D. E., & Magruder, K. M. (2009). Delayed-onset posttraumatic stress disorder among patients in Veterans Affairs primary care clinics. *British Journal of Psychiatry, 70*, 748–755.

Frueh, B. C., Hamner, M. B., Cahill, S. P., Gold, P. B., & Hamlin, K. (2000). Apparent symptom overreporting among combat veterans evaluated for PTSD. *Clinical Psychology Review, 20*, 853–885.

Gray, M. J., Bolton, E. E., & Litz, B. T. (2004). A longitudinal analysis of PTSD symptom course: Delayed-onset PTSD in Somalia peacekeepers. *Journal of Consulting and Clinical Psychology, 72*, 909–913.

Greenberg, S. A., & Shuman, D. W. (1997). Irreconcilable conflict between therapeutic and forensic roles. *Professional Psychology: Research and Practice, 28*, 50–57.

Hotopf, M., & Wessely, S. (2005). Can epidemiology clear the fog of war? Lessons from the 1990–1991 Gulf War. *International Journal of Epidemiology, 34*, 791–800.

Ikin, J. F., Sim, M. R., Creamer, M. C., Forbes, A. B., McKenzie, D. P., Kelsall, H. L., . . . Schwarz, H. (2004). War-related psychological stressors and risk of psychological disorders in Australian veterans of the 1991 Gulf War. *British Journal of Psychiatry, 185*, 116–126.

Ikin, J. F., Sim, M. R., McKenzie, D. P., Horsley, K. W. A., Wilson, E. J., Moore, M. R., . . . Henderson, S. (2007). Anxiety, post-traumatic stress disorder and depression in Korean War veterans 50 years after the war. *British Journal of Psychiatry, 190*, 475–483.

Institute of Medicine and National Research Council. (2007). *PTSD compensation and military service*. Washington, DC: National Academies Press.

Jackson, J. C., Sinnott, P. L., Marx, B. P., Murdoch, M., Sayer, N. A., Alvarez, J. M., . . . Speroff, T. (2011). Variation in practices and attitudes of clinicians assessing PTSD-related disability among veterans. *Journal of Traumatic Stress, 24*, 609–613.

Jones, E., & Wessely, S. (2007). A paradigm shift in the conceptualization of psychological trauma in the 20th century. *Journal of Anxiety Disorders, 21*, 164—175.

Lembke, J. (2000). *Spitting image: Myth, memory, and the legacy of Vietnam.* New York, NY: New York University Press.

LoPiccolo, C. J., Goodkin, K., & Baldewicz, T. T. (1999). Current issues in the diagnosis and management of malingering. *Annals of Medicine, 31*, 166—174.

McNally, R. J. (2003). Progress and controversy in the study of posttraumatic stress disorder. *Annual Review of Psychology, 54*, 229—252.

McNally, R. J. (2007). Revisiting Dohrenwend et al.'s revisit of the National Vietnam Veterans Readjustment Study. *Journal of Traumatic Stress, 20*, 481—486.

McNally, R. J., & Frueh, B. C. (in press). Why we should worry about malingering in the VA system: Comment on Jackson et al. *Journal of Traumatic Stress.*

Moering, R. G. (in press). Military service records: Searching for the truth. *Psychological Injury and Law.*

Mossman, D. (1996). Veterans Affairs disability compensation: a case study in counter-therapeutic jurisprudence. *Bulletin of the American Academy of Psychiatry and the Law, 24*, 27—44.

Poyner, G. (2010). Psychological evaluations of veterans claiming PTSD disability with the Department of Veterans Affairs: A clinician's viewpoint. *Psychological Injury and Law, 3*, 130—132.

Richardson, L. K., Frueh, B. C., & Acierno, R. (2010). Prevalence estimates of combat-related posttraumatic stress disorder: Critical review. *Australian and New Zealand Journal of Psychiatry, 44*, 4—19.

Rosen, G. M., & Taylor, S. (2007). Pseudo-PTSD. *Journal of Anxiety Disorders, 21*, 201—210.

Satel, S. L., & Frueh, B. C. (2009). Sociopolitical aspects of psychiatry: Posttraumatic stress disorder. In B. J. Sadock, V. A. Sadock, & P. Ruiz (Eds.), *Comprehensive textbook of psychiatry* (9th ed., pp. 728—733). Baltimore, MD: Lippincott, Williams & Wilkins.

Sayer, N. A., & Thuras, P. (2002). The influence of patients' compensation-seeking status on the perceptions of Veterans Affairs clinicians. *Psychiatric Services, 53*, 210—212.

Schnurr, P., Spiro, A., Vielhauer, M. J., Findler. M. N., & Hamblen, J. L. (2002). Trauma in the lives of older men: Findings from the Normative Aging Study. *Journal of Clinical Gero-psychology, 8*, 175—187.

Schnurr, P. P., Lunney, C. A., Sengupta, A., & Waelde, L. C. (2003). A descriptive analysis of PTSD chronicity in Vietnam veterans. *Journal of Traumatic Stress, 16*, 545—553.

Shephard, B. (2001). *A war of nerves: Soldiers and psychiatrists in the twentieth century.* Cambridge, MA: Harvard University Press.

Smith, T. C., Ryan, M. A. K., Wingard, D. L., Slymen, D. J., Sallis J. F., & Kritz-Silverstein, D. (2008). New onset and persistent symptoms of post-traumatic stress disorder self reported after deployment and combat exposures: Prospective population based US military cohort study. *British Medical Journal, 336*, 366–371.

Summerfield, D. (2001). The invention of post-traumatic stress disorder and the social usefulness of a psychiatric category. *British Medical Journal, 322*, 95–98.

Taylor, S., Frueh, B. C., & Asmundson, G. J. G. (2007). Detection and management of malingering in people presenting for treatment of posttraumatic stress disorder: Methods, obstacles, and recommendations. *Journal of Anxiety Disorders, 21*, 22–41.

Tuerk, P. W., Grubaugh, A. L., Hamner, M. B., & Foa, E. B. (2009). Diagnosis and treatment of PTSD-related compulsive checking behaviors in veterans of the Iraq war: The influence of military context on the expression of PTSD symptoms. *American Journal of Psychiatry, 166*, 762–767.

United States Government Accountability Office. (2007). *Veterans' disability benefits: Long-standing claims processing challenges persist* (#GAO-07-512T). Washington, DC: Author.

Wessely, S. (2005). War stories: Invited commentary on "Documented combat exposure of U.S. veterans seeking treatment for combat-related post-traumatic stress disorder." *British Journal of Psychiatry, 186*, 473–475.

Wessely, S., & Jones, E. (2004). Psychiatry and the "lessons of Vietnam": What were they, and are they still relevant? *War & Society, 22*, 89–103.

Wessely, S., Unwin, C., Hotopf, M., Hull, L., Ismail, K., Nicolaou, V., & David, A. (2003). Stability of recall of military hazards over time: Evidence from the Persian Gulf War of 1991. *British Journal of Psychiatry, 183*, 314–322.

Worthen, M. D., & Moering, R. G. (in press). A practical guide to conducting VA compensation and pension exams for PTSD and other mental disorders. *Psychological Injury and Law*.

Yehuda, R., Tischler, L., Golier, J. A., Grossman, R., Brand, S. R., Kaufman, S., & Harvey, P. D. (2006). Longitudinal assessment of cognitive performance in Holocaust survivors with and without PTSD. *Biological Psychiatry, 60*, 714–721.

CHAPTER 11

Working With Special Populations and Settings

As discussed previously, rates of posttraumatic stress disorder (PTSD) are notable in the general population, with point prevalence rates ranging from 6% to 9%. Here, we discuss the importance of recognizing and addressing PTSD in a range of special populations and settings. First, we discuss the importance of detecting PTSD in primary care settings, given the role of primary care providers as gatekeepers to specialized medical and psychiatric services, as well as the potential for PTSD to complicate the delivery of primary care services. Additionally, we discuss special populations and settings in which rates of traumatic event exposure or PTSD may be higher than what is found in the general population or where access to and course of PTSD treatment may be complicated. More specifically we discuss PTSD among individuals with severe and persistent forms of mental illness, in rural areas, and in prison settings—populations generally considered at risk for not accessing or receiving specialized PTSD services.

Primary Care Settings

Rates of PTSD in primary care settings typically range from 9% to 23%, with higher rates in urban or low-income practice settings (Gillock, Zayfert, Hegel, & Ferguson, 2005; Kartha et al., 2008; Liebschutz et al., 2007; Lowe et al., 2011; Magruder et al., 2005). As mentioned elsewhere, PTSD can be a chronic and debilitating condition if left untreated. Additionally, PTSD is often associated with a range of other psychiatric and medical conditions

(Liebschutz et al., 2007; Lowe et al., 2011; Schnurr & Green, 2004) that can complicate the delivery of appropriate primary care treatment. Although there have been significant strides in the recognition of depression in primary care settings, progress has been slower for anxiety disorders such as PTSD. Obviously, there are time constraints with regard to the number of psychiatric disorders primary care physicians can realistically screen for during the average patient encounter, which typically lasts about 15 minutes (Chen, Hollenberg, Michelen, Peterson, & Casalino, 2011). This is unfortunate, however, since most individuals do not volunteer their trauma histories or associated symptoms unless specifically asked and primary care providers generally serve as gatekeepers to specialized mental health services. In this regard, diagnostic screeners can be useful—either as routine clinical practice or when a provider suspects a trauma history and/or associated symptoms in his or her patient.

It may be impractical to routinely assess for PTSD in some primary care settings. However, all primary care providers should be aware of symptoms or comments that may be indicative of PTSD, particularly in higher risk primary care settings such as Veterans Affairs medical centers (VAMCs). Symptoms or behaviors that are consistent and relatively unique to PTSD include recurrent nightmares or mental images of the traumatic event, feeling on edge or overly alert, feeling jumpy or easily startled, feeling distant from other people, feeling emotionally numb and withdrawn, and anger or excessive irritability. Other nonspecific symptoms or conditions include feeling depressed or sad, more diffuse symptoms of anxiety, sleep difficulties, suppressed appetite, substance abuse, memory/concentration problems, chronic pain, and somatization or other unexplained physical symptoms, as well as excessive primary care use.

Instruments and strategies for assessing whether a patient has experienced a traumatic event are described in detail in Chapter 4. As noted in Chapter 4, measures of trauma exposure vary with regard to how comprehensive and detailed they are. For primary care settings, we recommend using one of the less comprehensive measures and assessing for the presence of those traumatic events that are most likely to result in a diagnosis of PTSD (rather than administering a trauma history questionnaire in it entirety). These include traumas such as childhood physical and sexual abuse, adult sexual assault, and combat exposure. If time permits, however, the trauma screen that is part of the Structured Clinical Interview (discussed in Chapter 4) is a relatively concise choice for assessing for a wider range of events.

Although useful to assess for a past history of these events, it is generally contraindicated to try to obtain a detailed account of these events unless the provider is experienced in trauma assessment and can adequately support the patient through this process. Specific assessment measures for PTSD symptoms are also discussed in detail in Chapter 4. Although significantly more brief than diagnostic interview measures of PTSD, self-report measures such as the PTSD Symptom Checklist take about 5 to 10 minutes for patients to fill out. This renders them impractical for most primary care settings given provider time constraints. As such, here we focus on PTSD screeners developed specifically for primary care settings. Again, as mentioned before, these screeners can be used to refer patients for further evaluation or treatment by a mental health provider or to recommend a course of pharmacological treatment in-house.

PTSD Screeners for Primary Care

Originally developed by Prins et al. in 2003, the PC-PTSD primary care screener has yielded the most empirical support and is currently being used by Veterans Affairs primary care clinics nationwide as a mandatory screening tool for PTSD. In fact, in a direct comparison with the two other screeners described in this section (Freedy et al., 2010), the PC-PTSD was found to be superior with regard to sensitivity (i.e., the proportion of patients *with* PTSD who test positive, "true positive") and specificity (the proportion of patients *without* PTSD who text negative, "true negative") relative to longer assessment measures of PTSD. This and other studies suggest that the optimal cutoff score of the PC-PTSD is a 3 (Bliese et al., 2008; Ouimette, Wade, Prins, & Schohn, 2008). Two other screening measures, the four-item SPAN, which represents **S**tartle, **P**hysiological Arousal, **A**nger, and **N**umbness, and Breslau et al.'s seven-item screener were both developed in 1999 (Breslau, Peterson, Kessler, & Schultz, 1999; Meltzer-Brody, Churchill, & Davidson, 1999) and tested in subsequent studies (Freedy et al., 2010; Kimerling et al., 2006; Yeager, Magruder, Knapp, Nicholas, & Frueh, 2007). The recommended cutoff scores are 5 and 4 for the SPAN and Breslau's measures, respectively.

Ideally, a patient who screens positive on a PTSD diagnostic screener would receive a more comprehensive assessment using a structured diagnostic interview such as the Clinician-Administered PTSD Scale (CAPS; discussed in Chapter 4). However, as we continue to stress, such an assessment is often impractical in primary care settings and will necessitate an outside referral, with which the patient may or may not be willing to comply. Whether assessed more comprehensively within primary care or referred out for further assessment, primary care providers should educate patients regarding PTSD and its course and discuss available treatment options, including psychotropic medications that could be prescribed in-house.

Treatment of PTSD in Primary Care

Consider the following two case examples within the context of a primary care visit:

Case 1: Patient T.W. presents to his primary care physician and reports that he has been having trouble sleeping and feels anxious and on edge. T.W.'s primary care physician astutely queries about her patient's onset of symptoms and discovers they started soon after T.W. was physically assaulted and robbed in the parking garage of his workplace 3 months prior to the appointment. T.W. also reports other symptoms consistent with a diagnosis of PTSD and feels that his symptoms are interfering with his ability to get things done at work and at home. T.W.'s primary care provider tells T.W. that she believes he has PTSD from the assault and discusses some of the available treatment options, including selective serotonin reuptake inhibitors (SSRIs) and psychotherapy.

Case 2: Patient J.B. has a documented history of alcohol abuse and a family history of alcohol dependence, and is currently taking an SSRI for chronic depressive symptoms. She admits to relapsing on alcohol in the past 6 months due to an increase in nightmares and intrusive thoughts related to a history of child sexual abuse. J.B. believes the nightmares have increased in intensity because her abuser tried to contact her recently to "try to make amends." J.B. is disappointed in herself because she believed that she had appropriately "hidden" those memories. She asks her primary care provider for an increase in her SSRI to deal with her anxiety and worry.

What is the ideal course of action in these two cases? Although there are no hard-and-fast rules, Case 1 is, by most accounts, a pretty straightforward case of PTSD. The index event is fairly recent, T.W.'s PTSD symptoms are in the moderate range, and he does not appear to have any other psychiatric diagnoses. For these reasons, medication as monotherapy is an appropriate treatment choice if that is T.W.'s preference. Case 2 is clearly more complicated in that J.B. suffers from depression and substance abuse issues that have worsened due to an increase in what is likely a chronic form of PTSD that has waxed and waned throughout J.B.'s lifetime. In this case, we would not necessarily disagree with increasing J.B.'s SSRI dosing, but we would also strongly encourage J.B. to receive a more formal mental health assessment and comprehensive treatment approach that includes a psychosocial intervention for PTSD.

In general, patient preference coupled with provider knowledge regarding the severity and complexity of the case should guide the initiation of a particular treatment course for a patient with PTSD. With regard to preference, some patients will elect not to receive any treatment at all, and thus should be educated regarding PTSD symptoms and given referrals for possible future use. Other patients may want some type of treatment for their symptoms but express a clear preference for psychotropic medications alone, which can be prescribed in-house; a psychosocial treatment alone, which will necessitate outside referral; or a combination of both. Generally speaking, more severe cases and those that involve comorbid psychiatric diagnoses (i.e., substance abuse) should be referred out to specialty providers. Treatment adherence, treatment response, and treatment side effects should then be used to determine if one modality of treatment should be intensified, changed, or combined with an adjunctive treatment strategy.

Psychopharmacological Treatment of PTSD

In many cases, primary care providers will choose to treat PTSD in-house with psychopharmacological agents. Medications used for the treatment of PTSD act primarily on the neurotransmitters associated with fear and anxiety, which include serotonin, norepinephrine, gamma-aminobutyric acid (GABA), and dopamine. Although there is support for their efficacy, particularly the SSRIs, medications used to treat PTSD do not typically alleviate all of the symptoms associated with this disorder, and it is generally recommended that patients take medications in conjunction with a psychotherapy specifically developed to treat PTSD, especially with more complex symptom presentations.

SSRIs are generally considered the pharmacological treatment of choice for PTSD, and this class of drugs include the only two medications that are currently Food and Drug Administration (FDA) approved for the treatment of PTSD—sertraline (Zoloft) and paroxetine (Paxil). SSRIs primarily affect the neurotransmitter serotonin, which is implicated in regulating mood, anxiety, and sleep. Consistent with this, studies generally support their efficacy in decreasing the anxiety and depression that is typically associated with PTSD (Stein, Ipser, & McAnda, 2009). SSRIs take about 6 to 8 weeks to reach maximum effectiveness and relapse of PTSD symptoms is less likely if the medication is taken for at least 1 year. Typical dosing recommendations for sertraline (Zoloft) generally range from 50 to 200 mg a day, and typical dosing recommendations for paroxetine (Paxil) generally range from 20 to 60 mg a day. As with depression or other anxiety disorders, some patients will respond sufficiently to an initial dosing recommendation for an SSRI, while others will need changes in dosing or additional care by a mental health provider. Thus, primary care providers should provide ongoing monitoring of PTSD symptoms (as they would for any other disease or condition) and modify treatment accordingly.

Other medications are considered "off-label" and have varying levels of empirical support with regard to the treatment of PTSD. These include citalopram (Celexa) and fluoexetine (Prozac), both of which are SSRIs, as well as venlafaxine (Effexor), a norepinephrine reuptake inhibitor; Nefazodone (Serzone), a phenylpiperazine antidepressant; and ulmirtazapine (Remeron), a tetracyclic antidepressant. Prazosin (Minipress), traditionally a hypertensive medication, has also been found useful for reducing or suppressing nightmares in individuals with PTSD through its effects on the neurotransmitter norepinephrine. In contrast to the above, some studies have yielded negative results with benzodiazepines, monoamine oxidase inhibitors (MAOIs), antipsychotics (as monotherapy), and lamotrigine (Lamictal). For a more comprehensive review of pharmacological treatments for PTSD, see Stein et al. (2009) and Ipser, Seedat, & Stein (2006).

Psychosocial Treatments for PTSD in Primary Care

As noted in Chapter 12, there are a number of empirically supported psychosocial interventions for PTSD. These interventions are typically infeasible to implement in primary care settings and require specialized training. Primary care providers should thus be prepared to provide their patients with trusted referral sources and to potentially coordinate care with their patients' mental health providers.

SEVERELY MENTALLY ILL PATIENT POPULATIONS

Although there is a great deal of research on the treatment of PTSD in the general population, we know much less about treating PTSD in patients with severe and persistent forms of mental illness (i.e., individuals with a psychotic disorder, bipolar disorder, or major depression coupled with severe functional impairment). What is well documented in the literature is that individuals with severe mental illness (SMI) report significantly higher rates of particular types of trauma across the lifetime, most notably physical and sexual assault, as well as PTSD relative to the general population (reviewed in Grubaugh, Zinzow, Paul, Egede, & Frueh, 2011). Not surprisingly, as in the general population, the presence of PTSD among individuals with SMI is strongly correlated with impaired functioning, decreased quality of life, and alcohol or drug use (reviewed in Grubaugh et al., 2011). Additionally, the presence of PTSD among individuals with SMI has been linked to transient living conditions or homelessness, higher disability ratings, suicidal ideation, and poorer psychosocial functioning. Other data suggest that the presence of PTSD among individuals with SMI is associated with exacerbations in the primary symptoms of psychosis such as delusions, hallucinations, and mood recurrence and polarity shifts (e.g., Kilcommons & Morrison, 2005; Lysaker & LaRocco, 2008; Meade al., 2009).

Assessment Issues

Due to the nature of psychotic disorders in particular, there are reasonable concerns that patients with SMI may not be able to accurately report on their traumatic memories and associated symptoms. Certainly, most instruments for assessing traumatic event exposure and PTSD symptoms were not initially normed on psychotic patients. However, recent studies generally support both the reliability and validity of trauma and PTSD assessments conducted in this population (reviewed in Grubaugh et al., 2011). In fact, studies comparing recognition of trauma and PTSD within routine clinical practice relative to systematic interview suggest that most individuals with SMI are unlikely to disclose trauma and abuse rather than overreport it and/or they may fail to perceive certain events as constituting abuse (e.g., Lab & Moore, 2005; McFarlane, Schrader, Bookless, & Browne, 2006; Picken, Berry, Tarrier, & Barrowclough, 2010). It is worth mentioning that these studies were conducted on patients who were relatively stable—thus, these findings do not extrapolate to patients who are floridly psychotic or manic, nor would we recommend assessing or treating a patient who is in this state.

What remains to be determined with PTSD is whether or not tailored instruments would significantly improve PTSD diagnostic accuracy in this population. Our clinical experience assessing for PTSD in patients with SMI suggests that it is feasible to use established diagnostic measures for PTSD. However, admittedly, some PTSD symptoms are more difficult than others to disentangle from the symptoms associated with a primary diagnosis of SMI. For example, when a patient with schizophrenia presents for a PTSD assessment, it can be tricky to distinguish concentration difficulties related to PTSD versus those related to the psychotic disorder—particularly in contexts where it is difficult to establish a temporal sequence with regard to the onset of PTSD and psychosis, such as with child sexual abuse. Additionally, some patients may report a restricted range of affect that is influenced, at least in part, by highly sedating medications. In these cases, after some probing, it may be helpful to simply ask patients whether they believe their symptoms are more due to PTSD or to their other symptoms and to not get mired in this level of detail.

Treatment Issues

Despite high rates of trauma and PTSD among individuals with SMI, the efficacy of PTSD-specific interventions for this patient population is far from established, as these individuals have historically been excluded from PTSD clinical trials. Although this exclusion was mostly guided by the desire to limit the impact of confounding factors on outcomes in clinical research settings, researchers and clinicians have expressed concerns that some frontline interventions for PTSD may be "overstimulating" for patients with SMI and potentially exacerbate patients' primary symptoms (Braiterman, 2004; Fowler, 2004). Our own exchanges with public-sector clinicians yielded similar concerns and were coupled with additional fears regarding their competence to effectively address trauma-related issues in their patients (Frueh, Cusack, Grubaugh, Sauvageot, & Wells, 2006). Although well intentioned, these beliefs are not founded in empirical evidence.

Due in part to the concerns noted above, the majority of the existing PTSD treatment outcome studies among individuals with SMI have focused on the use of cognitive restructuring without exposure, and only one published study used an exposure-based intervention. Studies using cognitive restructuring alone include single-case or small-case series designs (e.g., Hamblen, Jankowski, Rosenberg, & Mueser, 2004; Marcello, 2009), two pilot studies (Mueser et al., 2007; Rosenberg, Mueser, Jankowski, Salyers, & Acher, 2004), and a randomized controlled trial (Mueser et al., 2008). These studies have generally supported the effectiveness of cognitive restructuring in decreasing PTSD severity in this population. However, a number of patients retained a PTSD diagnosis at follow-up. The one published study using an exposure-based intervention for PTSD yielded stronger results, with 10 out of 13 treatment completers no longer meeting criteria for PTSD at follow-up (Frueh et al., 2009). Additional analyses from this trial suggested that clinicians can effectively implement an exposure-based intervention in this population with minimal compromise to the integrity of sessions or the therapeutic alliance (Long et al., 2010).

At this point, the literature base on the treatment of PTSD among adults with SMI is extremely limited. However, our own experience and that of others who have worked with this patient population suggest that it is feasible to treat PTSD in individuals with SMI, and there are growing data to support this contention (reviewed in Grubaugh et al., 2011). Some treatment considerations to keep in mind are the need to ensure that patients are relatively stable at the time they enter treatment. As noted earlier, patients should not be actively psychotic or manic during treatment. We also strongly recommend having patients wait for specialized PTSD treatment if they have had a recent psychiatric hospitalization or suicide attempt (i.e., within the past few months). Additionally, it is useful to coordinate specialized PTSD services with the patients other providers (i.e., psychiatrists, social workers). For example, patients' often bring up issues that derail from trauma-focused treatment but are obviously important, such as financial and housing difficulties. In this case, it is best to be supportive but to enlist the help of the individual's case manager in dealing more directly with these issues. Likewise, during the course of treatment, patients may comment that their medications are working suboptimally, and this would necessitate contact with the patient's psychiatrist. The goal with multiple provider coordination here is twofold: to ensure that the patient remains stable and to minimize any additional noise that could prevent the patient from fully engaging in trauma-focused treatment. Some additional issues to consider when treating PTSD in SMI patient populations include:

- *Patient concerns that they will not be able to handle trauma-intensive treatment.* This is a fairly common concern in any patient population and should be normalized. Patients should be told with confidence that such fears are normal and experienced by others but that the evidence base does not support the notion that individuals will "unravel" from treatment. Additionally, however, we have found it helpful at times to show, in graph form, other patients' decreases in within-session anxiety (as well as between-session PTSD symptoms) during treatment. Such graphs could later be replaced with patients' own scores to further demonstrate that treatment is working.

- *The need to involve family members to facilitate out-of-session exposure exercises.* We have found that with individuals with SMI, it is often useful to involve family members and friends in the treatment process—most notably during out-of-session exposure exercises. This serves as both a tool to maximize the likelihood that the patient will attempt the exercise but also to increase the likelihood that the assignment will be successful (i.e., that appropriate decreases in anxiety occur). The need to do this will obviously vary depending on the level of functioning of the individual as well as patient preference.

- *Oversedation due to psychiatric medication use.* Most patients with SMI are able to properly engage in treatment (or, as mentioned earlier, tend to be overengagers). However, if it does appear that a patient is oversedated or if she or he complains of oversedation, the therapist should coordinate care with the patient's psychiatrist to potentially titrate the dosing of particular medications that may be interfering with optimal treatment engagement.

- *Occasional lack of concordance between patients' subjective reports of anxiety and objective indicators of anxiety.* At times, patients may report extremely high ratings of distress and yet not appear commensurately distressed from direct observation (this also happens in non-SMI patient populations). In these cases, it is worth revisiting anchors for anxiety (as discussed in Chapter 12) to ensure that patients understand how to accurately rate their distress rating. Another strategy, if feasible, would be to measure blood pressure and heart rate during an exposure session and provide the patient with objective data on their arousal.

Overall, although there are some unique challenges related to treating PTSD among individuals with SMI, it is worth highlighting that these patients generally present and respond to PTSD treatment like patients in the general population. Also similar to patients in the general population, it is sometimes difficult to know who will adhere and respond to treatment. That is, at times, it is the patient with the most obstacles that best adheres and responds to treatment. Consider the following case:

Case 3: P.W. is a 62-year-old Vietnam veteran with PTSD related to child sexual abuse and bipolar disorder with psychotic features. For several years P.W. also suffered from alcohol abuse/dependence, which is currently in remission. At the time of his initial assessment for a PTSD study, P.W. was managing his bipolar disorder with medications and had been sober for 2 years, but also had severe and chronic symptoms of PTSD and was homeless and living in his car. Although he wanted PTSD specialty services at a VA PTSD clinic and received somewhat regular care at the VA (including medications for his bipolar disorder), he was resistant to staying in a shelter because of the "people and the noise." Research personnel were admittedly reluctant to randomize P.W. into the study trial as he was considered a high risk for drop out. Aside from fearing that his homelessness would hinder his ability to attend sessions, study staff were concerned about their ability to get in touch with P.W. between sessions (although this was mitigated somewhat in that P.W. had a prepaid cell phone). After some discussion among study staff, P.W. was admitted into the study. During the course of treatment, he missed two sessions but fairly promptly rescheduled. He participated fully in sessions and completed the majority of his out-of-session assignments and evidenced a significant decrease in PTSD symptoms after 10 sessions. In fact, he no longer met criteria for PTSD. Also, likely due to his PTSD symptom improvement, P.W. agreed to stay at a local shelter while his VA providers pursued housing options for him. By the time of his 6-month assessment, P.W. had moved to another state and was living with a relative. He reported doing well and no longer met criteria for PTSD on structured interview.

RURAL POPULATIONS

Individuals living in remote or rural locations face significant challenges in accessing appropriate mental health services, and it is anticipated that this problem will worsen in the future (New Freedom Commission on Mental Health, 2004). Although there are few studies specifically examining the role of rural living status on access to PTSD services, there is no doubt that in many areas of the nation, access to a variety of specialty providers is limited.

Telepsychiatry, or the use of videoconferencing technology to deliver mental health care, represents a way for addressing gaps in the availability of specialty PTSD services. That is, videoconferencing technology can provide a way for offsite clinicians to provide PTSD services to patients who suffer from ambulation difficulties or who live in remote or rural areas. The use of telepsychiatry in lieu of face-to-face care can also help circumvent other barriers to care that more directly bear on PTSD such as stigma or shame issues. To date, videoconferencing technology has brought a range of psychiatric services to both individuals and large-scale geographical areas (reviewed in Richardson, Frueh, Grubaugh, Egede, & Elhai, 2009).

With regard to PTSD specifically, there has been significant research, clinical, and program development efforts within the past decade. A primary leader in this area within the United States has been the Veterans Health Administration, which has significantly expanded the use of telepsychiatry to deliver specialized mental health services nationwide and has encouraged research testing the efficacy of PTSD services delivered via telehealth technology. To date, there are a number of studies, most of which consist of small samples of patients, testing the effectiveness of PTSD services delivered via telehealth technology (reviewed in Sloan, Gallagher, Feinstein, Lee, & Pruneau, 2011). Comparable to studies using telehealth technology for the treatment of other psychiatric disorders, data regarding PTSD suggest that treatment delivered via videoconferencing technology is superior to a waitlist control and results in either no worse or slightly worse clinical outcomes than face-to-face care.

Although more data along this theme are needed to make definitive conclusions, the use of videoconferencing for the treatment of PTSD appears to be a viable service delivery mode. Although there are some data to suggest that face-to-face care for PTSD may be superior to treatment delivered via telepsychiatry, it is important to note that this mode of service delivery was initially intended to expand the delivery of services to individuals or regions that otherwise would not receive any services at all. In this regard, we do not believe that it is essential to demonstrate that telepsychiatry is superior or even directly comparable to face-to-face care. Having stated this, however, there are a number of unique challenges and treatment issues to consider when delivering PTSD services via videoconferencing technology. These include:

- *Threats to the therapeutic relationship.* It is reasonable to be concerned that the therapeutic relationship might be dampened with the use of telepsychiatry. Surprisingly, however, the majority of studies examining this issue indicate that patients typically rate the quality and strength of the therapeutic relationship similarly in both face-to-face and telehealth modalities, and patients are generally satisfied with this modality of care (reviewed in Richardson et al., 2009). From our clinical experience, it usually takes patients and therapists just a couple of sessions to become familiar with the equipment and any initial awkwardness associated with the videoconferencing equipment.

- *Technological difficulties.* Technological difficulties can occur when using telehealth equipment, and these difficulties can be exacerbated when a patient lacks knowledge or confidence with technology. However, these problems are likely to become increasingly less relevant as more and more adults own a home computer, iPad, or other technological device that is generally more complicated than most videoconferencing equipment. In the case where a patient is unfamiliar or uncomfortable with technology, problems can usually be averted by providing the patient with basic education regarding the equipment and some form of exposure or onsite consultation. Although increasingly less relevant, it is also worth mentioning that slow connection speeds have hindered videoconferencing in the past. Most of these concerns, however, have been allayed as broadband and even cellular speeds have increased substantially in recent years. Using free programs such as Skype on the computer with a broadband connection, or even on a cell phone with a 3G connection, results in fairly stable and fast connections. More than likely, connectivity and speed issues will become a moot point in the near future.

- *Distance and patient safety.* Distance can potentially be a problem when a safety issue such as patient homocidality or suicidality arises. To date, there are already a number of studies reporting on the management of suicidality using home-based telehealth (for reviews, see Godleski, Nieves, Darkins, & Lehmann, 2008; Hailey, Roine, & Ohinmaa, 2008; Luxton, June, & Kinn, 2011). With regard to PTSD specifically, Gros, Veronee, Strachan, Ruggiero, and Acierno (2011) described a series of communications (all conducted using videoconferencing technology) between providers at a VA medical center, a veteran with suicidal ideation and intent, and the veteran's family. The intervention was successful in that an immediate safety plan was established and the patient was safely transported to an inpatient unit where he was subsequently hospitalized. Such data lend support for the feasibility of dealing with such issues safely and ethically.

- *Liability issues.* Providers should be aware of the legal and regulatory issues related to delivering mental health care remotely. These include licensing law requirements for delivering care out of state or even specific limitations associated with the use of telepsychiatry more broadly. Related to distance and patient safety issues, providers should also be aware of their responsibility and liability in cases of negligence or abandonment due to remote suicide intervention, and they should have a predetermined plan of action for dealing with suicidality, homocidality, and involuntary commitment.

PRISONERS

Prison populations tend to report high rates of trauma exposure, PTSD, and other mental health difficulties relative to the general population (e.g., Cristanti & Frueh, 2011; Steadman, Osher, Robbins, Case, & Samuels, 2009; Wolff et al., 2011). These rates in part reflect the disproportionate number of individuals in correctional settings from socially and economically disadvantaged backgrounds and the high rates of severe mental illness in this population—both of which place individuals at increased risk for victimization and PTSD.

The availability of mental health services, particularly psychosocial interventions, varies a great deal across different correctional settings. The reality is that most prison settings do not have the resources to provide specialized PTSD treatment. In this regard, telepsychiatry (described earlier) becomes relevant as a means of potentially delivering services to inmates if the necessary infrastructure is in place.

Circumventing the access barrier, there are a number of issues that would need to be considered when delivering services to this patient population. One issue regards the high prevalence of severe forms of mental illness in correctional settings. Thus, many of the issues relevant to SMI patient populations discussed earlier would apply to the treatment of incarcerated individuals. Additionally, however, interventions designed to treat comorbid diagnoses such as substance use and personality disorders (described in more detail in Chapter 12) are particularly relevant to this patient population. Finally, providers will face more pronounced deficits in motivation and insight, impulsive behaviors and aggressiveness, lack of trust of providers, feelings of hopelessness, and extreme feelings of isolation.

To date, there have been a few formal efforts to test the feasibility and effectiveness of PTSD interventions among inmates. These efforts are largely confined to women in correctional settings with a comorbid substance use disorder treated with a treatment intervention called Seeking Safety (SS; Wolff, Frueh, Shi, & Schumann, in press; Zlotnick, Johnson, & Najavits, 2009; Zlotnick, Najavits, Rohsenow, & Johnson, 2003). SS is a present-focused cognitive–behavioral therapy developed to target trauma/PTSD and comorbid substance use disorder that includes cognitive, behavioral, interpersonal, and case management components. SS also specifically targets the deficits common to incarcerated individuals, such as impulsiveness and emotional dysregulation. Extant studies suggest that the effects of SS on PTSD are modest but favorable (Najavits, Gallop, & Weiss, 2006; Wolff et al., in press; Zlotnick et al., 2003, 2009). To date, however, this intervention has not been disseminated more broadly.

Again, despite some promising treatment data, most correctional settings do not routinely provide empirically supported psychosocial interventions for PTSD. As such, the earliest opportunity to formally treat PTSD in this population may be at discharge. Inmates identified as having a mental illness typically receive a discharge plan detailing what services and treatment they will need to receive once they leave the correctional setting. Prior to discharge, psychotropic medications may represent a more viable and realistic treatment for PTSD in prison settings.

Conclusion

Without question, the toll of PTSD, if left untreated, is substantial at both the individual and societal levels. As gatekeepers to specialized services, primary care providers should be aware of the warning signs of PTSD and intervene appropriately to ensure their patients receive needed care. Additionally, however, mental health providers should be aware of patient populations that are at increased risk for trauma exposure and PTSD but who often "fall through the cracks" and do not receive specialized PTSD services.

References

Bliese, P. D., Wright, K. M., Adler, A. B., Cabrera, O., Castro, C. A., & Hoge, C. W. (2008). Validating the primary care posttraumatic stress disorder screen and the posttraumatic stress disorder checklist with soldiers returning from combat. *Journal of Consulting and Clinical Psychology, 76,* 272–281.

Braiterman, K. (2004). Commentary. *American Journal of Psychiatric Rehabilitation*, 7, 187–191.

Breslau, N., Peterson, E. L., Kessler, R. C., & Schultz, L. R. (1999). Short screening scale for *DSM-IV* posttraumatic stress disorder. *American Journal of Psychiatry*, *156*, 908–911.

Chen, M. A., Hollenberg, J. P., Michelen, W., Peterson, J. C., & Casalino, L. P. (2011). Patient care outside of office visits: A primary care physician time study. *Journal of General Internal Medicine*, *26*, 58–63.

Cristanti, A. S., & Frueh, B. C. (2011). Risk of trauma exposure among persons with mental illness in jails and prisons: What do we really know? *Current Opinion in Psychiatry*, *24*, 431–435.

Fowler, D. (2004). The case for treating trauma in severe mental illness: A commentary. *American Journal Psychiatric Rehabilitation*, 7, 205–212.

Freedy, J. R., Steenkamp, M. M., Magruder, K. M., Yeager, D. E., Zoller, J. S., Hueston, W. J., & Carek, P. J. (2010). Post-traumatic stress disorder screening test performance in civilian primary care. *Family Practice*, *27*, 615–624.

Frueh, B. C., Cusack, K. J., Grubaugh, A. L., Sauvageot, J. A., & Wells, C. (2006). Clinicians' perspectives on cognitive–behavioral treatment for PTSD among persons with severe mental illness. *Psychiatric Services*, *57*, 1027–1031.

Frueh, B. C., Grubaugh, A. L., Cusack, K. J., Kimble, M. O., Elhai, J. D., & Knapp, R. G. (2009). Exposure-based cognitive–behavioral treatment of PTSD in adults with schizophrenia or schizoaffective disorder: a pilot study. *Journal of Anxiety Disorders*, *23*, 665–675.

Gillock, K. L., Zayfert, C., Hegel, M. T., & Ferguson, R. J. (2005). Posttraumatic stress disorder in primary care: Prevalence and relationships with physical symptoms and medical utilization. *General Hospital Psychiatry*, *27*, 392–399.

Godleski, L., Nieves, J. E., Darkins, A., & Lehmann, L. (2008). VA telemental health: Suicide assessment. *Behavioral Sciences and the Law*, *26*(3), 271–286.

Gros, D. F., Veronee, K., Strachan, M., Ruggiero, K. J., & Acierno R. (2011). Managing suicidality in home-based telehealth. *Journal of Telemedicine and Telecare*, *17*, 332–335.

Grubaugh, A. L., Zinzow, H. M., Paul, L., Egede, L. E., & Frueh, B. C. (2011). Trauma exposure and posttraumatic stress disorder in adults with severe mental illness: A critical review. *Clinical Psychology Review*, *31*, 883–899.

Hailey, D., Roine, R., & Ohinmaa, A. (2008). The effectiveness of telemental health applications: A review. *Canadian Journal of Psychiatry*, *53*, 769–778.

Hamblen, J. L., Jankowski, M. K., Rosenberg, S. D., & Mueser, K. T. (2004). Cognitive–behavioral treatment for PTSD in people with severe mental illness: Three case studies. *American Journal of Psychiatric Rehabilitation*, 7, 147–170.

Ipser, J., Seedat, S., & Stein, D. J. (2006). Pharmacotherapy for post-traumatic stress disorder—a systematic review and meta-analysis. *South African Medical Journal*, *96*, 1088–1096.

Kartha, A., Brower, V., Saitz, R., Samet, J. H., Keane, T. M., & Liebschutz, J. (2008). The impact of trauma exposure and post-traumatic stress disorder on healthcare utilization among primary care patients. *Medical Care, 46,* 388–393.

Kilcommons, A. M., & Morrison, A. P. (2005). Relationship between trauma and psychosis: An exploration of cognitive and dissociative factors. *Acta Psychiatrica Scandinavica, 112,* 351–359.

Kimerling, R., Ouimette, P., Prins, A., Nisco, P., Lawler, C., Cronkite, R., & Moos, R. H. (2006). Utility of a short screening scale for *DSM-IV* PTSD in primary care. *Journal of General Internal Medicine, 21,* 65–67.

Lab, D. D., & Moore, E. (2005). Prevalence and denial of sexual abuse in a male psychiatric inpatient population. *Journal of Traumatic Stress, 18,* 323–330.

Liebschutz, J. M., Saitz, R., Brower, V., Keane, T. M., Lloyd-Travaglini, C., Averbuch, T., & Samet, J. H. (2007). PTSD in urban primary care: High prevalence and low physician recognition. *Journal of General Internal Medicine, 22,* 719–726.

Long, M. E., Grubaugh, A. L., Elhai, J. D., Cusack, K. J., Knapp, R., & Frueh, B. C. (2010). Therapist fidelity with an exposure-based treatment of PTSD in adults with schizophrenia or schizoaffective disorder. *Journal of Clinical Psychology, 66,* 383–393.

Lowe, B., Kroenke, K., Spitzer, R. L., Williams, J. B., Mussell, M., Rose, M., . . . Spitzer, C. (2011). Trauma exposure and posttraumatic stress disorder in primary care patients: Cross-sectional criterion standard study. *Journal of Clinical Psychiatry, 72,* 304–312.

Luxton, D. D., June, J. D., & Kinn, J. T. (2011). *Telemedicine Journal & E-Health, 17,* 50–54.

Lysaker, P. H., & LaRocco, V. A. (2008). The prevalence and correlates of trauma-related symptoms in schizophrenia spectrum disorder. *Comprehensive Psychiatry, 49,* 330–334.

Magruder, K. M., Frueh, B. C., Knapp, R. G., Davis, L., Hamner, M. B., Martin, R. H., . . . Arana, G. W. (2005). Prevalence of posttraumatic stress disorder in Veterans Affairs primary care clinics. *General Hospital Psychiatry, 27,* 169–179.

Marcello, S. C. (2009). Cognitive behavioral therapy for posttraumatic stress disorder in persons with psychotic disorders. *Clinical Case Studies, 8,* 438–453.

McFarlane, A. C., Schrader, G., Bookless, C., & Browne, D. (2006). Prevalence of victimization, posttraumatic stress disorder and violent behaviour in the seriously mentally ill. *Australian and New Zealand Journal of Psychiatry, 40,* 1010–1015.

Meade, C. S., McDonald, L. J., Graff, F. S., Fitzmaurice, G. M., Griffin, M. L., & Weiss, R. D. (2009). A prospective study examining the effects of gender and sexual/physical abuse on mood outcomes in patients with co-occurring bipolar I and substance use disorders. *Bipolar Disorders, 11,* 425–433.

Meltzer-Brody, S., Churchill, E., & Davidson, J. R. (1999). Derivation of the SPAN, a brief diagnostic screening test for post-traumatic stress disorder. *Psychiatry Research, 88,* 63−70.

Mueser, K. T., Bolton, E., Carty, P. C., Bradley, M. J., Ahlgren, K. F., Distaso, D. R., . . . Liddell, C. (2007). The trauma recovery group: A cognitive-behavioral program for posttraumatic stress disorder in persons with severe mental illness. *Community Mental Health Journal, 43*(3), 281−304.

Mueser, K. T., Rosenberg, S. D., Xie, H., Jankowski, M. K., Bolton, E. E., Lu, W., . . . Wolfe, R. (2008). A randomized controlled trial of cognitive-behavioral treatment for posttraumatic stress disorder in severe mental illness. *Journal of Consulting & Clinical Psychology, 76*(2), 259−271.

Najavits, L. M., Gallop, R. J., & Weiss, R. D. (2006). Seeking safety therapy for adolescent girls with PTSD and substance use disorder: A randomized controlled trial. *Journal of Behavioral Health Services and Research, 33,* 453−463.

New Freedom Commission on Mental Health. (2004) Subcommittee on Rural Issues: Background Paper. DHHS Pub. No. SMA-04-3890. Washington, DC: U.S. Department of Health and Human Services.

Ouimette, P., Wade, M., Prins, A., & Schohn, M. (2008). Identifying PTSD in primary care: Comparison of the Primary Care-PTSD screen (PC-PTSD) and the General Health Questionnaire-12 (GHQ). *Journal of Anxiety Disorders, 22,* 337−343.

Picken, A. L., Berry, K., Tarrier, N., & Barrowclough, C. (2010). Traumatic events, posttraumatic stress disorder, attachment style, and working alliance in a sample of people with psychosis. *Journal of Nervous & Mental Disease, 198,* 775−778.

Prins, A., Ouimette, P., Kimerling, R., Cameron, R. P., Hugelshofer, D. S., Shaw-Hegwer, J., . . . Sheikh, J. I. (2003). The primary care PTSD screen (PC-PTSD): Development and operating characteristics. *Primary Care Psychiatry, 9,* 9−14.

Richardson, L. K., Frueh, B. C., Grubaugh, A. L., Egede. L. E., & Elhai, J. D. (2009). Current directions in videoconferencing tele-mental health research. *Clinical Psychology: Science and Practice, 16,* 323−338.

Rosenberg, S. D., Mueser, K. T., Jankowski, M. K., Salyers, M. P., & Acher, K. (2004). Cognitive−behavioral treatment of PTSD in severe mental illness: Results of a pilot study. *American Journal of Psychiatric Rehabilitation, 7,* 171−186.

Schnurr, P. P., & Green, B. L. (Eds.). (2004). *Trauma and health: Physical health consequences of exposure to extreme stress.* Washington, DC: American Psychological Association.

Sloan, D. M., Gallagher, M. W., Feinstein, B. A., Lee, D. J., & Pruneau, G. M. (2011). Efficacy of telehealth treatments for posttraumatic stress-related symptoms: A meta analysis. *Cognitive Behaviour Therapy, 40,* 111−125.

Steadman, H. J., Osher, F. C., Robbins, P. C., Case, B., & Samuels, S. (2009). Prevalence of serious mental illness among jail inmates. *Psychiatric Services, 60*, 761–765.

Stein D. J., Ipser, J., & McAnda, N. (2009). Pharmacotherapy of posttraumatic stress disorder: A review of meta-analyses and treatment guidelines. *CNS Spectrums, 1* (Suppl 1), 25–31.

Wolff, N., Frueh, B. C., Shi, J., Gerardi, D., Fabrikant, N., & Schumann, B. E. (2011). Trauma exposure and mental health characteristics of incarcerated females self-referred to specialty PTSD treatment. *Psychiatric Services, 62*, 954–958.

Wolff, N., Frueh, B. C., Shi, J., & Schumann, B. E. (in press). Effectiveness of cognitive–behavioral trauma treatment for incarcerated women with mental illnesses and substance abuse disorders. *Journal of Anxiety Disorders.*

Yeager, D. E., Magruder, K. M., Knapp, R. G., Nicholas, J. S., & Frueh, B. C. (2007). Performance characteristics of the posttraumatic stress disorder checklist and SPAN in Veterans Affairs primary care settings. *General Hospital Psychiatry, 29*, 294–301.

Zlotnick, C., Johnson, J., & Najavits, L. M. (2009). Randomized controlled pilot study of cognitive–behavioral therapy in a sample of incarcerated women with substance use disorder and PTSD. *Behavioral Therapy, 40*, 325–336.

Zlotnick, C., Najavits, L. M., Rohsenow, D. J., & Johnson, D. M. (2003). A cognitive–behavioral treatment for incarcerated women with substance abuse disorder and posttraumatic stress disorder: Findings from a pilot study. *Journal of Substance Abuse Treatment, 25*, 99–105.

CHAPTER 12

PTSD Treatments and Treatment Planning

As previously noted, the majority of people who experience a traumatic event do not go on to develop PTSD. However, for the minority of people who do, there are fortunately a number of treatment options—largely psychosocial but also pharmacological in nature. In this chapter, we describe these interventions and additional treatment strategies for treating the comorbid symptoms/conditions that often accompany PTSD. As treatment strategies for children and adolescents are described in Chapter 8, we focus here primarily on describing treatment interventions for adults. We end with a discussion of a few novel interventions or approaches in need of further scientific investigation. In the spirit of evidence-based care approaches, we limit the majority of our discussion to PTSD interventions that have a significant empirical base and are supported by expert consensus panels and clinical practice guidelines. This will be followed by a consideration of treatment planning issues and feedback to patients.

EVIDENCE-BASED TREATMENTS

Psychosocial Treatments for PTSD

Clinical practice guidelines generally recommend cognitive–behavioral interventions as the most effective treatment approach for PTSD (Department of Veterans Affairs [DVA], 2010; Foa, Keane, & Friedman,

229

2009; Institute of Medicine & National Research Council, 2007; National Collaborating Centre for Mental Health, 2005). Treatments that fall under this umbrella typically include elements of psychoeducation, stress reduction, exposure to trauma-related cues and memories, and cognitive restructuring, with the latter two components being considered the "active ingredients" for PTSD symptom reduction.

Although there are a number of interventions that emphasize exposure and/or cognitive restructuring, the empirical data weigh heavily in support of two specific manualized treatments for adults with PTSD: Prolonged Exposure (PE; an exposure-based intervention; Foa, Hembree, & Rothbaum, 2007) and Cognitive Processing Therapy (CPT; predominantly a cognitive restructuring intervention but includes elements of exposure; Resick & Schnicke, 1993). Similarly, for children with PTSD, Trauma-Focused Cognitive Behavior Therapy (TF-CBT; Cohen, Mannarino, & Deblinger, 2006) has received substantial empirical support. The imbalance in the literature emphasizing PE and CPT for adults and TF-CBT for children over other similar treatments is not based on definitive research evidence of their superiority (Powers, Halpern, Ferenschak, Gillihan, & Foa, 2010; Seidler & Wagner, 2006) but rather the greater adoption of these specific interventions by health care agencies and systems (such as the DVA, Ruzek & Rosen, 2009; and the National Child Traumatic Stress Network; www.nctsnet.org).

Driving the successful dissemination of these treatments is their availability as manualized treatments with training workshops (in some cases complemented by Web-based introductory modules, e.g., http://tfcbt.musc.edu, or follow-up consultation, which has been shown to be important in ensuring fidelity and competence in implementation of psychosocial interventions; Henggeler, Sheidow, Cunningham, Donohue, & Ford, 2008). Other PTSD psychosocial treatments that have a scientific evidence base and are suitable for dissemination to clinicians are described in registries such as the National Registry of Evidence-Based Programs and Practices (NREPP; http://nrepp.samhsa.gov) in the United States and the National Institute for Health and Clinical Excellence (NICE; www.nice.org.uk/) internationally.

Exposure-based interventions broadly involve exposing patients to feared stimuli (i.e., objects, places, thoughts) within a safe environment in order to overcome or "extinguish" their fear reaction and can be traced back to Pavlovian fear conditioning models of animal behavior. Within this framework, extinction occurs when a previously learned response to a cue (e.g., fear response to food that is paired with an electric shock) is reduced when the cue (food) is presented in the absence of the previously paired aversive stimulus (shock). Though subtle differences may exist in the application of different types of exposure protocols for PTSD, the general underlying principles of these treatments involve repeatedly exposing an individual to feared traumatic memories and associated feelings in the absence of a negative outcome. This process ultimately results in a decrease in the patient's fear response to trauma-related cues and, as a result, a decrease in the avoidance behaviors that maintain PTSD. Put simply, exposure therapies help patients realize that thoughts and feelings about their traumatic memory are different from the trauma itself, are not inherently dangerous, and can be tolerated.

As already noted, PE is a specific brand of exposure therapy developed by Foa et al. that has generated the most empirical support of treatments within this category (Foa & Kozak, 1986; Foa et al., 2007). A recent meta-analysis of 13 randomized controlled trials for PE revealed a combined effect size of 1.08, suggesting that the average patient receiving PE fares better than 86% of patients who are assigned to a control group (i.e., do not receive what is considered an active treatment) (Powers et al., 2010). Another meta-analysis found a mean effect size of 1.26 for a range of exposure therapies relative to a control group suggesting that the average patient receiving an exposure-based intervention fares better than 90% of patients who are assigned to a control group (Bradley, Greene, Russ, Dutra, & Westen, 2005).

Similar to exposure therapies more broadly, the theoretical model of PE is based on conditioning principles: trauma-related cues have become conditioned stimuli that are avoided (Foa & Kozak, 1986). Exposure treatment requires that an individual be exposed to feared elements of the trauma memory and habituate to them through extinction principles. As habituation occurs, anxiety decreases. PE is also based on emotional processing theory, which suggests that traumatic events are incompletely and inaccurately encoded in memory as "fear networks." Within this framework, gradual exposure to corrective information through the confrontation of traumatic stimuli within a safe, therapeutic environment results in a competing and antithetical memory structure that inhibits the conditioned fear response and leads to a more organized, less distressing, and less intrusive traumatic memory.

PE, like the majority of exposure-based interventions, relies on two primary therapeutic tools: imaginal exposure and in vivo exposure. During imaginal exposure, patients "revisit" the index event, providing a detailed verbal account of the traumatic memory that includes sensory information, thoughts, feelings, and reactions experienced during the trauma (Foa et al., 2007). While recounting their traumatic memory in vivid detail, patients are instructed to verbalize subjective units of distress every 5 to 7 minutes on a scale from 0 to 100 or 0 to 10. These subjective units of distress scale (SUDS) ratings are then used to guide the pace and intensity of treatment in order to provide the patient with a therapeutic level of in-session anxiety (i.e., a level that is challenging yet not overwhelming), as well as provide patients with an ongoing awareness of how their anxiety will decrease over time if they tolerate the initial discomfort associated with confronting distressful memories (i.e., habituation). Similar to the principles of imaginal exposure, for in vivo activities outside of session, patients confront feared people, places, and things that remind them of the trauma but that are not dangerous. Patients work off a list previously constructed with the help of the therapist and patients are encouraged to start with an item that elicits a moderate level of anxiety (i.e., SUDS of 40), to monitor their SUDS, and to remain in the moment until they note a decrease in their distress.

Particularly anxious or avoidant patients may need to start with items that elicit less distress (i.e., SUDS of 25) in order to ensure they have some success with the exercise. Patients' awareness of how their distress decreases as they confront anxiety provoking stimuli and memories provides positive reinforcement for engaging in treatment. Treatment for PE typically ranges from nine to twelve 90-minute sessions. The first two sessions include information gathering and psychoeducation, with latter sessions focusing on imaginal exposure and monitoring of in vivo homework assignments.

Cognitive interventions for PTSD are based on cognitive therapy principles that can be traced to the work of Aaron Beck, MD and Albert Ellis, PhD. Cognitive interventions rely on the assumption that thoughts precede mood and that negative thoughts and beliefs are at the core of negative mood states. The goal of most cognitive therapies is to identify the negative and distorted beliefs that patients have and replace them with positive thoughts that are believed to be more balanced and healthy. With regard to PTSD, the focus of treatment is on identifying and targeting the negative cognitions that drive the core features of PTSD as well as other maladaptive cognitions common to trauma victims such as feelings of guilt, anger, shame, and self-blame.

There are very few randomized controlled trials of cognitive therapy that do not include elements of exposure or systematic desensitization (systematic desensitization is described later). Bradley et al. (2005) separated out cognitive behavior therapies with and without an exposure component and found comparable results in terms of efficacy. Cognitive–behavioral therapies without exposure yielded a mean effect size of 1.26 relative to a control group, suggesting that the average patient receiving a cognitive intervention fares better than 90% of patients who are assigned to a control group (Bradley et al., 2005), and these results are comparable to those reported earlier for exposure therapies.

As mentioned previously, Cognitive Processing Therapy (CPT) is a manualized cognitive therapy for PTSD with the most empirical support relative to other treatments in this category. Although classified here based on its emphasis on cognitive restructuring over exposure, it should be noted that CPT typically includes exposure through a written narrative component and is sometimes classified as an exposure-based intervention. Direct comparisons between the cognitive therapy and exposure components of CPT have failed to find significant differences across conditions (Resick, Nishith, Weaver, Astin, & Feuer, 2002).

CPT is based on information processing theory, which emphasizes the importance of how individuals encode and recall information. This process largely involves schemata (similar to cognitive therapies more broadly), which are frameworks for organizing and interpreting information. Schemata are generally useful in that they often save us time (i.e., they serve as cognitive shortcuts), but they can lead to errors if relevant information is not processed properly. In the context of a rape, a woman will try to process the assault given her existing schemata regarding sexual assault more broadly and her beliefs about herself. To the degree to which these conflict, she will have difficulty integrating the event into her belief system. This discrepancy is perhaps best highlighted by the just-world belief that is a central tenet of CPT and emerged from the social psychology literature.

The just-world belief is the common human tendency to believe that good things happen to good people and bad things happen to bad people. This tendency is not insensitive but, rather, is driven by the human need to feel more in control of random events, thereby decreasing feelings of vulnerability. A rape is generally discrepant with the just-world belief. Thus, when a woman is raped, she must struggle with integrating this event with her preexisting views of herself and her understanding of the world around her. In some cases, it may be easier for a woman to blame herself for the assault rather than to believe that she lives in a world where random acts of violence occur. Conversely, a woman may decide that the world is in fact a dangerous place and avoid places or people that remind her of the trauma or avoid social contact and social intimacy more broadly. Either view would be considered extreme and maladaptive and subsequently targeted in treatment.

CPT, like any cognitive therapy approach, emphasizes the importance of identifying and revising maladaptive beliefs about the trauma and promoting a more balanced integration of the traumatic event. Treatment generally consists of twelve 50-minute sessions. The initial session includes education about PTSD and a rationale for the treatment. Patients are then instructed to write an impact statement prior to the next session on the meaning of the rape, including the effects of the rape on their beliefs about themselves, others, and the world more broadly. They are also instructed to consider themes such as trust, safety, competency, and so on, when writing their statement. Subsequent sessions (sessions 3 through 7) focus on identifying maladaptive thoughts (stuck points), increasing the patient's awareness between their thoughts and feelings, and processing of the traumatic event.

Processing the traumatic event typically involves writing and reading a detailed narrative account of their worst traumatic memory and Socratic questioning designed to help patients challenge their faulty thinking patterns when they reexamine the memory by reviewing and elaborating or modifying their narrative description of it. Thus, through a series of questions, the therapist encourages patients to essentially "weigh the evidence" and reevaluate their maladaptive thoughts. In so doing, patients tend to revise the narrative description of the trauma memory, changing it from a largely implicit and therefore intrusive memory to an explicit and therefore more complete and objective account of the event. This process, if successful, leads patients to a more balanced view of themselves, others, and the world. Sessions 8 through 12 follow a similar strategy of Socratic questioning but focus more specifically on the distinct themes of safety, trust, power and control, esteem, and intimacy issues.

Eye movement desensitization and reprocessing (EMDR), sometimes classified separately, is discussed here as another variant of a cognitive–behavioral intervention for PTSD. EMDR was developed in the late 1980s and early 1990s from the personal observation of Francine Shapiro, PhD, and subsequently manualized in 1995 (Shapiro, 1995). Dr. Shapiro noticed that rapid back-and-forth eye movements had a desensitizing effect on her own unpleasant/distressing thoughts. In further observing that lateral eye movements in isolation did not yield therapeutic effects, she then integrated lateral eye movements (and subsequently other variations of bilateral audio/visual stimulation) into a more comprehensive treatment package for PTSD that includes elements of exposure and cognitive restructuring.

EMDR is a somewhat controversial treatment in that proponents of EMDR have historically argued that lateral eye movements facilitate the cognitive processing of traumatic memories (via their effect on dampening the distress associated with traumatic memories), while other researchers simply view EMDR as another variant of exposure therapy. Consistent with the latter view, a meta-analysis and other subsequent studies suggest that the lateral eye movements in EMDR do not offer any additional treatment benefits over exposure alone (Davidson & Parker, 2001). Currently, the EMDR Institute has a more tempered view of lateral eye movements, asserting that the success of EMDR is due to its many treatment components—all of which contribute somewhat equally to treatment efficacy. Regardless of whether EMDR is considered a unique treatment approach or whether lateral eye movements are essential to the efficacy of EMDR, a number of practice guidelines support its use in the treatment of PTSD. The average effect sizes for EMDR relative to control or nonspecific therapies are $d = 1.25$ and $d = 0.75$, respectively (Bradley et al., 2005). These numbers suggest that the average patient receiving EMDR fares better than 90% of patients who are assigned to a control group and 79% of those who are assigned to a nonspecific therapy group. These findings also suggest that EMDR is similar in efficacy to other cognitive–behavioral interventions.

EMDR involves an eight-phase treatment approach that includes

Phase 1: Information gathering and treatment planning.

Phase 2: Preparation (teaching the patient self-care techniques they can use throughout the course of treatment).

Phase 3: Assessment (identification of the trauma scene, identification of negative beliefs, and development of positive beliefs to counter negative beliefs).

Phases 4–6: Processing the trauma using EMDR.

Phase 7: Closure and debriefing.

Phase 8: Reevaluation of progress and ensuring adequate processing of the memory.

Starting with Phase 3, the patient is instructed to identify and focus on a specific traumatic memory. Next, the therapist prompts for negative belief statements about the memory ("I can't protect myself"). The patient is then asked to rate the memory and negative beliefs (i.e., negative cognitions) on an 11-point SUDS and to identify the bodily location of their distress. The therapist then has the patient generate positive statements (i.e., "I'm safe now") that can replace the negative beliefs and rate how strongly they believe the positive statement on a 7-point scale (Validity Cognition Scale; VOC). The therapist subsequently guides the patient through Phases 4 through 6 (described next), which include the Desensitization, Installation, and Body Scan phases, respectively.

In Phase 4, the Desensitization phase, the patient is instructed to focus on the traumatic image, negative thoughts, and physiological sensation of distress while at the same time moving his or her eyes back and forth (or using an alternate bilateral form of audio, visual, tactile, or kinesthetic stimulation) for concentrated sets of approximately 15 to 30 seconds. The patient is then instructed to "blank out" the memory and take a deep breath. After this, the patient is instructed to recall the memory/thought and give a SUDS rating. Sets of eye movements are repeated until the patient's SUDS rating is a 0 or 1. In Phase 5, the Installation phase, the patient is instructed to focus on the positive cognition he or she generated previously while again tracking the therapist's finger. The goal of this phase is to help the patient replace negative beliefs with positive ones. In Phase 6, Bodily Scan, the patient is instructed to scan his or her body for any lingering tension/sensations, which are then targeted using the same bilateral stimulation. Session lengths vary significantly across EMDR studies.

The bottom line with PE and CPT is that they are both indicated for the treatment of PTSD based on sufficient efficacy data as described in the section in Chapter 2 on evidence-based clinical practice guidelines. EMDR likewise has generated sufficient evidence of efficacy by most guidelines, but studies have failed to demonstrate that the saccadic eye movements unique to this intervention are necessary. In this regard, EMDR more likely represents another variant of exposure therapy that, similar to PE, has been successfully disseminated and marketed. Although some providers advocate for one approach over the other based on personal preference, there are no conclusive data to suggest one is superior to the other. In fact, most meta-analyses suggest that cognitive–behavioral interventions for PTSD are comparable in efficacy (Powers et al., 2010; Seidler & Wagner, 2006).

Some cognitive–behavioral treatments for PTSD heavily emphasize *anxiety management skills* training. Stress Inoculation Training (SIT) is the intervention under this framework with the most empirical support. As the name suggests, SIT was developed to help "inoculate" patients from their PTSD anxiety and reactivity by providing patients with anxiety management skills training prior to exposure. SIT places more emphasis on anxiety management techniques such as systematic desensitization (progressive muscle relaxation) and breathing retraining (teaching patients to breathe deeply from their diaphragms). However, it also includes cognitive techniques (i.e., positive thinking/reframing techniques/thought stopping) and exposure. After patients master the necessary anxiety management skills, they confront feared stimuli from a hierarchical list of fear-inducing items starting with the least feared item and working up the list. Although considered an efficacious treatment approach for PTSD in some treatment guideline reports (DVA, 2010; Foa et al., 2009), SIT and other anxiety management approaches have not experienced the widespread dissemination of the other psychosocial interventions described in this chapter. Rather, elements of anxiety management approaches are often integrated into more comprehensive cognitive–behavioral packages. Because of this, there are fewer more recent treatment outcome studies using SIT or similar approaches.

Psychopharmacological Treatment of PTSD

As mentioned in Chapter 11, the medications used for the treatment of PTSD act primarily on the neurotransmitters associated with fear and anxiety, which include serotonin, norepinephrine, gamma-aminobutyric acid (GABA), and dopamine. Selective serotonin reuptake inhibitors (SSRIs) are generally considered the pharmacological treatment of choice for PTSD, and this class of drugs includes the only two medications that are currently Food and Drug Administration (FDA) approved for the treatment of PTSD—sertraline (Zoloft) and paroxetine (Paxil). As such, we describe these two medications here and refer the reader to other sources (DVA, 2010; Ipser, Seedat, & Stein, 2006; Stein, Ipser, & McAnda, 2009) for information on medications for PTSD that are considered "off-label" due to varying levels of empirical support.

SSRIs primarily affect the neurotransmitter serotonin, which is implicated in regulating mood, anxiety, and sleep. Consistent with this, studies generally support their efficacy in decreasing the anxiety and depression that is typically associated with PTSD (Stein et al., 2009). SSRIs take about 6 to 8 weeks to reach maximum effectiveness, and relapse of PTSD symptoms is less likely if the medication is taken for at least 1 year. Typical dosing recommendations for sertraline (Zoloft) generally range from 50 to 200 mg a day, and typical dosing recommendations for paroxetine (Paxil) generally range from 20 to 60 mg a day. As with depression or other anxiety disorders, some patients will respond sufficiently to an initial dosing recommendation for an SSRI, while others will need changes in dosing or additional care by a mental health provider. Thus, primary care providers should provide ongoing monitoring of PTSD symptoms (as they would for any other disease or condition) and modify treatment accordingly. Of note, with children there is no evidence that SSRIs add to the benefit of psychosocial therapies such as TF-CBT (Cohen, Mannarino, Perel, & Staron, 2007).

Although there is some support for their efficacy, particularly the SSRIs, not all practice guidelines support the use of psychotropic medications for the treatment of PTSD. For example, after a review of 37 PTSD pharmacotherapy trials, the Institute of Medicine (2007) determined that there was insufficient evidence in support of any psychotropic medications for PTSD including SSRIs. Additionally, psychotropic medications do not typically alleviate all of the symptoms associated with this disorder, and it is generally recommended that patients take medications in conjunction with a psychotherapy specifically developed to treat PTSD, particularly with more complex symptom presentations.

Variability in Treatment Response

It is worth noting that there is some variability in treatment response across different patient populations. Historically, women have responded better to PTSD treatments than men. To be clear, however, these gender differences are likely better explained by the nature of the traumas experienced by men and women in these studies. That is, male samples have predominantly consisted of men with combat-related PTSD, and female samples have predominantly consisted of female sexual assault survivors. More specifically, treatment outcome studies on combat-related PTSD have consisted of veterans from the Vietnam era. It could be that combat-related PTSD is more resistant to treatment than other types of trauma. It could also be that there are factors unique to the Vietnam War experience or to the environment Vietnam veterans faced postdeployment that complicated treatment delivery/success in this subpopulation of trauma survivors. Yet another possibility is the role of disability within the VA health care system and the potential for it to discourage symptom recovery (see Chapter 7 for a discussion of this issue). Among children and adolescents, there is no corresponding gender difference in response to evidence-based treatments such as TF-CBT (Cohen, Mannarino, & Iyengar, 2011; Lang, Ford, & Fitzgerald, 2011): Boys with abuse- or violence-related PTSD appear to benefit as much as girls from cognitive–behavioral psychosocial therapy.

The recent conflicts in Iraq and Afghanistan represent an opportunity for better understanding of treatment response differences between combat- and non-combat-related PTSD and between women and men. That is, the Veterans Health Administration is much more prepared to treat combat-related PTSD in Operation Iraqi Freedom/Operation Enduring Freedom (OIF/OEF) veterans relative to the Vietnam era, and OIF/OEF veterans are more educated regarding the warning signs of PTSD and available treatment options and have greater access to empirically supported interventions for PTSD than their Vietnam predecessors. Thus, clinical researchers will hopefully be able to treat OIF/OEF veterans before PTSD becomes a more pervasive and disabling condition. Additionally, however, Iraq and Afghanistan represent the first military conflicts to include women in combat duties. Thus, it may be possible to make meaningful gender comparisons in treatment response more broadly and to combat-related stress more specifically.

PTSD Interventions for Patients With Comorbid Conditions

Historically, patients with comorbid conditions have been excluded from PTSD clinical trials for the sake of increased internal validity. As a result, despite the high overlap between PTSD and some psychiatric conditions, treatment approaches for dual disorders remain underdeveloped and there are insufficient data to classify these treatments as frontline interventions for PTSD consistent with the guidelines discussed in Chapter 2. There are also limited data to inform the optimal sequence of care with regard to the treatment of PTSD and comorbid conditions (i.e., whether treatment should be integrated and both disorders targeted simultaneously or whether it is better to treat one disorder first and then the other)—though more recent clinical wisdom leans toward an integrated treatment approach.

Substance Abuse Seeking Safety (SS) is an integrated treatment approach for PTSD and substance use disorders and is one of the most researched dual-diagnosis PTSD interventions (Najavits, Gallop, & Weiss, 2006; Zlotnick, Johnson, & Najavits, 2009; Zlotnick, Najavits, Rohsenow, & Johnson, 2003). In recent guidelines from the International Society for Traumatic Stress Studies on the treatment of PTSD and comorbid conditions, SS was the only integrated treatment for comorbidity to receive a Level A rating (Foa et al., 2009). Level A ratings are based on the Agency for Health Care Policy and Research (AHCPR) Guidelines and represent the highest possible grade on the scale.

SS is a present-focused cognitive–behavioral therapy developed to target trauma/PTSD and comorbid substance use disorder that includes cognitive, behavioral, interpersonal, and case management components. It is a flexible treatment designed to be delivered in both individual and group format and has been used in both inpatient and outpatient settings with a range of substance-abusing patient populations. SS consists of 25 topics that can be covered in any order. Representative topics include Coping With Triggers (a more behavioral topic where patients are encouraged to fight their triggers), Recovery Thinking (a more cognitive topic where patients are encouraged to explore the role of honesty in their lives and role play with other members), Asking for Help (a more interpersonal topic where patients learn how to ask for and receive help), and Getting Others to Support Your Recovery (a more interpersonal topic that encourages patients to identify people in their lives who are positive influences on their recovery and to explore ways to solicit support from these individuals). Across topics, the overarching goal of SS is to promote patients' sense of safety in their thoughts, behaviors, and feelings.

More recently, a cognitive–behavioral therapy designed to treat co-occurring PTSD and substance use disorders, Trauma Affect Regulation: Guide for Education and Therapy (TARGET; Ford & Russo, 2006), has shown evidence of efficacy in randomized clinical trials as a group therapy with adults (Frisman, Ford, Lin, Mallon, & Chang, 2008) and an individual psychotherapy with women (Ford, Steinberg, & Zhang, 2011) and girls (Ford, Steinberg, Hawke, Levine, & Zhang, 2012). TARGET is manualized, with 10 to 12 sessions that teach how the biological changes involved in PTSD and addiction can be managed and potentially modified with a seven-step sequence for "focused" thinking that integrates cognitive–behavioral and acceptance/mindfulness-based interventions to reduce experiential avoidance and enhance emotion regulation. The focusing skills component of TARGET provides a practical way for the patient to "stop and think" when experiencing posttraumatic stress reactions that lead to drinking or substance use. They are summarized in the acronym FREEDOM: Focusing the mind on one thought that you choose based on your core values and hopes; Recognizing current triggers for "alarm" reactions; distinguishing alarm-driven ("reactive") versus adaptive ("main") Emotions, thoughts (Evaluations), goal Definitions, and behavioral Options; and dedicating oneself to Make a positive contribution to the world by gaining control of "alarm reactions." The FREEDOM steps are learned and practiced incrementally in therapy sessions and in self-monitoring exercises in the natural environment, particularly in situations or contexts that are high risk for relapse due to eliciting automatic patterns of drinking or substance use, or the urge to do so. A structured FREEDOM practice exercise template is provided for the client to review recent or historical experiences, similar to the narrative reconstruction approaches in CPT. TARGET also includes a creative arts component using personalized "lifelines" (constructed with collage, drawing, poetry, and writing) to apply the FREEDOM steps to constructing a life narrative that includes traumatic and stressful events but does not involve repeated retelling of traumatic events.

Severe and Persistent Mental Illness Refined since its development, Trauma Management Therapy (TMT) is based on a multicomponent intervention for social phobia (Turner, Beidel, Cooley, Woody, & Messer, 1994) and chronic combat-related PTSD among Vietnam veterans (Beidel, Frueh, Uhde, Wong, & Mentrikoski, 2011; Frueh, Turner, Beidel, Mirabella, & Jones, 1996; Turner, Beidel, & Frueh, 2005). TMT has been tested in an open trial for the treatment of PTSD among patients with severe and persistent forms of mental illness with significant decreases in PTSD symptoms and diagnoses from pre- to posttreatment (Frueh et al., 2009). TMT typically consists of 27 sessions of psychoeducation, social skills and anger management training, imaginal exposure, and in vivo homework activities. Exposure sessions are delivered in individual format, and social skills and anger management training is delivered in a group context. Relative to other exposure-based interventions for PTSD, TMT places a heavy emphasis on social skills building and emotion regulation. This emphasis was developed in response to data indicating that exposure treatment is often not as effective at treating the negative symptoms of PTSD (e.g., avoidance, social withdrawal, and emotional numbing) and aspects of emotion management (e.g., anger, hostility) relative to other features of PTSD such as arousal. The essential elements of the social skills training component of TMT consists of instruction, modeling, behavioral rehearsal or "role-plays," feedback, and reinforcement. Following each group session, patients are assigned practice exercises to further refine and consolidate their skills.

Another PTSD cognitive–behavioral treatment for individuals with SMI, which more heavily emphasizes cognitive restructuring, has been tested in two pilot studies (Mueser et al., 2007; Rosenberg, Mueser, Jankowski, Salyers, & Acher, 2004) and a randomized controlled trial (Mueser et al., 2008) with promising results. In the most recent, and the only randomized controlled test of the intervention, Mueser et al. (2008) found that although CBT was not more effective than treatment-as-usual (TAU) at eliminating PTSD diagnostic status at post, 3-, and 6-month follow-ups, it was significantly better than TAU at decreasing PTSD severity and negative trauma-related cognitions, depressive symptoms, other anxiety symptoms, and health-related concerns. The strongest effects were for patients with more severe PTSD symptoms.

This CBT program is a 12- to 16-week cognitive–behavioral therapy consisting of psychoeducation about PTSD, breathing retraining, and cognitive restructuring. Specific treatment modules include an introduction (one session); crisis plan review (one session); psychoeducation about the core symptoms of PTSD (one to two sessions); breathing retraining (one or more sessions); psychoeducation about the associated symptoms of PTSD (one or two sessions); cognitive restructuring: common styles of thinking (one to three sessions); cognitive restructuring: the five steps of cognitive restructuring (seven or more sessions); and generalization training and treatment termination (two sessions). The cognitive restructuring sessions are similar to other CBT approaches in that they focus on teaching patients (a) about the connection between their thoughts and feelings, (b) to identify their maladaptive thoughts, and (c) to use cognitive restructuring when distressed using a step-by-step process. As part of generalization training, patients explain what cognitive restructuring is to their case manager.

Although the CBT programs described above lend themselves to addressing the more complicated deficits found in individuals with severe forms of mental illness, it remains to be seen whether this population can benefit sufficiently from shorter and less intensive cognitive–behavioral interventions for PTSD. It is hoped that recent increased efforts to treat

PTSD in patients with severe mental illness will generate the data that are needed to establish a clear course of clinical action for this patient population.

Comorbid Anxiety Disorders Multiple Channel Exposure Therapy (M-CET) for PTSD and panic disorder is a manualized 12-session treatment that integrates Cognitive Processing Therapy (CPT) and exposure for panic. Compared to patients assigned to a minimal attention control group, patients who received M-CET experienced greater reductions in PTSD and panic (Falsetti, Resnick, & Davis, 2005). Although promising, M-CET has yet to be sufficiently replicated and/or tested in a randomized controlled trial.

Altogether, it is a bit surprising that more progress has not been made in the treatment of complicated patient populations such as those with comorbid psychiatric conditions. Fortunately, however, there has been a growing emphasis in the past decade on expanding clinical research to more representative patient populations and practice settings—that is, a growing emphasis on external validity versus internal validity and the importance of developing treatments that will disseminate effectively outside of the research lab. As such, it is likely that the evidence base for treating patients with PTSD and comorbid psychiatric conditions will evolve sufficiently in the next decade.

Providing Feedback

Once a comprehensive assessment of the patient has been conducted (as detailed in Chapter 4) and a diagnosis of PTSD is confirmed (or the presence of sufficient symptoms to warrant specialized PTSD treatment), it is important to provide feedback to patients about their symptoms and the treatment options that are available to them. Generally speaking, this process involves describing PTSD and normalizing patients' symptoms, instilling hope for recovery, describing the treatment approach and ground rules for treatment, and ensuring adequate buy-in. One of the most critical elements of this process is the instillation of hope in the patient and getting buy-in. Providers should be very explicit in stating that PTSD, relative to many other psychiatric disorders, is a curable condition that can be effectively treated. Additionally, the therapist should acknowledge that the very symptoms that drive and maintain PTSD, will at times make attending treatment sessions or engaging in out-of-session assignments aversive. However, patients should be reminded that avoidance does not work. In fact, avoiding trauma-related thoughts and feelings is exactly what most patients presenting for PTSD treatment have been doing without success for months and sometimes years. Patients should be told with confidence that if they ride out the initial discomfort of treatment, their symptoms will get better.

In the initial session, the use of metaphors can be particularly useful for getting buy-in from the patient. One that we particularly like is that of trying to push a large beach ball under water (source unknown). No matter how hard one tries to do this, the ball just keeps popping back up. This is obviously a metaphor for trying to push away feelings and thoughts about the trauma. The more a person tries not to think about and avoid his or her traumatic memories, the more they will keep resurfacing because it is almost impossible to not think about an event that is by definition distressing. Patients should be told that if they deal with their upsetting memories straight on, they can get rid of them and free themselves of the exhaustion of trying to keep them away—and, more importantly, not have to fear them anymore. Also, by not fighting the memories, patients can learn that the memories are distinct from the trauma and will not cause them harm. Put more simply, the choice to engage in treatment is one of mild temporary discomfort on the part of the patient as opposed to an ongoing and exhaustive cycle of avoidance and anxiety.

Another part of the feedback process is selling the treatment, which should not be hard to do given the strong evidence base for a number of specific treatment approaches. Within a practice, providers should review data on the effectiveness of PTSD treatments more broadly and perhaps include materials the patient can take home. This review is most helpful when it includes a review of the theoretical principles of the treatment (or treatments if the specific treatment approach has not already been decided) as well as the evidence base with regard to recovery. Additionally, we find it helpful among more reluctant patients to show them, in graph form, how our other practice patients with similar fears and concerns improved during the course of treatment (similar to what is detailed in Chapter 13).

Treatment Planning   Often, the choice of one PTSD psychosocial modality over another is generally one of provider preference and choice. **Case 1:** Patient B.G. is an Operation Enduring Freedom (OEF) veteran who was tasked with removing land mines that were placed by the Soviets 20 years previously and the Taliban in recent years. While performing the hazardous duty of mine clearing, B.G. received incoming fire from insurgents on multiple occasions and witnessed one of his fellow soldiers being fatally wounded. B.G. believed on several occasions that he would not live to the end of the day. He currently has a number of intrusive thoughts about that day and others that leave him keyed up and on edge, and he often wakes up screaming from nightmares, momentarily losing track of where he is upon awakening. **Case 2:** Patient S.W. is an Operation Iraqi Freedom (OIF) veteran. Although he reports some symptoms of arousal and avoidance, he is most bothered by feelings of guilt for failing to detect an improvised explosive device that left two of his platoon members injured and one dead. S.W. stays up late at night playing through the events leading to the explosion, punishing himself with what-ifs and wrought with feelings of self-loathing and remorse.

What psychosocial intervention is most appropriate for B.G. and S.W.? From our experience, it is sometimes easier to treat a patient with a primary symptom presentation of arousal and avoidance with a cognitive–behavioral intervention that heavily emphasizes exposure (such as patient B.G.). Conversely, patients who present more strongly with cognitive-based distortions and ruminations such as guilt or shame are often more easily treated with a cognitive–behavioral intervention that emphasizes cognitive restructuring (such as patient S.W.). However, as mentioned earlier, there are no systematic differences between the two treatments in terms of efficacy. Additionally, however, only in some research contexts would it be proscribed to blend effective PTSD treatment elements. That is, in clinical settings, providers are free to use whatever treatment elements make the most sense given their patients' symptom presentation. So, with the preceding case examples, one could just as easily argue that the provider could start S.W. with exposure, exhaust all possible progress in terms of what could be targeted in imaginal and in vivo exposure exercises, and then move into targeted cognitive restructuring for addressing his feelings of guilt and shame.

Treating Patients With Comorbid Psychiatric Conditions   Treatment determinations with regard to patients with comorbid psychiatric conditions should often be done on a case-by-case basis, depending on the symptom severity of the patient and the temporal sequence of the patient's symptom presentation. Some case examples, including patient J.B. discussed in Chapter 11, are provided next for elaboration of this point.

Case 3: J.B. has a documented history of alcohol abuse and family history of alcohol dependence. She admits to relapsing on alcohol in the past 6 months—drinking the equivalent of a fifth of vodka and a few beers daily—due to an increase in nightmares and intrusive thoughts related to a history of child sexual abuse. J.B. believes her nightmares have increased in frequency and intensity because her abuser (family member with whom she had cut off ties) tried to contact her recently to "make amends." J.B. is disappointed in herself because she believed that she had successfully pushed away those memories.

Case 4: M.C. is a police officer who recently intervened in an armed robbery of a local convenience store. After avoiding being hit by two bullets, he was forced to shoot the assailant, who subsequently died in the hospital 2 days later. Since the incident, M.C. has been "cued up" while on patrol and sometimes has to isolate himself to try to calm the beating in his chest. He has nightmares about the incident and isn't sleeping well. He admits to recently having a few beers to help him fall asleep—though he invariably wakes in the middle of the nightly and sometimes does not go back to sleep. Prior to the shooting, M.C. was primarily a social drinker and rarely drank alone or frequently.

Case 5: K.V. was sexually assaulted by an acquaintance. Since the assault, she has suffered from intrusive memories of the assault and is avoiding all of her friends and most of her usual activities for fear that she will run into her perpetrator. She has not been to work in over a week and fears she will lose her job. She spends most of the day isolated in her apartment sleeping. She is frequently tearful and has been having thoughts of suicide but has no clear plan of action.

Although there are no hard-and-fast rules with regard to treatment course in the preceding examples, some recommendations can be made based on the severity and nature of these patients' symptoms. M.C. would likely respond well to an intervention that focuses exclusively on addressing his PTSD symptoms, given the clear link between his drinking behaviors and the onset of his PTSD symptoms. In this case, clinical wisdom would suggest that his drinking will likely abate once the symptoms driving him to drink (his PTSD symptoms) are taken care of. J.B. is clearly a more complicated case, and there is no clear temporal sequence with regard to the drinking. Additionally, the drinking is more severe, suggesting clear abuse and the potential for dependence. J.B.'s symptom presentation and history suggest that she would be best served by one of the combined interventions for substance abuse described earlier, or by attending AA (or another substance abuse program) in addition to receiving PTSD services. Finally, K.V. is an example of a patient who would respond best to combined psychotherapy and pharmacotherapy given the severity of her depression. K.V.'s symptom presentation places her at high risk for poor treatment engagement.

PTSD Interventions in Need of Further Testing

Despite the efficacy of a number of cognitive–behavioral interventions for PTSD and FDA approval for SSRIs, there is still room to develop novel strategies and interventions to improve treatment response in this population. That is, across all psychosocial interventions for PTSD, roughly 33% of patients who complete treatment and 44% of the intent-to-treat group (the group that includes those who complete treatment as well as those who drop out) retain their PTSD diagnosis (e.g., Bradley et al., 2005). Likewise with SSRIs, a significant number of patients are nonresponders or partial responders (Stein et al., 2009). These individuals more than likely continue to suffer from significant PTSD-related symptoms and impairment. Also, as noted above, some groups do not fare as well in treatment relative to others.

Currently, promising treatment approaches with varying degrees of empirical support include the use of virtual reality enhancement for combat-related PTSD, imagery rescripting and prazosin for the treatment of PTSD-related nightmares, clinician-assisted Web-based interventions for PTSD, and combined psychosocial/pharmacological treatment for PTSD (see Cukor, Spitalnick, Difede, Rizzo, & Rothbaum, 2009, for a review of these and other novel treatment approaches). With regard to pharmacotherapies for PTSD, there is a need for more data directly comparing the efficacy of medications versus psychosocial treatment as monotherapies, as well as the efficacy of combined/integrated treatments.

CONCLUSION

There are a number of treatment options for individuals suffering from PTSD. These options have emerged from a fairly large and convincing body of data that suggest that most patients with PTSD who engage and adhere to treatment will recover or experience meaningful symptom reduction. Although empirically supported interventions for PTSD are generally considered comparable in efficacy, clinicians should be mindful of each patient's unique symptom prepresentation and select the approach or blend of treatment elements that will provide the most immediate symptom relief for their patients. They should also remain watchful of their patients' treatment progress, using some of the strategies discussed in Chapter 13, and appropriately modify the intensity of the treatment approach or the combination of treatment elements in order to optimize treatment response. Across all treatment approaches, the message from providers to patients should be one of hope and recovery, as PTSD is broadly considered a curable condition.

REFERENCES

Beidel, D. C., Frueh, B. C., Uhde, T. W., Wong, N., & Mentrikoski, J. M. (2011). Multicomponent behavioral treatment for chronic combat-related posttraumatic stress disorder: A randomized controlled trial. *Journal of Anxiety Disorders, 25,* 224–231.

Bradley, R., Greene, J., Russ, E., Dutra, L., & Westen, D. (2005). A multidimensional meta-analysis of psychotherapy for PTSD. *American Journal of Psychiatry, 162,* 214–227.

Cohen, J., Mannarino, A., & Deblinger, E. (2006). *Treating trauma and traumatic grief in children and adolescents.* New York, NY: Guilford Press.

Cohen, J. A., Mannarino, A. P., & Iyengar, S. (2011). Community treatment of post-traumatic stress disorder for children exposed to intimate partner violence: a randomized controlled trial. *Archives of Pediatric and Adolescent Medicine, 165*(1), 16–21.

Cohen, J. A., Mannarino, A. P., Perel, J. M., & Staron, V. (2007). A pilot randomized controlled trial of combined trauma-focused CBT and sertraline for childhood PTSD symptoms. *Journal of the American Academy of Child and Adolescent Psychiatry, 46*(7), 811–819.

Cukor, J., Spitalnick, J., Difede, J., Rizzo, A., & Rothbaum, B. O. (2009). Emerging treatments for PTSD. *Clinical Psychology Review, 29*, 715–726.

Davidson, P. R., & Parker, K. C. H. (2001). Eye movement desensitization and reprocessing (EMDR): A meta-analysis. *Journal of Counseling and Clinical Psychology, 69*, 305–316.

Department of Veterans Affairs. (2010). *Programs for veterans with PTSD* (VHA Handbook No. 1160.03).

Falsetti, S. A., Resnick, H. S., & Davis, J. (2005). Multiple channel exposure therapy: Combining cognitive–behavioral therapies for the treatment of posttraumatic stress disorder with panic attacks. *Behaviour Modification, 29*, 70–94.

Foa, E. B., Hembree, E. A., & Rothbaum, B. O. (2007). *Prolonged exposure therapy for PTSD: Therapist guide.* New York, NY: Oxford University Press.

Foa, E. B., Keane, T. M., & Friedman, M. J. (2009). Effective treatments for PTSD: *Practice guidelines from the International Society for Traumatic Stress Studies* (1–388). New York, NY: Guilford Press.

Foa, E. B. & Kozak, M. J. (1986). Emotional processing of fear: Exposure to corrective information. *Psychological Bulletin, 99*, 20–35.

Ford, J. D., & Russo, E. (2006). Trauma-focused, present-centered, emotional self-regulation approach to integrated treatment for posttraumatic stress and addiction: Trauma adaptive recovery group education and therapy (TARGET). *American Journal of Psychotherapy, 60*(4), 335–355.

Ford, J. D., Steinberg, K., Hawke, J., Levine, J., & Zhang, W. (2012). Evaluation of Trauma Affect Regulation—Guide for Education and Therapy (TARGET) with traumatized girls involved in delinquency. *Journal of Clinical Child and Adolescent Psychology, 41*(1), 27–37.

Ford, J. D., Steinberg, K. L., & Zhang, W. (2011). A randomized clinical trial comparing affect regulation and social problem-solving psychotherapies for mothers with victimization-related PTSD. *Behavior Therapy, 42*(4), 560–578.

Frisman, L. K., Ford, J. D., Lin, H., Mallon, S., & Chang, R. (2008). Outcomes of trauma treatment using the TARGET model. *Journal of Groups in Addiction and Recovery, 3*, 285–303.

Frueh, B. C., Grubaugh, A. L., Cusack, K. J., Kimble, M. O., Elhai, J. D., & Knapp, R. G. (2009). Exposure-based cognitive-behavioral treatment of PTSD in adults with schizophrenia or schizoaffective disorder: A pilot study. *Journal of Anxiety Disorders, 23*, 665–675.

Frueh, B. C., Turner, S. M., Beidel, D. C., Mirabella, R. F., & Jones, W. J. (1996). Trauma management therapy: A preliminary evaluation of a multicomponent behavioral treatment for chronic combat-related PTSD. *Behaviour Research & Therapy, 34,* 533–543.

Henggeler, S. W., Sheidow, A. J., Cunningham, P. B., Donohue, B. C., & Ford, J. D. (2008). Promoting the implementation of an evidence-based intervention for adolescent marijuana abuse in community settings: Testing the use of intensive quality assurance. *Journal of Clinical Child and Adolescent Psychology, 37*(3), 682–689.

Institute of Medicine & National Research Council. (2007). *Treatment of PTSD: An assessment of the evidence.* Washington, DC: National Academies Press.

Ipser, J., Seedat, S., & Stein, D. J. (2006). Pharmacotherapy for post-traumatic stress disorder—a systematic review and meta-analysis. *South African Medical Journal, 96,* 1088–1096.

Lang, J. M., Ford, J. D., & Fitzgerald, M. M. (2011). An algorithm for determining use of trauma-focused cognitive-behavioral therapy. *Psychotherapy, 47*(4), 554–569.

Mueser, K. T., Bolton, E., Carty, P. C., Bradley, M. J., Ahlgren, K. F., DiStaso, D. R., . . . Liddell, C. (2007). The trauma recovery group: A cognitive–behavioral program for posttraumatic stress disorder in persons with severe mental illness. *Community Mental Health Journal, 43,* 281–304.

Mueser, K. T., Rosenberg, S. D., Xie, H., Jankowski, M. K., Bolton, E. E., Lu, W., . . . Wolfe, R. (2008). A randomized controlled trial of cognitive–behavioral treatment for posttraumatic stress disorder in severe mental illness. *Journal of Consulting & Clinical Psychology, 76,* 259–271.

Najavits, L. M., Gallop, R. J., & Weiss, R. D. (2006). Seeking safety therapy for adolescent girls with PTSD and substance use disorder: A randomized controlled trial. *Journal of Behavioral Health Services and Research, 33,* 453–463.

National Collaborating Centre for Mental Health. (2005). Clinical Guideline 26. PTSD: The management of PTSD in adults & children in primary & secondary care. London, UK: National Institute for Clinical Excellence.

Powers, M. B., Halpern, J. M., Ferenschak, M. P., Gillihan, S. J., & Foa, E. B. (2010). A meta-analytic review of prolonged exposure for posttraumatic stress disorder. *Clinical Psychology Review, 30,* 635–641.

Resick, P. A., Nishith, P., Weaver, T. L., Astin, M. C., & Feuer, C. A. (2002). A comparison of cognitive-processing therapy with prolonged exposure and a waiting condition for the treatment of chronic posttraumatic stress disorder in female rape victims. *Journal of Consulting and Clinical Psychology, 70,* 867–879.

Resick, P. A., & Schnicke, M. K. (1993). *Cognitive processing therapy for rape victims: A treatment manual.* Newbury Park, CA: Sage.

Rosenberg, S. D., Mueser, K. T., Jankowski, M. K., Salyers, M. P., & Acher, K. (2004). Cognitive–behavioral treatment of PTSD in severe mental illness: Results of a pilot study. *American Journal of Psychiatric Rehabilitation, 7,* 171–186.

Ruzek, J. I., & Rosen, R. C. (2009). Disseminating evidence-based treatments for PTSD in organizational settings: A high priority focus area. *Behaviour Research & Therapy, 47*, 980–989.

Seidler, G. H., & Wagner, F. E. (2006). Comparing the efficacy of EMDR and trauma-focused cognitive–behavioral therapy in the treatment of PTSD: A meta-analytic study. *Psychol Med, 36*, 1515–1522.

Shapiro, F. (1995). *Eye movement desensitization and reprocessing: Basic principles, protocols, and procedures.* New York, NY: Guilford Press.

Stein, D. J., Ipser, J., & McAnda, N. (2009). Pharmacotherapy of posttraumatic stress disorder: A review of meta-analyses and treatment guidelines. *CNS Spectrums, 1*(Suppl 1), 25–31.

Turner, S. M., Beidel, D. C., Cooley, M. R., Woody, S. R., & Messer, S. C. (1994). A multicomponent behavioral treatment for social phobia: Social effectiveness therapy. *Behaviour Research & Therapy, 32*, 381–390.

Turner, S. M., Beidel, D. C., & Frueh, B. C. (2005). Multicomponent behavioral treatment for chronic combat-related posttraumatic stress disorder: Trauma management therapy. *Behavior Modification, 29*, 39–69.

Zlotnick, C., Johnson, J., & Najavits, L. M. (2009). Randomized controlled pilot study of cognitive–behavioral therapy in a sample of incarcerated women with substance use disorder and PTSD. *Behavioral Therapy, 40*, 325–336.

Zlotnick, C., Najavits, L. M., Rohsenow, D. J., & Johnson, D. M. (2003). A cognitive–behavioral treatment for incarcerated women with substance abuse disorder and posttraumatic stress disorder: Findings from a pilot study. *Journal of Substance Abuse Treatment, 25*, 99–105.

CHAPTER 13

Follow-Up With Evaluation and Support

During the course of therapy, it is important to continue to monitor patient progress and to adjust treatment as necessary to maximize posttraumatic stress disorder (PTSD) symptom reduction. As such, in this chapter, we will review strategies for ongoing assessment of symptoms and treatment progress. More specifically, we review strategies for monitoring within-session and between-session decreases in PTSD-related distress as well as provide strategies for systematically tracking PTSD-related symptoms throughout the course of treatment—both as an aid for ongoing treatment planning and as a tool for increasing treatment engagement and instilling hope.

STRATEGIES FOR ONGOING ASSESSMENT AND FOLLOW-UP

Within-Session Tracking

As discussed in Chapter 12, most psychosocial treatments for PTSD are considered cognitive–behavioral and involve some form of therapeutic "exposure" to the traumatic memory and associated symptoms. Also discussed in more detail in Chapter 12, exposure-based interventions for PTSD are based on conditioning principles where trauma-related cues have become conditioned stimuli that are avoided. Based on these principles, exposure treatment requires that an individual be exposed repeatedly to feared aspects of the trauma memory in order to habituate to them. As habituation occurs, anxiety decreases. Consistent with this theoretical rationale, we typically find tracking within-session habituation (i.e., subjective units of distress scale [SUDS]) useful for assessing treatment progress.

During treatment sessions, therapists should be alert to increases and decreases in anxiety (i.e., clinical indications of habituation). This can be done by tuning in to patients' nonverbal cues (i.e., nervous hand rubbing/wringing, sweating, nervous tapping of the feet) as well as by directly asking patients to rate and describe their anxiety using SUDS.

Although there are some data to suggest that within-session habituation is not necessary for treatment gains (Baker et al., 2010; van Minnen & Foa, 2006), the usefulness of SUDS ratings as a general index of patient distress cannot be underscored in that they help guide the pace (i.e., intensity) of the session. SUDS ratings typically range from 0 to 10 or from 0 to 100, with higher scores indicating greater anxiety or distress. The key to successfully using SUDS ratings is to ensure that patients appropriately anchor their physiological reactivity to the scale. Thus, therapists should spend sufficient time explaining the scale and detailing that a 10 or 100 score would indicate the most anxious they are capable of feeling. Patients often respond that this is how anxious they felt during the actual trauma. A 0, however, would reflect a time or situation when the patient is the most relaxed. A 5 or 50 would then logically represent a moderate level of distress.

Foa, Hembree, and Rothbaum (2007) recommend having the patient identify anchor points for their SUDS and to refer to these anchor points until the patient is familiar with the ratings. For example, one patient may say that she is a 0 when she is at the beach lying in the sand, a 5 or 50 when she is asking for a raise from her boss, and that she was a 10 or 100 during the actual experience of the trauma. Everyone's SUDS will vary somewhat, but, in general, it is important to reinforce the point that ratings of 10 or 100 should be reserved for instances of extreme anxiety.

Once it appears that the patient understands SUDS ratings, let him or her know that you will be referring to these both within and outside of sessions to monitor distress and titrate the intensity of the treatment sessions as well as in vivo exercises. During imaginal exposure, the therapist should record patients' SUDS approximately every 5 to 7 minutes. In addition to

FIGURE 13.1   **ADEQUATE SUDS DECREASE OVER COURSE OF ONE SESSION**

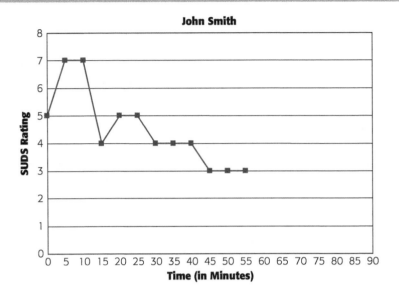

monitoring SUDS during sessions, therapists may find it useful to graph their patients' scores (as demonstrated in this chapter) to better monitor habituation and treatment progress and to demonstrate within-session gains. Traditional wisdom in line with theoretical models of PTSD suggests that patients should experience some reduction in anxiety prior to the conclusion of the imaginal exercise in order to break the cycle of anxiety and avoidance and prevent further reinforcement of avoidance behaviors. The graph in Figure 13.1, with a fictional name for the patient, indicates adequate habituation within session, with a starting SUDS rating of 5, a peak of 7, and a decrease to 3 by the end of the exposure session.

The graph in Figure 13.2, however, potentially reflects a lack of sufficient habituation toward the end of the imaginal exercise/session. Consider the following scenario:

Case 1: Ms. Johnson is a 32-year-old woman who was involved in a near-fatal car collision 3 months prior to initiating treatment. She has frequent nightmares of the moments prior to the accident, the impact, and her time trapped in the car before the medics could evacuate her. She refuses to drive herself, preferring to have her husband or other relatives

FIGURE 13.2   **INSUFFICIENT SUDS DECREASE OVER THE COURSE OF ONE SESSION**

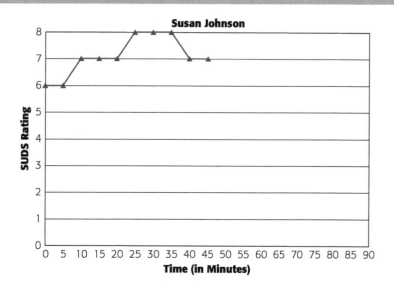

drive her to and from work or to other places. While in the car with her husband or other drivers she is extremely anxious, has physiological symptoms of anxiety such as sweating and heart palpitations, and is easily startled by other drivers and noises. During the session depicted in Figure 13.2, the therapist and patient are focused on the moment when Ms. Johnson awoke from the collision and discovered blood coming from an injury above her eye and felt excruciating pain in her back and abdominal area. This causes an immediate increase in Ms. Johnson's ratings of anxiety, but as she and her therapist focus exclusively on this aspect of the memory, her ratings start to decrease. After a couple of cycles, Ms. Johnson reports a SUDS of 7, a decrease from her previous rating of 9. The therapist terminates the session, believing that her patient's distress has decreased sufficiently. However, in keeping with theoretical models of exposure therapy, we prefer to err on the side of caution and continue the exposure so that patients are experiencing the maximum amount of decrease in their anxiety ratings as time permits. In this case, we would thus suggest having Ms. Johnson continue processing her traumatic memory until her SUDS ratings decrease to preferably a 5 or at least 6.

In Vivo SUDS Tracking

Similar to within-session SUDS monitoring, it will be important to have patients track and record their out-of-session (in vivo) exposure SUDS ratings. Similar to the method outlined by Foa et al. (2007), we instruct patients to record a pre-, post-, and peak SUDS and to remain in the exposure exercise until there is an appreciable decrease from the peak SUDS rating. If patients report difficulty with out-of-session assignments, the therapist should problem-solve ways to ensure that patients are successful on subsequent trials. One strategy may be to select an activity from the patient's in vivo hierarchy (their previously constructed list of anxiety-provoking cues and activities ordered from least to most distressing) that elicits less anxiety, and thus is more likely to result in the successful completion of the exercise. Alternatively, the therapist and patient could enlist the help of a family member or friend. For example, if a patient could not tolerate remaining in a crowded food court at the mall because it cued overwhelming feelings of vulnerability, a less anxiety-provoking alternative (but one that will have a higher likelihood of success) would be to have a trusted friend accompany the patient. Once the patient gains success with this, he or she could then attempt the same activity alone. Similarly, the therapist could also accompany the patient on this assignment as part of a treatment session. The overarching goal with any out–of–session assignment is to maximize the patient's likelihood of success.

Between-Session Tracking

For any treatment modality, we find self-report measures of PTSD such as the PTSD Symptom Checklist (PCL; discussed in Chapter 4) useful for tracking PTSD severity during the course of treatment. Tracking PTSD symptoms between sessions can help determine whether, and how well, the patient is responding to treatment and to identify specific symptoms that need additional focus—that is, in administering the PCL, the therapist may notice that a few specific symptoms are significantly more pronounced than others and problem-solve around those symptoms in subsequent sessions. Although there is no hard-and-fast rule, we recommend assessing patients' PTSD symptoms at least every 2 or 3 weeks if the patient is being seen at least once a week. Particularly useful are those symptoms

FIGURE 13.3 **STEADY DECLINE IN PCL SCORES OVER THE COURSE OF TREATMENT**

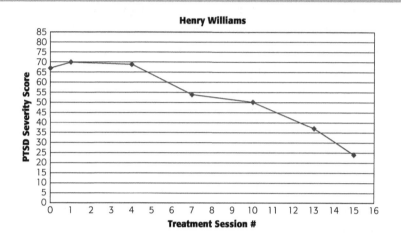

that can be directly targeted during imaginal and in vivo exercises such as Cluster B and Cluster C symptoms (e.g., recurrent and distressing memories; intense physiological distress at exposure to internal cues or external cues; avoidance of thoughts and feelings; or avoidance of activities, people, places associated with the trauma, etc.).

Also, if patients are doing well, it is often beneficial to give them concrete evidence of their PTSD symptoms decreasing over time for additional encouragement and reinforcement of treatment gains. Figure 13.3 shows a graph demonstrating adequate between-session gains over the course of treatment. In this case, the patient started with a PCL score of 67 and ended treatment with a PCL of 24. For context, the PCL ranges from 17 to 85 and a score of 45 or 50 on the PCL are usually considered indicative of a diagnosis of PTSD.

Early in treatment, patients may sometimes demonstrate temporary spikes in their PCL scores (demonstrated in Figure 13.4). In these cases, it is important for the therapist to reinforce that this is not unusual and that the increase in symptoms is temporary as new aspects of the traumatic memory are being uncovered and dealt with. Alternatively, the therapist should explore whether something occurred during the week that may have increased the patient's symptoms. Consider the following scenario for context:

FIGURE 13.4	**TEMPORARY INCREASE ON PCL SCORES OVER THE COURSE OF TREATMENT**

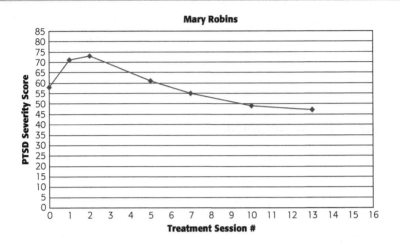

Case 2: Mary Robins is a 25-year-old woman who was sexually assaulted by a stranger while in her home. She presented for treatment due to depression and severe symptoms of PTSD including a number of intrusive memories of the assault, difficulty concentrating at work, feeling emotionally numb, and feeling isolated from others. Although compliant in treatment, Ms. Robins reports more severe symptoms of PTSD after the third treatment session focused on imaginal exposure. After some probing by the therapist, Ms. Robins shares a particularly distressing incident that happened at work. Ms. Robins reported being in the break room at work when she was overwhelmed by feelings of panic and distress at smelling her perpetrator's cologne. Apparently, a new employee at the office was wearing the same cologne her assailant wore during the assault. She reported leaving the break room abruptly and then going to the restroom to calm down before leaving work altogether for that day. Since then, she has called in sick to work, fearful of "losing it" if she goes back.

Aside from the PCL, it may prove useful to also assess for changes in patients' maladaptive cognitions over time—particularly in the context of an intervention that is primarily cognitive in nature. A few measures, developed specifically for trauma survivors, include the Posttraumatic Cognitions Inventory (Foa, Ehlers, Clark, Tolin, & Orsillo, 1999), The Posttraumatic

Maladaptive Cognitions Scale (Vogt, Shipherd, & Resick, 2010), and the Trauma-Related Guilt Inventory (Kubany et al., 1996). Higher scores on these measures correspond to higher endorsement of negative/maladaptive beliefs, and similar to the SUDS and the PCL, can be used as general indices of treatment progress. Also similar to the PCL, these cognitions scales could be used to identify specific maladaptive thoughts that can be further addressed in treatment.

Pharmacological Treatment

Patients receiving psychotropic medications for PTSD should likewise be monitored for adequate response or worsening of symptoms. In situations where a patient is unresponsive, appropriate titration of an existing medication or change to another medication should be made—of course, this is after the physician has adequately assessed for medication adherence to the current regimen. Additionally, however, the potential benefits of psychotherapy should be revisited and appropriate referrals and assistance to obtain recommended services should be provided. Since patients do not typically see their primary care provider as often as they would see a psychotherapist, PTSD symptoms should be assessed at every visit in order to obtain a valid trajectory of symptoms over time.

Monitoring of Other Psychiatric Conditions or General Functioning

As mentioned in previous chapters, comorbid psychiatric conditions are common among patients with PTSD, and the presence of these conditions can affect treatment priorities and the use of one intervention over another. Psychiatric conditions most often comorbid with PTSD include substance use problems, depression, and other forms of anxiety. Fortunately, as outlined in Chapter 4, there are a number of empirically supported assessment measures (many of them brief) for these psychiatric conditions. There are data to suggest that, when PTSD is effectively treated, many of these associated symptoms decrease or disappear. However, in some cases, additional comorbid diagnoses will require specialized care. This is most often the case with more severe forms of comorbidity.

As with any other treatment condition, providers should be alert to suicidal ideation or intent in their patients and address this directly. In the case of either, a thorough assessment of risk should be conducted and the next step managed accordingly. Although there is some data debating the usefulness of "no harm contacts" we find it helpful to have patients at least verbally commit to contacting their provider or emergency department if they feel at risk for harming themselves. Of course, in the case of clear suicidal intent, treatment should follow state-specific legal guidelines that generally involve immediate hospitalization of the patient.

At least every few months, if not already addressed within the course of treatment, it may also be worthwhile for therapists to assess the overall mental health status of their patients, including impairments in social and occupational functioning, patient perceptions of treatment gains or difficulties, and areas in which patients would like to see further improvement.

TREATMENT ADJUSTMENTS

Ideally, patients will adhere to their treatment, and treatment gains will be made. In some cases, however, patients with PTSD do not improve or perhaps worsen despite the best efforts of the therapist. In these cases, the therapist should first probe regarding treatment compliance. That is, is the patient regularly attending sessions and is the patient completing out-of-session exercises? Are comorbid psychiatric conditions interfering with the patient's ability to fully engage or benefit from treatment? In the case of pharmacotherapy, is the dosing sufficient? Is general life chaos interfering with compliance, and do these issues need to be addressed directly?

Assuming the lack of treatment gains is not due to poor treatment compliance, it may be useful to intensify the same treatment modality or to consider incorporating an adjunctive treatment. In some cases, a switch in treatment modalities or approach may be indicated. This is most obvious in the case of insufficient pharmacotherapy reaction. After a psychiatrist or primary care provider has titrated and adjusted her patient's psychiatric medications to no avail, psychotherapy is the next likely course of action. Similarly, if a therapist using psychotherapy is struggling to get his patient to complete out-of-session exercises because the patient is severely depressed, it would be useful to talk to the patient about taking a selective serotonin reuptake inhibitor (SSRI) or other antidepressant. Inclusion of an adjunctive strategy may also prove useful when a comorbid psychiatric condition is interfering with the patient's ability to fully engage in treatment. Similarly, in the context of treating a patient with an exposure-based treatment such as prolonged exposure, it may be useful to spend some time in session using cognitive restructuring if there are guilt or shame issues that appear to warrant specialized attention.

In cases where patient distress is high and functioning is significantly impaired and there continues to be very little treatment progress despite trying all of the preceding strategies, it may be worthwhile to discuss more intense treatment options with the patient. These could include partial hospitalization or inpatient PTSD programs.

CONCLUSION

There are a number of tools therapists can use to monitor the treatment of their patients. Ongoing assessment is critical for both tracking treatment progress and providing patients with evidence of their treatment gains. Although there is no hard-and-fast rule regarding the frequency of ongoing assessment, most providers would agree that this should be done on a regular basis, varying somewhat depending on the treatment context. This information can then be used to adjust treatment or refer the patient for other services that may maximize their response and recovery. The key throughout this process is for the provider to remain open to any additional strategies that could benefit the patient.

REFERENCES

Baker, A., Mystowski, J., Culver, N., Yi, R., Mortazavi, A., & Craske, M. G. (2010). Does habituation matter? Emotional processing theory and exposure therapy for acrophobia. *Behaviour Research and Therapy, 48,* 1139–1143.

Foa, E. B., Ehlers, A., Clark, D. M., Tolin, D. F., & Orsillo, S. M. (1999). The Posttraumatic Cognitions Inventory (PTCI): Development and validation. *Psychological Assessment, 11,* 303–314.

Foa, E. B., Hembree, E. A., & Rothbaum, B. O. (2007). *Prolonged exposure therapy for PTSD: Emotional processing of traumatic experiences: therapist guide.* New York, NY: Oxford University Press.

Kubany, E. S., Haynes, S. N., Abueg, F. R., Manke, F. P., Brennan, J. M., & Stahura, C. (1996). Development and validation of the Trauma-Related Guilt Inventory (TRGI). *Psychological Assessment, 8*, 428–444.

van Minnen, A., & Foa, E. B. (2006). The effect of imaginal exposure length on outcome of treatment for PTSD. *Journal of Traumatic Stress, 19*, 427–438.

Vogt, D. S., Shipherd, J. C., & Resick, P. A. (2010, July 21). Posttraumatic maladaptive beliefs scale: Evolution of the Personal Beliefs and Reactions Scale. *Assessment, 19*, 308–317.

CHAPTER 14

Going Forward

NEW FRONTIERS AND FUTURE DIRECTIONS

The sequence of chapters in this book have provided you, the reader, with summarized information from over three decades of research on posttraumatic stress disorder (PTSD) and other posttraumatic reactions. This research has greatly advanced our ability to clinically evaluate and treat people suffering psychological difficulties in the aftermath of traumatic events. Prior chapters in this book have addressed a wide range of clinical issues and provided practical guidance for mental health clinicians practicing in a variety of clinical settings and serving a wide range of patient populations. These prior chapters have covered historical and conceptual aspects of the PTSD diagnosis; evidence-based practice in mental health; general clinical issues in working with trauma survivors; assessment approaches to PTSD and related comorbid conditions; ethnocultural considerations; forensic evaluations; clinical work with children and adolescents, veterans, and other special populations and settings; treatment planning and patient feedback; and treatment follow-up assessment. Collectively, these issues provide direction on how we, as clinicians, can better conceptualize and assess our patients' PTSD-related problems, construct case formulations that address PTSD and associated psychiatric and psychosocial problems, and plan treatment interventions to reduce or even eliminate trauma-related distress and dysfunction.

There are a number of critical issues of which we must always remain mindful. Within the current *Diagnostic and Statistical Manual of Mental*

Disorders (*DSM*) diagnostic system, psychiatric diagnoses are largely mere descriptive categories. That is, modern psychiatry consists of a diagnostic system that requires clinicians to assess, classify, conceptualize, and treat their patients according to presenting signs and symptoms that are thought to be the manifestations of underlying psychopathology—without any basis for understanding the causes or mechanisms that produce the psychopathology. This is generally an atheoretical taxonomic approach, rather than a hypothesis-driven scientific search for how or why problems such as PTSD occur or persist. One benefit of this framework to psychiatric disorders is that it provides a reliable common language for organizing, describing, and defining clusters of symptoms that commonly hold together. This facilitates research (basic, clinical, and translational) and allows for the development of accepted standards of practice. Yet, this approach is not without flaws. The diagnostic categories of the *DSM* distinguish psychiatric disorders on the basis of manifest appearance, rather than on actual or potential etiological distinctions—such as environmental, behavioral, biological, and genetic factors. Rosen, Frueh, Lilienfeld, McHugh, and Spizter (2010, pp. 269–270, 272) addressed this issue:

> Several commentators have discussed how diagnostic categories within the *DSM* identify subjects using a "top down" method (e.g., McHugh, 2005; McHugh & Treisman, 2007). This approach, in which patients are diagnosed in checklist fashion, is graphically demonstrated in the diagnostic "trees" appended to the *DSM*. Within this framework, if a shared symptom is given diagnostic priority, patients who may actually suffer from distinct disorders can be drawn into what becomes an over-inclusive category. Ideally, and contrary to the top-down approach, clinicians want to understand their patients by considering psychiatric disorders within the full context of individuals and their situational circumstances. By this method, a psychiatrist draws diagnostic formulations from a "bottom-up" approach that evaluates an individual's full biography and takes into account his or her previous psychological problems, temperament, mental state, and situational contexts. When thinking "bottom up," a diagnostician considers all forms of psychological maladjustments that people can experience and express with mental symptoms. . . . (T)he creation of the PTSD diagnosis in 1980 has shaped how we conceptualize an individual's reactions in the aftermath of

trauma. On the one hand, the diagnosis offers several advantages over opposing frameworks, foremost of which is that the diagnosis is parsimonious. With the use of a single diagnostic construct, an individual's presenting problems are accounted for, an etiological model is provided, and treatment goals can be defined. On the other hand, the diagnosis is not without its limitations. Of greatest concern, the PTSD diagnosis encourages a "top-down" assessment model that lumps most posttraumatic reactions under the rubric of a single term. Essentially normal reactions are joined with more severe symptoms of disorder, contributing to confusion as to what is adaptive and what is maladaptive. Multiple processes (e.g., conditioned fear, grief, family dynamics) are conceptualized as largely "caused" by a singular event that is hypothesized to contribute to an underlying pathogenesis, such as fragmented memory or deregulated stress hormones. Finally, the diagnosis of PTSD creates the illusion that a disorder in nature has been identified: a disorder that accounts for and even "explains" an individual's problems.

Of course, much of the preceding quote from Rosen et al. (2010) also applies to virtually all psychiatric disorders as they are currently conceptualized in *DSM-IV*, and as they are expected to be conceptualized in *DSM-5*. What sets PTSD slightly apart from most other psychiatric disorders is the defining etiological event—trauma—that precedes, and is generally accepted to have caused, the disorder. Therefore, there is the presumption of a causal mechanism, although exactly how exposure to traumatic stressors leads to PTSD symptoms, and why this is highly variable from trauma to trauma, symptom to symptom, and individual to individual, is not stated or explained. The risk, then, is that well-intentioned practitioners may begin to apply PTSD diagnoses to a widening array of stressful events (a phenomenon termed "bracket creep"; McNally, 2003), as well as emotional and behavioral reactions. Thus, the disorder, which has gradually moved into the public's awareness, risks the "medicalization" of human reactions to adversity and loss. If significantly misused, the results could be profoundly iatrogenic. For example, PTSD could become (mistakenly) thought of as an incurable disease due to irreversible changes in the brain caused by traumatic stressors. Or PTSD could be (again mistakenly) viewed as responding only to certain specific therapies, like a medical illness that can be treated successfully only by drugs that change the specific pathophysiology of the disease. This could drastically limit the sense of hope and the therapeutic options available to patients with PTSD and clinicians who treat them.

We hope the information provided and discussed in this volume will help practicing clinicians ensure the accuracy, sensitivity, and effectiveness of their clinical efforts with people—both children and adults—experiencing psychological difficulties after traumatic and life-altering experiences. In the remainder of this final chapter, we conclude this book with a very brief comment on new frontiers and future directions, a consideration of the proposed criteria changes for PTSD in *DSM-5*, and a few final remarks.

NEW FRONTIERS IN THE FIELD RELEVANT TO ASSESSMENT AND TREATMENT PLANNING

Data obtained from genetic and neuroscience research is rapidly changing the field of mental illness, and PTSD is no exception. A growing empirical database is quickly advancing our understanding of the significant role that genetics appears to play in the development of PTSD (Afifi, Asmundson, Taylor, & Jang, 2010; Galea et al., 2006; Kilpatrick et al., 2007; Koenen et al., 2009). Studies on genetic mutations, candidate genes, and the degree of variance contributed by heredity over and above environment have begun to show that most psychiatric disorders have underlying genetic bases, although frequently they are the same ones across different mood and anxiety disorders. At the same time, data from studies using various forms of neuroimaging and other biological approaches have also advanced our understanding of the brain aspects of PTSD.

All of this gives rise to the question of whether there are clear and specific biological markers for PTSD. Certainly, the field of traumatology has gone through a number of phases with respect to answering this question. In the 1990s, the "cortisol hypothesis" generated some excitement when preliminary studies found that patients with chronic PTSD exhibited lower than normal urinary cortisol levels (Yehuda, Southwick, Nussbaum, Giller, & Mason, 1990). However, subsequent studies have not consistently revealed lower cortisol levels among individuals with exposure to trauma and PTSD (Young & Breslau, 2004) and many people with disorders other than PTSD also exhibit lower cortisol levels (Fries, Hesse, Hellhammer, & Hellhammer, 2005). The neuroanatomy has also drawn considerable attention. For example, in the mid-1990s, there was preliminary data to suggest reduced hippocampal volumes among traumatized people (Bremner et al., 1995) leading to a widely accepted (at least for a time) hypothesis that stress damaged the brain, shrinking the hippocampus. However, this notion gradually fell away as subsequent studies failed to replicate initial findings or showed that it is more likely that a smaller hippocampus is a risk factor or vulnerability that preexists PTSD rather than the result of exposure to trauma or PTSD (e.g., Bonne et al., 2001). Other ideas have also come and gone in the search for a biological "signature," including the belief that PTSD might have a specific genetic cause (Koenen et al., 2009). These are all worthy areas for continued research, but for the clinician the crucial implication is that biology plays a definite, but as yet not well understood role in PTSD.

At this point, efforts to identify sensitive and specific laboratory-based tests or objective biological markers, such as cortisol levels, neuroanatomical markers (e.g., hippocampal volume), genetic profiles, or brain activity (e.g., amygdala reactivity), have all fallen far short of being useful diagnostic tests or clinical markers for PTSD (Zhang, Li, Benedek, Li, & Ursano, 2009). Thus, at this point we are left with the conclusion of the Institute of Medicine (IOM, 2006) that: "No biomarkers are clinically useful or specific in diagnosing PTSD, assessing the risk of developing it, or charting its progression (p. 46)." Clinicians therefore need to be wary about expecting any form of biological data to provide much clinical utility or using oversimplified analogies with their patients about ways in which stress or trauma damage the brain. Perhaps the lone exception to this is the promising use of psychophysiological data (e.g., heart rate reactivity) with some patients to measure reactivity to cues during and after treatment. For a more in-depth review of this issue see Rosen, Lillienfeld, and Orr (2010).

Proposed Criteria for **PTSD** in *DSM-5*

As of this writing the proposed *DSM-5* criteria changes for PTSD have been available for review for almost 2 years and the *DSM-5* field trials, sponsored by the American Psychiatric Association, have been completed, and the publication of the new *DSM* is expected in 2013. Here, we summarize these proposed changes, review some of the empirical bases for or against them, address forensic implications, and consider wider implications for epidemiology, assessment, and treatment of PTSD. Please be mindful, however, that by the time *DSM-5* is actually published the criteria for PTSD may change further or be somewhat different than we expect at the time of this writing.

Proposed Criteria Changes to *DSM-5*

The proposed PTSD criteria for *DSM-5* include the following changes:

1. Further specification regarding criteria for the traumatic event (A1), including that learning of deaths of close relatives or close friends must have involved events of a violent or accidental nature, and that exposure through electronic media does not (usually) qualify.
2. Elimination of the prior requirement that the traumatic event be accompanied by a reaction of fear, helplessness, or horror (A2).
3. Spreading the three symptom clusters (B–D) of *DSM-IV* into four symptom clusters, mainly by separating avoidance and numbing into two separate clusters.
4. The numbing symptom cluster (D) is characterized by negative alterations in cognitions and mood associated with the traumatic event.
5. Cluster D includes two new symptoms, including persistent distorted blame of self or others about the causes or consequences of the traumatic event, and a pervasive negative emotional state.
6. The arousal and reactivity symptom cluster (now E) includes a new symptom described as reckless or self-destructive behavior.
7. Elimination of the acute versus chronic specification.

In our reading of them, these proposed changes are incremental in nature and do not fundamentally alter the core concept of the PTSD diagnosis or the general approach to how the diagnosis is considered and made. The proposed changes mean the disorder will remain absolutely familiar to experienced clinicians and it should be easy for them to adapt to the new criteria. We next discuss some of the evidence base related to several of the important diagnostic issues with this disorder.

Criterion A: The Traumatic Stressor

As noted throughout this book, the diagnostic criteria for PTSD begin with Criterion A, the traumatic stressor criterion. Criterion A requires exposure to a traumatic event involving actual or threatened death, actual or threatened serious injury, or violation of one's bodily integrity (A1). Exposure can involve directly experiencing the event, witnessing it happening to others, or learning about it happening to a close associate. Also required in *DSM-IV* is that the individual experienced intense fear, helplessness, or horror during or immediately after the event (A2). There are several problems with this, however (Long & Elhai, 2009). First of all, Criterion A1 is extremely diverse with respect to the types of events that can apply to meet the criteria. It can be met by exposure to high magnitude, catastrophic events, such as combat, sexual assault, or a life-threatening accident. However, it can also be satisfied by low-magnitude events that are not even directly experienced, such as learning that a family member died unexpectedly or witnessing a fight. Note that these indirectly experienced events are not consistent with how the PTSD diagnosis was originally intended and framed in *DSM-III*. That is, they were initially conceived as major, life-threatening traumatic stressors that fell outside the usual range of human experience (Spitzer, First, & Wakefield, 2007).

In addition to the above, it is worth reminding readers that the diagnosis of PTSD represents a relatively new and novel approach that rules "traumatic" events are unique and distinct from less severe, more general life stressors. However, research findings consistently show strong associations between PTSD symptoms and general life stressors, including bereavement, divorce, and financial hardship. In other words, the assumption that exposure to life-threatening stressors is the primary cause of a *unique* set of stress response symptoms is somewhat problematic. Bruce Dohrenwend (2010) recently proposed a typology of stressful situations and events to be empirically tested for their relation to PTSD and other posttraumatic reactions.

Criterion A1 is also somewhat ambiguous in its meaning. Among both researchers and clinicians there is often wide divergence of opinion as to which experiences satisfy the criterion and which do not. One of the most controversial examples occurred after the terrorist attacks on September 11, 2001. Some PTSD experts held that viewing the horrific images of the death and destruction on television, especially repeated images of the sort that filled the news coverage for days and even weeks after the events, were sufficient to meet the A1 criterion. And, indeed, some research seemed to suggest an increase in PTSD symptomatology among some people far away from the actual sites of the attacks. Others, of course, were highly critical of this notion, arguing that such an interpretation trivializes the much more traumatizing experiences of those who had survived the attacks or were directly involved in rescue and other first responder efforts. According to this view, including stressful events that are not "traumatic" in the strictest sense dilutes the PTSD diagnosis and redirects treatment and service resources away from those who are genuinely suffering PTSD.

Ultimately, the epidemiological research has supported the latter position, with posttraumatic reactions being strongly associated with proximity to the events. But one can quickly see there are a host of reasonable questions regarding implementation of A1. If a soldier stationed on a military base in a war zone hears the sound of distant explosions and fears the possibility of coming under direct threat, does this satisfy Criterion A1? Does losing a home to a hurricane satisfy the criterion if the individual is not home at the time? What about sexual harassment of a nonphysical nature? How do we consider stressful or sad experiences such as losing a job, coping with a serious illness that is not life threatening, or learning that an elderly family member has died of natural causes?

Criterion A1's ambiguity does not effectively address such examples, and there is no universally agreed upon list of events or conditions that would satisfy Criterion A1 available for us to refer to. Encouragingly, the proposed changes to PTSD's diagnosis for *DSM-5* do address some of these questions by providing slightly more detailed parameters. For example, according to the current proposed changes, viewing potentially horrific events on television or movies explicitly would not typically qualify as a traumatic event (American Psychiatric Association *DSM-5* Development, 2010).

Another aspect of PTSD's trauma criterion (A2) has also been scrutinized. The psychologist Richard J. McNally has argued that including A2 within Criterion A "confounds the response with the stimulus" in behavioral terms, and "it confounds the host with the pathogen" in medical terms (McNally, 2009, p. 598). Studies have demonstrated that the vast majority of individuals who meet Criterion A1 also meet Criterion A2; and among individuals who meet Criterion A1 and all PTSD symptom criteria, almost all meet A2 (Brewin, Andrews, & Rose, 2000; Creamer, McFarlane, & Burgess, 2005; Karam et al., 2010). Therefore, many experts believe that Criterion A2 is essentially unnecessary to the diagnosis of PTSD. When PTSD is assessed, the determination of A2 relies upon the individual's memory, which is likely to be heavily influenced by current symptoms; this may account for much of the apparent relationship between A2 and other PTSD symptoms. Accordingly, the proposed PTSD criteria for *DSM-5* no longer include this element (American Psychiatric Association *DSM-5* Development, 2010). However, for treatment planning purposes, and for the effective delivery of therapies such as Prolonged Exposure (PE), helping patients to recall their emotional and cognitive reactions at the time of, and soon after, traumatic experiences remains very important. The change in the *DSM* is a reminder that what the patient recalls is less likely to be an exact replica of their actual mental state at the time of trauma than a reconstruction based on how they are feeling now—and often will emphasize a sense of fear, helplessness, or horror to the exclusion of other equally important feelings and thoughts that may be important to include in a full therapeutic reconstruction of the memory.

Other Considerations Regarding the Proposed PTSD Criteria for *DSM-5*

Symptom Overlap With Other Psychiatric Disorders   Over the years many experts have expressed concern about symptom overlap between PTSD and other mood and anxiety disorders (McHugh & Treisman, 2007; Spitzer et al., 2007). Symptoms of anhedonia (Criterion C4), sleep difficulty (D1), and concentration difficulty (D3) are common features of major depressive disorder (MDD), and several of these symptoms (along with irritability, D2), are prominently shared with generalized anxiety disorder. Other PTSD symptoms of arousal and anxiety are consistent with many cardinal features of panic disorder. Not surprisingly, PTSD is almost always found with co-occurring mood and anxiety disorders, most frequently major depressive disorder. While there is support for the notion that PTSD's observed comorbidities are not simply the result of "double counting" individual symptoms, it should be a relatively distinct disorder that is free from symptom overlap with other disorders. Unfortunately, isolating PTSD's symptom criteria appears not to have been considered with regard to the *DSM-5*'s proposed diagnostic revisions. Instead, the current proposal makes the PTSD diagnosis even less distinct, by including additional symptoms that are related to depression: exaggerated negative expectations about oneself, other, or future; distorted blame of oneself or others regarding the causes or consequences of the trauma; and a pervasive negative emotional state (American Psychiatric Association *DSM-5* Development, 2010).

Symptom Structure   Prior versions of the *DSM* have stipulated a tripartite PTSD symptom structure consisting of reexperiencing, avoidance/numbing, and hyperarousal. However, substantial evidence from exploratory and confirmatory factor analyses symptoms demonstrates that a three-factor PTSD symptom model does not adequately capture PTSD's actual underlying dimensions (Asmundson et al., 2000; Cox, Mota, Clara, & Asmundson, 2008; Elhai & Palmieri, 2011; McWilliams, Cox, & Asmundson, 2005; Taylor, Kuch, Koch, Crockett, & Passey, 1998). The proposed new criteria for PTSD address this by dividing the symptoms among four clusters now, separating avoidance and numbing, placing each into their own symptom cluster (American Psychiatric Association *DSM-5* Development, 2010).

Clinically Significant Distress or Impairment: Criterion F   Like all psychiatric disorders, PTSD is more than a simple checklist of symptoms. It is a *disorder*, which means it also includes the requirement that the constellation of symptoms cause clinically significant distress or impairment in social, occupational, or other important areas of functioning. This is a critical element of the disorder. However, current *DSM* criteria are vague about how this distress or impairment is defined and where the clinical threshold is set. The criteria proposed for *DSM-5* are not different from *DSM-IV* in these regards and, therefore, do not provide clarity to either of these concerns.

Delayed Onset A problematic construct in PTSD is the notion of "delayed-onset," which has special relevance in recent years as Veteran Affairs (VA) disability applications from veterans whose military service ended years, even decades, ago have soared dramatically. A systematic review examining the evidence for the existence of this construct concluded there is "no consensus emerging as to its prevalence" (p. 1319) and that studies demonstrating delayed-onset PTSD in the absence of prior symptoms are quite rare, whereas clinically presumed delayed-onset defined as an exacerbation or reactivation of prior symptoms is relatively common (Andrews, Brewin, Philpott, & Stewart, 2007). As we discussed in Chapter 1, large-scale epidemiological studies report zero or extremely low rates of delayed-onset PTSD (Breslau, Davis, Andreski, & Peterson, 1991; Frueh, Grubaugh, Yeager, & Magruder, 2009). One problem with the research on this construct is a lack of clarity regarding the conceptual definition of "delayed onset." The fact that a disorder is recognized many years after the etiological event is not evidence that onset of the disorder was "delayed." PTSD diagnosed more than 6 months after a traumatic event could indicate delayed treatment or disability seeking, delayed onset of *any* symptoms of PTSD, or delayed onset of the full disorder such that a change in one or two symptoms alters PTSD diagnostic status. Another issue is the actual time interval from traumatic exposure to onset, with "delayed onset" counting as any PTSD onset that occurs from 7 months to 50 or more years posttrauma. Spitzer et al. (2007) proposed revised PTSD diagnostic criteria, changing the onset criterion to read as either "the symptoms develop within a week of the event" or "if delayed onset, the onset of symptoms is associated with an event that is thematically related to the trauma itself (e.g., onset of symptoms in a rape survivor when initiating a sexual relationship)" (p. 235). The current proposed revisions to the *DSM-5* criteria provide a different approach to the problem. The suggested definition has been changed from "if onset of symptoms is at least 6 months after the stressor" to "if diagnostic threshold is not exceeded until 6 months or more after the event(s) (although onset of some symptoms may occur sooner than this)." This is more clear and precise, though likely does not address the problem identified in epidemiological studies that delayed-onset PTSD is at best exceedingly rare, if it exists at all.

Forensic Implications As discussed in Chapter 8, perhaps the most significant forensic context of PTSD is its use in VA disability claims by veterans seeking financial compensation for psychiatric disability putatively caused by traumatic event exposure occurring during their military service (e.g., combat). Recent legislative changes have been made to the VA's consideration of Criterion A, namely, that the evidentiary standard for establishing the required in-service stressor has been liberalized (Department of Veterans Affairs, 2010). There is no longer a requirement for corroboration of the claimed in-service stressor if it is related to the veteran's fear of hostile military or terrorist activity. This appears to mean that merely serving in hazardous areas, such as any military base in a war zone is now categorized as a "traumatic event." This interpretation does not seem consistent with the *DSM-IV* definition of trauma, although the VA claims that it is. It is possible that this legislative amendment will not be consistent with the new and tighter A1 criteria proposed in *DSM-5*. Wording in *DSM-IV* counsels that "Malingering should be ruled out in those situations in which financial remuneration, benefit eligibility, and forensic determinations play a role" (p. 427). It is not clear if or how this will be revised in *DSM-5*.

Conclusions on the Near Future of PTSD in the *DSM*

As of this writing, our view is that the current proposed changes for *DSM-5* represent only a modest revision from current *DSM-IV* criteria. They likely represent a slight improvement in several ways discussed earlier, although they are incremental and relatively minor in nature. They do not indicate any fundamental shifts in how the disorder is conceived, classified, or defined. As such, they are unlikely to have meaningful impact on obtained prevalence rates, clinical evaluation approaches, intervention strategies, or forensic applications of the disorder. The proposed criteria revisions do address several of the empirical limitations inherent in *DSM-IV* that are discussed earlier in this chapter and in preceding chapters. These improvements include reformulating the A1 criterion so that it is more precise and specific, eliminating the A2 criterion, and changing the symptom structure from three to four clusters, making it more consistent with the empirical data derived from factor analytic studies. The proposed criteria revisions also include the addition of several new symptoms to the disorder. It is unclear whether these new added symptoms are empirically supported and what impact, if any, they are likely to have on prevalence rates or clinical approaches to the disorder, though we expect the likely impact will be minor.

FINAL REMARKS

In conclusion, we remind clinicians that individual reactions to traumatic event exposure vary widely. Although the general qualitative response is most commonly negative in valence, most people show tremendous resilience, and the disorder we term *PTSD* is found in only a small percentage. We must also be careful to remember that even significant emotional and behavioral posttraumatic reactions are not necessarily evidence of disorder in all cases. Psychologist Ron Acierno summarized several implications of this nicely (in Frueh, Elhai, & Acierno, 2010, pp. 266−267):

> The concept that extreme and negative emotional responses are not necessarily indicative of a psychopathological state is clarified by considering these responses in the environmental context from which they originate. From this perspective, that to which we refer to as "symptoms" might actually often constitute normal, expected, and even adaptive responses to a traumatic event or situation. Whereas the "normality" of response is relatively simple to understand in the immediate time frame of an event (e.g., hypervigilance and exaggerated startle during street combat in Iraq could keep you alive and is thus not only normal, but highly adaptive), it might be less clear one or two months post-event; or when the environmental context changes to the extent that these responses are no longer adaptive (e.g., when a soldier returns home). . . .
>
> In the *DSM-IV*, the point at which the response set moves from "normal, expected, and nonpathological" to PTSD is considered when 1 month has elapsed; however, we maintain that it should be when functional impairment becomes and remains significant. Moreover, this impairment as functional impact is contextually defined because many responses that comprise PTSD are adaptive on the battlefield or in the immediate aftermath of disaster, and decidedly maladaptive once the traumatic situation is well past.

The advantages of conceptualizing PTSD in this way, that is, as a product of initially predictable behavioral learning acquired in a manner similar to most other environmental episodes of learning, followed by a failure to unlearn or to change responding when the context changes to one of less danger, is important when developing treatment options and estimating prognosis.

It is empirically well established that general life stressors, especially those occurring at critical developmental time points, play a significant role in the development of mood and anxiety disorders (Post, 2007). The "kindling" theory, as this phenomenon is known, offers a perspective on the interaction between stress and psychiatric disorder episodes over time (Monroe & Harkness, 2005; Post, 2007; Stroud, Davila, & Moyer, 2008). According to this theory, life stressors play two etiological roles: first, as an acute pathophysiological agent in the immediate aftermath of stress; and second, as a stimulus that leaves long-lasting vulnerabilities that lower the threshold of stress required to trigger episodic recurrences. Traumatic stressors, as defined by the *DSM-IV* A1 criterion, can be viewed as representing an extreme point along a stressor continuum. Moreover, as we have noted in several places throughout this book, although PTSD has always been classified as an anxiety disorder in *DSM*, and there is certainly much evidence to support this, its position within this category is not necessarily secure—or at least pure. Strong arguments have been made that it is a mood disorder, a disorder of emotional dysregulation, of dissociation, of anger, guilt, and shame, and so on.

All of this is presented to suggest that the evolution of our understanding of PTSD, and posttraumatic reactions in general, is far from complete. It also points toward the value of considering the new transdiagnostic models, assessment practices, and treatment approaches, which may effectively address concerns of symptom overlap and diagnostic comorbidity in PTSD and related disorders. A transdiagnostic treatment approach, combining treatment components from various disorders, has been gaining traction in the field (Barlow et al., 2010; Gros, Magruder, Ruggiero, Shaftman, & Frueh, 2012). In the trauma field, researchers have combined the exposure-based practices common in the fear disorders with the behavioral activation, anger management, emotion regulation training, or other relevant components common in the distress disorders to treat patients with PTSD (Beidel, Frueh, Uhde, Wong, & Mentrikoski, 2011; Ford, Steinberg, & Zhang, 2011). These multicomponent treatments for PTSD apply different specific elements to target specific aspects of the clinical syndrome associated with PTSD. This is likely to be the future path of clinical services for a large percentage of people with PTSD.

REFERENCES

Afifi, T. O., Asmundson, G. J., Taylor, S., & Jang, K. L. (2010). The role of genes and environment on trauma exposure and posttraumatic stress disorder symptoms: A review of twin studies. *Clinical Psychology Review, 30*, 101–112.

American Psychiatric Association *DSM-5* Development. (2010). Proposed draft revisions to *DSM* disorders and criteria. Retrieved from www.dsm5.org/ProposedRevisions/

Andrews, B., Brewin, C. R., Philpott, R., & Stewart, L. (2007). Delayed-onset posttraumatic stress disorder: A systematic review of the evidence. *American Journal of Psychiatry, 164*, 1319–1326.

Asmundson, G. J., Frombach, I., McQuaid, J., Pedrelli, P., Lenox, R., & Stein, M. B. (2000). Dimensionality of posttraumatic stress symptoms: A confirmatory factor analysis of *DSM-IV* symptom clusters and other symptom models. *Behavior Research and Therapy, 38*, 203–214.

Barlow, D. H., Fachione, T. J., Fairholme, C. P., Boisseau, C. L., Allen, L. B., & Ehrenreich-May, J. (2010). *Unified protocol for transdiagnostic treatment of emotional disorders.* New York, NY: Oxford University Press.

Beidel, D. C., Frueh, B. C., Uhde, T., Wong, N., & Mentrikoski, J. (2011). Multicomponent behavioral treatment for chronic combat-related posttraumatic stress disorder: A randomized controlled trial. *Journal of Anxiety Disorders, 25*, 224–231.

Bonne, O., Brandes, D., Gilboa, A., Gomori, J. M., Shenton, M. E., Pitman, R. K., & Shalev, A. Y. (2001). Longitudinal MRI study of hippocampal volume in trauma survivors with PTSD. *American Journal of Psychiatry, 158*, 1248–1251.

Bremner, J. D., Randall, P., Scott, T. M., Bronen, R. A., Seibyl, J. P., Southwick, S. M., . . . Innis, R. (1995). MRI-based measurement of hippocampal volume in patients with combat-related posttraumatic stress disorder. *American Journal of Psychiatry, 152*, 973–981.

Breslau, N., Davis, G. C., Andreski, P., & Peterson, E. (1991). Traumatic events and posttraumatic stress disorder in an urban population of young adults. *Archives of General Psychiatry, 48*, 216–222.

Brewin, C. R., Andrews, B., & Rose, S. (2000). Fear, helplessness, and horror in posttraumatic stress disorder: Investigating *DSM-IV* criterion A2 in victims of violent crime. *Journal of Traumatic Stress, 13*, 499–509. doi: 10.13/ A:1007741526169

Cox, B. J., Mota, N., Clara, I., & Asmundson, G. J. (2008). The symptom structure of posttraumatic stress disorder in the National Comorbidity Replication Survey. *Journal of Anxiety Disorders, 22,* 1523–1528.

Creamer, M., McFarlane, A. C., & Burgess, P. (2005). Psychopathology following trauma: The role of subjective experience. *Journal of Affective Disorders, 86,* 175–182.

Department of Veterans Affairs. (2010). Stressor determinants for posttraumatic stress disorder (38 CFR Part 3). *Federal Register, 75,* 39843–39852.

Dohrenwend, B. P. (2010). Toward a typology of high-risk major stressful events and stituations in posttraumati stress disorder and related psychopathology. *Psychological Injury and Law, 3,* 89–99.

Elhai, J. D., & Palmieri, P. A. (2011). The factor structure of posttraumatic stress disorder: A literature update, critique of methodology, and agenda for future research. *Journal of Anxiety Disorders, 25,* 849–854.

Ford, J. D., Steinberg, K. L., & Zhang, W. (2011). A randomized clinical trial comparing affect regulation and social problem-solving psychotherapies for mothers with victimization-related PTSD. *Behavioral Therapy, 42,* 560–578.

Fries, E., Hesse, J., Hellhammer, J., & Hellhammer, D. H. (2005). A new view of hypocortisolism. *Psychoneuroendocrinology, 30,* 1010–1016.

Frueh, B. C., Elhai, J. D., & Acierno, R. (2010). The future of posttraumatic stress disorder in the *DSM. Psychological Injury and Law, 3,* 260–270.

Frueh, B. C., Grubaugh, A. L., Yeager, D. E., & Magruder, K. M. (2009). Delayed-onset posttraumatic stress disorder among veterans in primary care clinics. *British Journal of Psychiatry, 194,* 515–520.

Galea, S., Acierno, R., Ruggiero, K., Resnick, H., Tracy, M., & Kilpatrick, D. (2006). Social context and the psychobiology of posttraumatic stress. *Annals of New York Academy of Sciences, 1071,* 231–241.

Gros, D. F., Magruder, K. M., Ruggiero, K. J., Shaftman, S. R., & Frueh, B. C. (2012). The categorization of the symptoms of posttraumatic stress disorder: A comparison with the distress disorders and fear disorders. [Manuscript submitted for publication]

Institute of Medicine. (2006). *Posttraumatic stress disorder: Diagnosis and assessment.* Washington, DC: National Academies Press.

Karam, E. G., Andrews, G., Bromet, E., Petukhova M., Ruscio, A. M., Salamoun, M., . . . Kessler, R. C. (2010). The role of criterion A2 in the *DSM-IV* diagnosis of posttraumatic stress disorder. *Biological Psychiatry, 68,* 465–473.

Kilpatrick, D. G., Koenen, K. C., Ruggiero, K. J., Acierno, R., Galea, S., Resnick, H. S., . . . Gelernter, J. (2007). The serotonin transporter genotype and social support and moderation of posttraumatic stress disorder and depression in hurricane-exposed adults. *American Journal of Psychiatry, 164,* 1693–1699.

Koenen, K. C., Aiello, A. E., Bakshis, E., Amstadter, A. B., Ruggiero, K. J., Acierno, R., . . . Galea, S. (2009). Modification of the association between serotonin transporter genotype and risk of posttraumatic stress disorder in adults by county-level social environment. *American Journal of Epidemiology, 169*, 704–711.

Long, M. E., & Elhai, J. D. (2009). Posttraumatic stress disorder's traumatic stressor criterion: History, controversy, clinical and legal implications. *Psychological Injury and Law, 2*, 167–178. doi: 10.1007/s12207-009-9043-6

McHugh, P. R. (2005). Striving for coherence: Psychiatry's efforts over classification. *Journal of the American Medical Association, 293*, 2526–2528.

McHugh, P. R., & Treisman, G. (2007). PTSD: A problematic diagnostic category. *Journal of Anxiety Disorders, 21*, 211–222.

McNally, R. J. (2003). Progress and controversy in the study of posttraumatic stress disorder. *Annual Review of Psychology, 54*, 229–252.

McNally, R. J. (2009). Can we fix PTSD in *DSM-V*? *Depression and Anxiety, 26*, 597–600.

McWilliams, L. A., Cox, B. J., & Asmundson, G. J. (2005). Symptoms structure of posttraumatic stress disorder in a natinally representative sample. *Journal of Anxiety Disorders, 19*, 626–641.

Monroe, S. M., & Harkness, K. L. (2005). Life stress, the "kindling" hypothesis, and the recurrence of depression: Considerations from a life-stress perspective. *Psychological Review, 112*, 417–445.

Post, R. M. (2007). Kindling and sensitization as models for affective episode recurrence, cyclicity, and tolerance phenomena. *Neuroscience and Biobehavioral Reviews, 31*, 858–873.

Rosen, G. M., Frueh, B. C., Lilienfeld, S. O., McHugh, P. R., & Spitzer, R. L. (2010). Afterword: PTSD's future in the *DSM*: Implications for clinical practice. In G. M. Rosen & B. C. Frueh (Eds.), *Clinician's guide to posttraumatic stress disorder* (pp. 263–276). Hoboken, NJ: Wiley.

Rosen, G. M., Lilienfeld, S. O., Frueh, B. C., McHugh, P. R., & Spitzer, R. L. (2010). Reflections on PTSD's future in *DSM-5*. *British Journal of Psychiatry, 197*, 343–344.

Rosen, G. M., Lilienfeld, S. O., & Orr, S. P. (2010). Searching for PTSD's biological signature. In G. M. Rosen & B. C. Frueh (Eds.), *Clinician's guide to postttraumatic stress disorder* (pp. 3–31). Hoboken, NJ: Wiley.

Satel, S. L., & Frueh, B. C. (2009). Sociopolitical aspects of psychiatry: Posttraumatic stress disorder. In B. J. Sadock, V. A. Sadock, & P. Ruiz (Eds.), *Comprehensive textbook of psychiatry* (9th ed.; pp. 728–733). Baltimore, MD: Lippincott Williams & Wilkins.

Spitzer, R. L., First, M. B., & Wakefield, J. C. (2007). Saving PTSD from itself in *DSM-V*. *Journal of Anxiety Disorders, 21*, 233–241.

Stroud, C. B., Davila, J., & Moyer, A. (2008). The relationship between stress and depression in first onsets versus recurrences: A meta-analytic review. *Journal of Abnormal Psychology, 117*, 206–213.

Taylor, S., Kuch, K., Koch, W. J., Crockett, D. J., & Passey, G. (1998). The structure of postraumatic stress symptoms. *Journal of Abnormal Psychology, 107,* 154–160.

Yehuda, R., Southwick, S.M., Nussbaum, G., Giller, E.L., & Mason, J.W. (1990). Low urinary cortisol excretion in PTSD. *Journal of Nervous and Mental Disease, 178,* 366–369.

Young, E. A., & Breslau, N. (2004). Cortisol and catecholamines in posttraumatic stress disorder: An epidemiologic community study. *Archives of General Psychiatry, 61,* 394–401.

Zhang, L., Li, H., Benedek, D., Li, X., & Ursano R. (2009). A strategy for the development of biomarker tests for PTSD. *Medical Hypotheses, 73,* 404–409.

Author Index

Subject Index